BUSINESS

Across Cultures

For Hasan Ozbekhan
Because he started to give us the essence of organizational and
system thinking

FONS TROMPENAARS
PETER WOOLLIAMS

BUSINESS

→ → → → *Across Cultures*

CAPSTONE

Copyright © 2003 by Fons Trompenaars and Peter Woolliams

The right of Fons Trompenaars and Peter Woolliams to be identified as the authors of this work has been asserted in accordance with the Copyright, Designs and Patents Act 1988

First published 2003 by
Capstone Publishing Ltd (a Wiley Company)
The Atrium
Southern Gate
Chichester
West Sussex PO19 8SQ
England
www.wileyeurope.com

CIP catalogue records for this book are available from the British Library and the US Library of Congress

ISBN 1-84112-474-5

Typeset by Forewords, 109 Oxford Road, Cowley, Oxford

Printed and bound by T.J. International Ltd, Padstow, Cornwall

This book is printed on acid-free paper responsibly manufactured from sustainable forestry in which at least two trees are planted for each one used for paper production.

Substantial discounts on bulk quantities of Capstone Books are available to corporations, professional associations and other organizations. For details contact John Wiley & Sons: tel. (+44) 1243 770441, fax (+44) 1243 770517, email corporatedevelopment@wiley.co.uk

Contents

INTRODUCTION

As business becomes more global and the workforce ever more diverse, the issue of "culture" becomes increasingly important for leaders and managers and their organizations. Of course many researchers and authors have already written about culture. Models and frameworks have been developed and described, ranging from early anthropological investigations through to studies of national and organizational culture. However, most existing works have tended to focus on knowledge *of* cultures. This book, and others in the series, is concerned with knowledge *for* cultures, and provides a new conceptual framework for dealing with the business implications of culture. Our aim is to provide a practical toolkit for managers and leaders by helping them develop a new mindset for working with and across cultures. As readers will discover, there is an entirely different logic flowing throughout this book, one breaking away from traditional management texts which are often overly influenced by Anglo-American research and thinking.

The readers of our previous books and publications, together with audiences from conference presentations, have told us that they need an organized body of knowledge beyond simple recognition of cultural differences in a business context. The advantage of the earlier works was that they helped managers structure their own experiences and understand that they were seeing the world not as it is, but from the perspective of who they were. Increasingly, however, they have demanded a generic-solution framework to help them develop their cross-cultural competence, and enable them to be more effective in doing business and managing across cultures.

The new thinking and knowledge presented in this book has resulted from a synergistic mix of a number of sources. The first is our own rigorous research. This has included fundamental, applied, and strategic research conducted by our team and extended network, one that has included many PhD students. Then there is our own multi-cultural consulting practice, Trompenaars Hampden-Turner, which has a diverse range of interventions across the globe. We have enjoyed and benefited from collecting, analyzing, and working with leaders and managers on many "real world" critical incidents and cases that owe their origin to culture. And, not least, we continue to monitor and evaluate the work of other authors to validate and triangulate with our own work, although we would claim that their solutions to dealing with cultural differences are limited.

In our previous publications we have emphasized the importance of having sound models to structure and explain the complexity of the multicultural world that surrounds us. In our previous work we have initially helped managers to recognize that there are cultural differences, helped them perceive their importance and understand how they impact on main business processes. In *Riding the Waves of Culture*, a conceptual model based on seven bi-polar dimensions was used to represent the diversity of values. In *Seven Cultures of Capitalism*, we applied this framework to seven major national themes in order to make capitalism meaningful. In *21 Leaders for the 21st Century*, we explored the cultural dilemmas faced by leaders in large international organizations.

However, we were aware that, like many other cultural models that have been published since, these tools were seeking to model cultures across the world by scoring them on bi-polar scales. For such cultural profiling tools, each dimension is based on the single-axis continuum. When seeking to apply this sort of typology, or indeed any other associative model in an international context, we find that being restricted to the extremities of each scale is constraining. The fundamental limitation of such models is that it is implicit that the more a culture tends to one end of a bi-polar dimension, the less it must tend to the other. What if we need to consider the possibility of both extremes being present in a single culture?

Increasingly we have found limitations to classifying cultural differences in this way – especially when trying to help managers and leaders deal with these differences. As much as anything, bi-polar models often produce stereotypical descriptions that fail to explain many facets of the actual culture they are trying to represent.

So we might hear comments like this:

"Obviously the Japanese are not creative! They are highly communitarian and they don't dare to stick their necks out, as they are worried about jeopardizing their team spirit,"

or this:

"Now I understand why the culture in the US breeds all these lawyers. They have become so universalistic because they need rules that govern their individualistic relationships,"

and this:

"What's more, their specificity has to do with the fact that they're so mobile. They don't have time to develop relationships they trust. So lawyers and their specific contracts take their place."

What about the following explanation of the French and Italians?

"Isn't it amazing how relaxed they are with appointments and deadlines? They turn up 20 minutes late and don't even bother making an excuse! They can do things in parallel, they're from synchronic cultures, while we North-West Europeans are sequential. We'd rather wait."

This has been the unintended consequence of mapping cultures with linear models. The quantitative support and exhaustive statistical analysis gave these the scientific flavor that the 70s and 80s business communities wanted. Let us recall that in those times the Anglo-Saxon business model was so dominant that showing cultural differences, and the consequences for the application of Anglo-Saxon models, was thought to be a great step forward.

So how did this thinking develop to try to explain why the French couldn't cope with the matrix organization or that the Japanese were unlikely to take MBO (management by objectives) seriously? In fact, very little. Hofstede, for example, wrote article after article to "prove" that cultures were dissimilar – to the point where this impeded the development of alternative thinking and constrained the understanding and development of Anglo-American business theory. But he was a pioneer and we shouldn't blame him. It is rather his followers, blindly citing his work, who should be those getting a warning memo. Too many academic studies and publications have followed this linear thinking, trying to prove that there are cultural differences and that they affect the applicability of standardized business practices. We have found that since the mid-90s there has been an increased need to develop an alternative logic and overcome the limitation of this outdated thinking.

Through this Culture for Business series we want to offer an alternative to simply recognizing cultural differences and develop ways of crossing these differences and thus satisfying the many requests from our clients and readers. They have suggested several main areas that we will summarize in this book, but which will be extended one-by-one in the full series.

We have also developed a new set of tools to capture cultural differences in an alternative paradigm that overcomes the limitations of the linear bi-polar models. The new logic is largely explained by the theory of complimentarity – that no value can flow if it lacks a tension with its opposite. Traffic lights stuck on red and green don't help traffic negotiate a junction – only the constant changing through the red-amber-green cycle sustains the system. If individuals are disconnected from the community, they become egoists. If the community isn't in contact with individuals, we could speak of communism. And both egotism and communism (on their own) do not seem to work in the long run.

RECOGNIZE, RESPECT AND RECONCILE

Back to school now, but with *our* three R's. This is the essence of our new approach based on the need to **R**ecognize, **R**espect and then **R**econcile cultural differences. The reader will be aware of the first requirement to *recognize* cultural differences. At least the earlier models have achieved that and help managers avoid being ethnocentric. Accepting the theory of complimentarity is the beginning of the next step, which is to *respect* cultural differences.

As supported by our extensive research evidence, all values are fundamentally within each of us but they manifest themselves as a series of dilemmas. While the dilemmas themselves are beyond culture, the way people approach and resolve them are culturally determined. Respect starts from within. Once you know there is something "Japanese-like" in you, but that it is your own culture inside your head which silently whispers this to you, this is where respect starts.

Fons writes:

I remember that I was in love with a girlfriend (now my wife, obviously). It was 25 years ago and we were spending a weekend in London. One Sunday morning, she showed me a dress that she had bought the day before and asked what I thought of it. She added that she had bought it to please me. The dress, in my opinion, was awful, but I told her that I liked it. Doesn't this sound familiar? When we're in love an honest "no" becomes a tactful "yes." We suddenly realize that we are partly Japanese. But in the Netherlands, we have to be in love to have a relationship prevail over an opinion about a material object.

Peter adds:

In turn, the British would say "interesting" to indicate their disgust.

It is very difficult to realize that we are being ethnocentric far too often.

Did you hear about the man who wanted to take his kids to the local swimming pool one Saturday afternoon, so he telephoned first to check whether they were open? When the telephone was answered, he asked if he was speaking to someone at the local swimming pool. "Well, that depends on how far away you are," said the voice at the other end.

Once you are aware of and respect cultural differences, the way is open for the third step, which is *reconciliation*. We often hear that the world of business and management does not need more proof that people are difficult. The question now is to ask what we can do with the differences to make our businesses more effective once we cross cultural or diversity boundaries. Reconciling cultural differences is the answer.

This book and other titles in the series will all explicitly and/or implicitly follow the same three steps of recognition, respect and reconciliation. While this first book describes the common model across all the major disciplines, the functionally specific books that follow will cover areas in much more detail, with more cases and examples for the specialist.

First, we will consider how culture pervades business and then look at this from both national and organizational perspectives. In subsequent chapters, we will demonstrate how our general model is applied to Marketing, Accounting and Finance, Human Resource Management and leadership. We will conclude with our paradigm of the reconciling organization, in which the principles we discuss are embedded in both the mindset and actions of leaders and their organizational systems.

You will find more information and material at the series' website: www.cultureforbusiness.com.

CHAPTER 1

The organization as a cultural construct

n order to explore the future for global business, we should first reflect on where the past has brought us. When we look at work that was done in the late nineteenth century and at the beginning of the twentieth, we can clearly see how social theory in general and organization theory in particular have attempted to explain the developments that the industrial revolution had initiated.

Among the grand theories that have stood the test of time, we find the works of Durkheim, Tönnies and Weber that seek to explain large societal developments. Emile Durkheim focused on the transition from mechanical to organic solidarity as a result of the division of labor. Ford Tönnies observed a movement from *Gemeinschaft* to *Gesellschaft*, while Max Weber discussed the unavoidable evolution of the bureaucratic "ideal type" as a logical conclusion of the "spirit of Protestantism." In the field of organization theory, we can see serious efforts by Taylor and Fayol to find reliable, reproducible and transferable principles that would help management and workers to become more efficient. Frederick Taylor is credited with developing Scientific Management (although he never used this term to describe what he called "managing scientifically") and his account of the Pennsylvania Dutch is well known. By simply observing movements of physical labor and advising workers how to become more efficient, productivity was significantly affected. In parallel, attention was given to effective systems of variable pay, so that workers were motivated to apply more efficient work methods. Henri Fayol focused on organizational structure, looking at things like the most ideal team size and the optimal "span of control." However, the assumption on which these ideas were based is clearly that of a purely rational individual – an "actor" – in a closed organizational system.

With increasing organizational efficiency, growth was spectacular. So much so that private owners had to go public, not simply because the stock market was now a fact, but because the split between ownership and management developed. A new shareholder logic was introduced which kept the individual rational but opened the organizational system. Simultaneously, Scientific Management continued to experiment on how one could increase worker productivity by changing "hygiene factors" such as the intensity of light in the work environment. The so-called Hawthorne experiments on this led to results which surprised the theorists: people did not operate like mechanical systems. From this, Elton Mayo and Dick Roethlisberger, the two main experimenters, started what was to become the Human Relations School. Workers were more motivated by the fact they got attention and felt part of an elite than by the level of the lighting on their work bench. This opened up new attention to the actor as a full social individual, in sharp contrast to the uni-dimensional, materialistic, rational actor that was assumed to exist under the Scientific Management School.

However, organizational systems and thinking remained far too closed. Many social psychologists of the 1950s followed similar assumptions. Unfortunately these models are too often cited by more recent writers seeking to legitimize their own commentaries.

Motivational Scope	Organizational System	
	Closed	Open
Rational	• Scientific Management (strictly "managing scientifically")	• Functionalism • Early Systems Theory • Contingency Theory
Social	• Human Relations School of Social Psychology	• Modern Systems Theory • Symbolic Interactionism • Chaos Theory

Functionalism and systems theory as methodologies were developed to obtain better insights into the interaction between the organizational system and its environment. By considering an organization as an open system and introducing concepts such as input, output, feedback, and lag, many new linkages were discovered to be in need of attention. Systems jargon – like Entropy, the Principle of Equifinality, and the Law of Requisite Variety – was introduced or copied from other disciplines. Writers like Parsons, Merton, and von Bertalanffy were criticized because they looked at an organizational system in the same way that a natural scientist would look at a molecule. The systems movement culminated in the Club of Rome (Limits to Growth) which predicted the end of the economic world from the vicious circle of growth producing waste and depleshing raw materials. Today, a version of this open systems approach is still very popular; for example, look at contingency theory. This has some following because it has been subject to critical and rigorous research by academics such as Harvard professors Paul Lawrence and Jay Lorsch. Essentially contingency theory was a revenge and counter-argument to the "one best way of organizing" so implicit in Scientific Management. Contingency theorists like Derek Pugh and Paul Hickson (the so-called Aston Group of researchers) demonstrated that optimal organizational structure was contingent upon main environmental characteristics such as the inter-linkage between technology and market.

Lawrence and Lorsch found significant correlation between the degrees of differentiation and interpretation of organizational processes in industries that were operating in different environments. Others found relationships between the number of hierarchical levels and the complexity of technology. Attempts were made to quantify the cause-and-effect relationships of environmental factors, such as complexity of market and technology by using R&D expenditure/turnover ratios or the average life span of a product. The search was on for variables, co-variables, and transfer (input–output) functions. In turn, the structural characteristics of an organization were quantified through counting hierarchical levels and the average span of control. In some cases, scores of job-evaluations were entered into computer manpower planning models. And indeed, the claimed optimal organization structure was dependent on those quantifiable environmental characteristics that could be modeled!

The motives for such research and claimed findings were varied. Thinking often followed the notion that if the optimum organization structure could be designed and implemented, then a lean, efficient organization would enable management to deliver the shareholders' goals. And in this optimal organization, management could motivate and control the work force in order to deliver the results if they knew which levers to pull (or push) – levers such as pay for performance.

Let us remind ourselves once again that most of this published research, the host organizations in which the research was undertaken, and the researchers themselves were Anglo-American – or were at least dominated by such thinking. But then came a quantum shift: the beginning of globalization during the 1970s.

Organizational theorists added the cultural factor. Studies were conducted in large multinational role-driven organizations, like Shell and IBM, operating in global markets. The immediate advantage of such market settings was that factors such as financial, technological, and market conditions were similar since the companies sold global products. In fact, the only significant difference was the cultural environment in which the company operated. Some early results at the time showed that the cultural factor was an insignificant influence on the way the organization was structured – especially where the HQ or parent structure had been exported without any local adaptation. It was commonly held that "the organization is (national) culture-free" and in some regard this is still evident from our consulting practice today – more so than one might expect.

Fons remarks:

In my earlier career at Shell, while I was doing my PhD, I clearly remember my encounter with the Dutch General Manager of the refinery in Singapore. I asked him how the refinery had adjusted itself to Singaporean culture. He immediately asked whether I was working with Personnel! Indeed at the time I was, so he invited me into the real world of management and gave me a tour. Amid the whispering of steam from hot metal, he asked me if I could understand that "things could not easily be adapted to Singaporean culture. If Singaporeans do not like working in shifts, can we simply adjust our approach? Obviously not." Cynically enough, this revealed that the way the organization was set up was very similar to the refinery in Rotterdam-Pernis. In fact the organizational schemes were developed there and "exported" to Singapore, even including the descriptions for the large majority of jobs. In short, the technology of production was so dominant that culture was deemed irrelevant.

What about the financial analysts or market traders of today and their approaches? When they cut a deal for a merger or acquisition, do they ever raise the possibility of a cultural misfit in the organizations they marry? No, because the financial factor dominates. This was well illustrated by one analyst who whispered to us: "We are in the business of weddings, not in long-term marriages!"

So why the Culture for Business series? Both in theory and in practice, culture is a factor that, unlike technology, market or financial conditions, cannot easily be quantified or shown to be a major causal variable. And yet the greatest management thinkers and practitioners keep on bringing up this subject of culture. How come? What is the fallacy in the existing debates on culture? What is the limitation of the logic within which these conclusions have been drawn? We offer an answer.

CULTURE AS THE CONTEXTUAL ENVIRONMENT

Although the preceding arguments sound very logical, they are only logical within an illogical system. The assumptions on which these perceptions of reality are based come straight from the natural sciences. The quest was for scientific rather than ontological truth. The Contingency School also interpreted reality as scientists would study cells. There were no alternative ways of imposing meaning on what was observed. It was Alfred Schutz, the phenomenologist, who said it so clearly: "The advantage of a natural scientist over a social scientist is that atoms and molecules don't talk back." The researcher has often taken the observed individual as a purely rational actor, following exactly the same motives as the observer would follow. This is not only true for the definition of the environment but for the interpretation of organizational structure as well. Let us return to the definition of complexity of the technology in use or to the number of hierarchical levels in the organization. The former was defined by indices or ratios such as R&D/Turnover. If we were to ask a modern teenager – without a calculator – what the square root of 144 multiplied by 13 and divided by 10 was, they might well answer that the sum was impossible for them to solve. In contrast, a third year math student might laugh about its simplicity. What is complex and/or makes things complex?

In order to approach the answer we need to include the perception of those who perceive this reality. When asking a Singaporean how many levels of authority he had above him and how many below him, he answered three above and five below. We were surprised because Fons had interviewed a process operator in Rotterdam with exactly the same job description, but in a very much larger refinery. His answer was two levels above him and three below. What accounted for the difference was that an older colleague of the Singaporean was seen as hierarchically senior, despite the fact that they had a similar job group level; furthermore, the fact that a woman was at the same formal level didn't mean much to the interviewee in Singapore. Both internal and external environments are created in the minds of those who observe them. In fact, as the systems thinker Russ Ackoff would have put it, the contingency theorist observes behavior, while a modern systems theorist needs to explain action. If we observe a mouse and see it running for a piece of cheese, then we can guess that the cheese is the goal. But it is difficult to check whether the mouse is aware of this goal or has set this goal. It might just be an automatic reaction. And what about a computer? Like the mouse – the animal – it seems to be goal-seeking, but not goal-setting. And that accounts for behavior rather than action. It is purposive behavior and not purposeful behavior or action. Action is motivated behavior. It is behavior where the individual is not only seeking goals but also setting them.

In combining the full spectrum of an individual's range of possible behaviors and to include the environment, the organizational scientist has major dilemmas to reconcile. That is why in the early 80s so many alternative methods were developed to help the observer make sense out of all this. Much underlying rationale was about trying to make employees behave in ways deemed to be effective. But the problem with seeking to simply hire a pair of hands is that there is always a person on the other end!

The dilemma is clear. Social psychologists can make useful generalizations about human and organizational behavior, but the environment is often excluded. On the other hand, when the early open systems thinkers and functionalists introduced the environment, the behavioral perspective still dominated. We have been influenced by all these theorists but especially by the later systems thinkers like Russ Ackoff and Eric Trist, by symbolic interactionists like Mead, by elusive management thinkers like Charles Handy and by the beginnings of Chaos Theory.

Once we take the goal-seeking and goal-setting individual seriously as the core of our debate in framing organizational behavior, we realize that we immediately face a whole series of organizational dilemmas. When we introduce people in organizations as purposeful individuals who interact with an environment of choice, who are also displaying free will, how can we ever conceive of an organization in a larger community asking for discipline and control?

Action is motivated behavior and therefore a basic principle of motivation needs to be introduced. Etymologically speaking, the word "motivation" is derived from what makes a person move. Why not go back to Aristotle who introduced three basic motives: *causa ut*, *causa quod* and *causa sui*? the *causa ut* or "in order to" motive is the motivation that individuals derive from the pre-designed pictures which they make; these can range from a very detailed short-term project or a fuzzy long-term vision. The *causa quod* or "because" motive refers to the moving force of a situation that has happened to an individual. Finally, the *causa sui* refers to the fact that the actor is "self causing." in every act, the three motives are united, but one or more might prevail. Why all this fuss? Because it helps us approach the central dilemma of management or being managed – namely the differentiation of thoughts and feelings open to free will and integration through being organized. The causes that motivate our behavior from the past and the design of our visions are both socially constructed. Once we understand that, we start to understand that there is an evolution of sharing between people enabling them to be organized.

Let's add another logic of interactionism. If we review the definitions of organizational structure, we find the basic one is "a set of relationships among the parts and between the parts and the whole." Natural scientists would decide on the type of relationships they were looking for and how these were dictated by the whole. Social scientists cannot but include the individuals that have made up this structure. If we simply said that we have observed a flat organization in Singapore and that the individuals making up that structure did not agree, then who is right? In fact it doesn't matter, as long as we know that "what is defined as real is real in its consequences." We should never forget that the essence of relationships between the parts are individuals communicating. Communication is the exchange of information. Information is the carrier of meaning. So if we agree that culture is essentially a system of shared meaning, we begin to understand that every organization is a cultural construct.

We have sought to justify that culture is not just a factor that we can introduce next to ones such as technology, socio/political, financial, and other elements making up the transactional environment. Culture is rather the contextual environment, defining much of the essence of the relationships between an organization and the environment in which it operates.

CHAPTER 2

The organization of meaning: introducing value dimensions

RECOGNIZING CULTURAL DIFFERENCES

Culture, like an onion, consists of layers that can be peeled off. We can distinguish three main layers.

Firstly, the outer layer is what people primarily associate with culture: the visual reality of behavior, clothes, food, language, the organizational chart, the handbook for HR policies, etc. This is the level of explicit culture and it deals with the expressed manifestations of culture. On this level one has to be careful since initial observations often reveal more about you than about the culture you're observing. So where the French will almost always have an opinion about food the English may have a tendency to ignore it.

Some argue that with the globalization of business and TV networks across the world, cultural differences converge and gradually disappear. We see McDonald's hamburgers, Gucci bags, Lexus Cars, Coca-Cola, AOL, and Microsoft Windows in London, Moscow, Rio de Janeiro and Lagos. True. But be careful. These are only the artifacts that we observe. To see the cultural effects we have to go deeper into the onion and ask about the reasons why people purchase these products. We get quite different answers when we look at the value of the hamburger in different cultures, for example. A New Yorker might buy a Big Mac because it was a quick bite for a quick buck, whereas a Muscovite might buy one and keep the packaging as proof of having eaten there.

Secondly, the middle layer refers to the norms and values that an organization holds: what is considered right and wrong (norms) or good and bad (values). Values are the shared orientations of a group of what people define as the things they like and desire. Norms are shared orientations of what people believe should be done. Do you dress down and not wear a smart business suit on Friday? Values are what you would prefer to do and feel comfortable doing. Norms are how most of the other people in the organization would dress on Friday – the dress code. When a culture is successful, values become norms. When there is a tension between them, then this is the source of energy for change.

If we asked you what the norms and values of your country were, you would be likely to seek clarification: "In the North or South, urban or rural?" Once you are part of a culture, there is a tendency to see the differences within it. This is because things shared in a culture are not seen. The shopping mall in the US goes unnoticed and so does the clock in Switzerland. Only a visitor to the US from a country that does not have large shopping malls finds them worthy of notice and comment.

This is best represented by considering culture as a normal distribution. There are differences under the bell-shaped curve in all cultures, but even more between cultures. Where do these cultural differences come from? Why are the French more relaxed with time than the Americans and why do Americans breed so many lawyers? How come the Dutch go for consensus, while Koreans tend to decide more quickly? We have to go back to the etymological root of the word "culture" – cultivation. It deals with human interaction with nature. Culture is the values and norms that people hold to be more effective in surviving in a hostile natural environment. But we forget that what has become routine goes unnoticed. During presentations and workshops we ask the audience to hold their breath. We had to stop doing this in Germany because people tried too hard. Why do we do this experiment? To show that breathing has become a routine reaction to a lack of oxygen. Oxygen is a value that has become a norm; that's why we forget about it. It has become a basic assumption. It is only when oxygen is not available to us, as when holding our breath or swimming underwater, that we remember how important it is.

Thirdly, there is the deepest inner layer of the cultural onion: the level of unquestioned, implicit culture. This is the result of human beings organizing to reconcile frequently occurring dilemmas. It consists of basic assumptions, many series of routines and methods developed to deal with the regular problems that people face. These methods of problem-solving have become so basic that, like breathing, we no longer think about how we do it. For an outsider these basic assumptions are very difficult to recognize. Understanding the core of the cultural onion is the key to successfully working with other cultures and achieving successful alliances and cross-border collaboration.

Thus, while we instantly recognize explicit cultural differences, we may not recognize implicit cultural differences. This explains why the need for cultural due diligence in pre- and post-merger/acquisition management is usually absent from the agenda. Our research and experience has led us to develop and validate models and diagnostic instruments to reveal and measure these basic assumptions. They are based on the seven dimensions model of cultural differences developed over the last fifteen years and are at the core of both our new cultural due diligence model and reconciliation framework.

Thus we can summarize that culture is about meaning, about what meaning is given to things, actions and behaviors. Although a wedding is the start of a marriage, it has different meanings in different cultures. In some it is tax efficient to be married, in others it is the union of two families and their businesses, not just the bride and groom. Thus the motive is different in different cultures even though a wedding might look similar from the outside – a gathering of relatives and friends in a party atmosphere after an official ceremony. It is a different because it has a different meaning in different cultures.

We can begin by using the seven dimensions model, which enables managers to learn to recognize these cultural differences, to be prepared for them, and to check where and how they might exist and manifest themselves.

RESPECT FOR CULTURAL DIFFERENCES

Different cultural orientations and views of the world are not right or wrong – they are just different. It is all too easy to be judgmental and distrust those who give different meaning to their world from the meaning you give to yours. Thus the next step is to respect these differences and accept the right of others to interpret the world in the way they have chosen. Respect is easiest when we recognize that all cultural differences are in ourselves. We don't see the world as it is, only as we are. It is as though we are wearing cultural glasses all the time. And the lenses another person wears are different to yours.

Once we get beyond the simple differences in artifacts and are faced with differences in meaning, then, because of the different views of the world and the different meaning given to things which are apparently the same, we find the that these differences manifest themselves as dilemmas. We have two seemingly opposing views in us. As long as we remember that respect must come automatically, then once we recognize differences and respect them the real trouble starts. We remember IBM managers telling us only a couple of years ago that at IBM they trained people according to three steps: 1 – recognition, 2 – respect, and 3 – ignore the differences. They called it globalization.

We would like to propose an alternative. This alternative is a reconciliation of differences, which is the integration of seemingly opposing values and which leads to the true sense of the word integrity.

RECONCILING CULTURAL DIFFERENCES

Much attention has been given to recognition and respect for cultural differences. However, if we stop at only these first two stages, we run the risk of supporting only stereotypical views of cultures. In our extensive cross-cultural database at Trompenaars Hampden-Turner, we have found enough variation in any one country to know that it is very risky to speak of a national, corporate, or even functional culture in terms of simple stereotypes. We claim that our work is unique in that our focus has been to extend research on culture to giving much more attention to the reconciliation of differences rather than to their simple identification.

We have accumulated a significant body of evidence that wealth through effective business is created by reconciling values. This is true for alliances (including mergers and acquisitions) and in recruitment. It is true in leadership[1] as well as for nations speaking peace unto nations.[2]

Our new approach helps to identify and define behaviors that vary across the world and across companies. This approach will show managers how to guide the "people side" of reconciling any kind of values. It has a logic that integrates differences and is a series of behaviors that enables effective interaction with those of contrasting value systems. It reveals a propensity to share understanding of the other's position in the expectation of reciprocity and requires a new way of thinking that is initially difficult for Westerners.

But first, what are these major dilemmas in need of reconciliation? As mentioned earlier, we've developed a model to structure the differences around us in seven basic bi-polar orientations. This

What do we mean by dilemmas?

We define a dilemma as "two propositions in apparent conflict." In other words a dilemma describes a situation whereby one has to choose between two good or desirable options.

For example: On the one hand, we need flexibility, whilst on the other hand, we also need consistency.

So a dilemma describes the tension that is created due to conflicting demands.

What is not a dilemma? Here are some examples:

- A description of a current and ideal state: "We have good communication tools, but we need to use them better."
- An either/or option: "Should we start hiring new employees now or wait till next year?"
- A complaint: "We make good strategic plans, but due to lack of leadership we are not able to follow them through."

In order to formulate dilemmas, avoid the above negative examples. Think in terms of both sides of the dilemma (e.g., individual versus group; objective versus subjective; logic versus creativity; analytical versus intuitive; formal versus informal; rules versus exceptions, etc.). Also, always describe the dilemma by using the words "on the one hand...on the other hand..."

seven-dimensional model is a means to elicit, describe, and frame the major dilemmas organizations must resolve when faced with integration of people and systems. In our globalizing world "life as taken for granted" within our own nations or organizations is abruptly challenged by this alternative logic.

A CLASSIFICATION OF DILEMMAS

As well as simply demonstrating cultural differences, the seven dimensions model of culture also enables us to characterize commonly occurring dilemmas from the tensions between the values from which they originate. We can consider the dilemmas that arise across each of the following dimensions:

1. Universalism–Particularism. Do people in the organization tend to follow standardized rules or do they prefer a flexible approach to unique situations?

2. Individualism–Communitarianism. Does the culture foster individual performance and creativity or is the focus on the larger group leading to cohesion and consensus?

3. Neutral–Affective. Are emotions controlled or do people display emotions overtly?

4. Specific–Diffuse. What is the degree of involvement in personal relationships (high = diffuse, low = specific)? Does a specific business project come easily, out of which a more diffuse relationship may develop or do you have to get to know your business partners before you can do any business with them?

5. Achievement–Ascription. Is status and power based on your performance or is it more determined by which school you went to or your age, gender, and family background?

6. Sequential–Synchronic. Do you organize time in a sequential manner, doing one task at a time, or in parallel, keeping many things active at once?

7.   Internal–External Control. Are you stimulated by your inner drive and sense of control or are you adaptive to external events that are beyond your control?

When faced with cultural differences, one effective approach is to compare the two profiles based on the linear seven dimensions model to identify where the major differences originate. In practice, the major origin of cultural differences between your organization and a new business partner may lie predominantly in one or two cultural dimensions. By reconciling the dilemmas deriving from the differences on the orientations, organizations can begin to reconcile their cultural orientations. Recognition of these differences alone is insufficient. However, it is very important that these are taken into consideration before and during the processes in which different cultures meet.

Cultural Diversity expresses itself in viewpoints and values in operational priorities and ways of doing things that result in dilemmas. They cannot be resolved simply by deciding to go for one of the advocated propositions and ignoring alternative viewpoints. This is why we need to reconcile differences, that is, to be ourselves, but at the same time see and understand how others' perspectives can help our own. We define leadership as the propensity to reconcile dilemmas. Once you are aware of your own mental models and cultural predispositions, and once you can respect and understand that those of another culture are legitimately different, then it becomes possible to reconcile these differences. We invite you to continuously seek to improve and develop your capacity to deal with dilemmas at both the personal level (those dilemmas you face when working with other people) and at the level of your organization. Your capacity to reconcile dilemmas is how we define intercultural leadership competence and is a direct measure of your leadership potential relevant to the twenty-first century.

Through our questionnaires, structured interviews, focus groups, and consulting practice, we are accumulating hard evidence that confirms that this new competency correlates highly with effectiveness in environments where one party needs to deal with a diversity of values. In short, where parties can reconcile and integrate, the expected benefits of the intercultural encounter are delivered and even exceeded.

Once players in intercultural interactions are aware of their own mental models and cultural predispositions, and once they can respect and understand that those of another culture are legitimately different, then it becomes possible to reconcile differences, yielding positive business benefits.

For convenience we have chosen to define these based on the seven dimensions on which the values of diverse cultures vary, described briefly above.

UNIVERSALISM VERSUS PARTICULARISM

More universalist cultures tend to feel that general rules and obligations are a strong source of moral reference. Universalists tend to follow the rules even when friends are involved and look for "the one best way" of dealing equally and fairly with all cases. They assume that the standards they hold dear are the right ones and they attempt to change the attitudes of others to match.

Particularist societies are those where "particular" circumstances are much more important than the rules. Bonds of particular relationships (family, friends) are stronger than any abstract rule and the response may change according to circumstances and the people involved.

In order to test these extreme definitions, we have asked 65,000 managers world-wide to consider the following dilemma.

You are a passenger in a car driven by a close friend. He hits a pedestrian. You know he was going at least 35 miles per hour in an area of the city where the maximum speed allowed is 20 miles per hour. There are no witnesses. His lawyer says that if you are prepared to testify under oath that he was only driving at 20 miles per hour it may save him from serious consequences.

What right has your friend to expect you to protect him?

1: *My friend has a* definite *right, as a friend, to expect me to testify to the lower figure.*

2: *He has* some *right, as a friend, to expect me to testify to the lower figure.*

3: *He has* no *right, even as a friend, to expect me to testify to the lower figure.*

Would you help your friend in view of the obligations you feel towards society?

This dilemma, along with others, is discussed further in Fons' book *Did the Pedestrian Die?* The story, originally created by Stouffer and Toby, is a powerful, discriminating and provoking exercise used in our workshops. It takes the form of a dilemma which measures and challenges universal and particularistic responses.

Figure 2.1 shows the responses from a selection of countries (our database of 65,000 managers contains a wide distribution of answers across 100 different ones). We find that North Americans and Northern Europeans are almost totally universalistic in their approach to the problem. The proportion falls to under 70 percent for Latins,

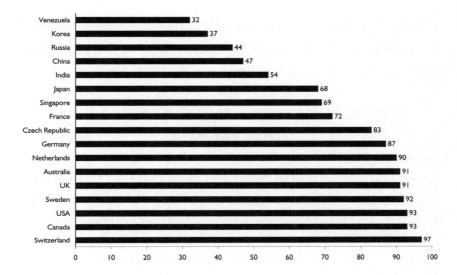

Figure 2.1 The car and the pedestrian: percentage of respondents indicating that their friend has no or only some right to expect help, and that the respondent would not help their friend.

Africans, and Asians. They would tend to lie in order to protect their friend.

Time and again, universalists respond in such a way that as the seriousness of the accident increases – if the pedestrian is fatally injured – the obligation to help their friend decreases. They seem to be saying to themselves "the law was broken and the serious condition of the pedestrian underlines the importance of upholding the law." This suggests that universalism is rarely used to the exclusion of particularism, but rather that it forms the first principle in the process of moral reasoning. Particular consequences remind us of the need for universal laws.

By asking respondents further questions about other universalistic–particularistic dilemmas, we can combine the answers on a scale that measures the relative degree to which people are universalistic or particularistic. The scales were developed after extensive testing of alternative questions and wording of questions and only accepted when Cronbach's Alpha Test of reliability and consistency gave significant results (Woolliams and Trompenaars, 1998).

UNIVERSALISM VERSUS PARTICULARISM ACROSS OTHER VARIABLES

We have explored the relationship on each dimension scale – including universalism versus particularism and a range of other variables including gender, age, experience of working abroad, industry, job function, etc. This analysis has followed both conventional statistical tests and data mining. We were careful to use non-parametric methods for rank order or nominal data and avoided adopting the Central Limit Theorem to justify the application of parametric methods, which is a mistake made by too many researchers. Thus we used variations of Correspondence Analysis and Multi-dimensional Scaling rather than simple correlation. Data mining was based on entropy analysis using the ID3 algorithm to assess the variety explained by each variable. While, with all of the dimensions, the national culture of the participants explained most of the variety, industry often appeared as a second source of variety (for all dimensions except for individualism, where religion scored highest).

Based on the above methods of analysis, the tables in this chapter (and the next) show the relative significance of each variable.

Variety in value differences

Entropy	Universalism–Particularism
Lowest (the more important variable)	Country
	Industry
	Religion
	Job function
	Age

	Corporate Climate/Culture
	Education
Highest (the least important variable)	Gender

An example analysis of the database indeed shows interesting differences (see Figure 2.2). Mining, sports goods, and equipment industries show the highest universalistic scores, shortly followed by pharmaceuticals, banking, and governmental services. On the particularistic scale, we find motor industry and petroleum/refining as the highest representatives, shortly followed by detergents, photographic products, and telecoms. This group is very much influenced by marketing activities, while the top universalists are more concerned about being right first time.

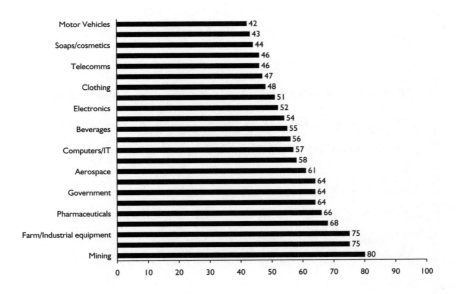

Figure 2.2 Universalism – average score by industry

UNIVERSALISM VERSUS PARTICULARISM IN INTERNATIONAL MANAGEMENT

Whilst we have often used dilemmas such as the car accident (which everyone can relate to), there are many equivalent real-world dilemmas that have an impact on international managers. The most dominant and frequently occurring is the global–local dichotomy. Shall we have one standardized approach or shall we try the local, more particular approach? If we have a single universal model that appears to work in our own country, can we just replicate it across the globe? The Ford Mondeo (meaning "world car"), for example, was envisaged as a model to be both made and sold in an identical way across the world.

There are differing views on whether we are becoming more globally universal and alike or whether we are becoming more influenced by particular and unfamiliar national cultures.

In hindsight, this dilemma was one which very much jeopardized the success of the KLM–Alitalia alliance. The Protestant Dutch were

Uniform dress and behavior for staff at Euro Disney

With regard to personnel, the American management of Euro Disney took a universalistic approach. Employees were not allowed to have beards or wear eye shadow. Furthermore, they had to dress the same and behave in certain standard ways (i.e., smile a lot). Staff training at Disney University aimed at homogeneity; Disney stood for core American values. This approach was not accepted by the particularistic French employees, and the result was a staff turnover of 50 percent in the first 16 months of operation.

sticklers for following the contract. The prepayment of some $100 million for the development of Malpensa airport was one of the central conditions. The Italians saw it as a sign of the seriousness of the alliance, rather than of the financial evaluation of the investment. When the investment failed to go according to schedule, the Dutch began discussing prepayments; a contract is a contract. The Italians had all kinds of reasons why it was not going as planned. Life is hectic and might offer unexpected particular exceptions: "What's the problem? We'll do it in another way."

The bounding outcome behaviors in intercultural encounters can be identified as the following:

Ignoring other cultures

One type of behavior is to ignore the other orientation. You are sticking to your own (cultural) standpoint. Your style of decision making is to either impose your own way of doing things because it is your belief that your way of doing things and your values are best, or because you have rejected other ways of thinking or doing things because you have either not recognized them or have no respect for them. Our aim is to help you to both recognize and respect cultural differences as the first step to reconciling the differences.

Abandon your own orientation

The second type of response is to abandon your orientation and go native. Here you adopt a "when in Rome, do as the Romans do" approach. Acting or keeping up such pretences won't go unnoticed – you will be very much an amateur. People from the other culture will mistrust you, and you won't be able offer your own strengths to any alliance.

Compromise

Sometimes do it your way. Sometimes give in to the others. But this is a win/lose solution or even a lose/lose solution. Compromise cannot lead to a solution in which both parties are satisfied; something has to give.

Reconciliation

What is needed is an approach where the two opposing views can come to fuse or blend – where the strength of one extreme is extended by considering and accommodating the other. This is reconciliation and, as we have stated earlier, is the approach that leads to you becoming more effective, especially in situations of diversity or working across cultures. One approach is to start from your own natural orientation but to accommodate the alternate viewpoint to achieve reconciliation. An alternative approach is to start from the opposite orientation to your normal values, but then to embrace your own orientation and thus achieve the reconciliation you need.

Hence a company can adopt a global strategy in the extreme – by ignoring other cultures and replicating its original and successful universal approach across the world. It may run into problems, for example when trying to sell beef hamburgers in countries where religion may forbid beef. Or it can adopt a multi-local approach, where it adapts to each particular location in which it is trading. But as a consequence of this latter course, costs may rise because of loss of economies of scale to support different particular systems. In addition, the organization may well lose any single corporate identity.

At the corporate level, an organization needs to reconcile the single universalistic global approach with the multi-local particularistic approach. As we have demonstrated above, compromise, as in a multinational company, is not enough.

What is needed is the reconciliation between the universal and the particular. In general, international success depends upon discovering special veins of excellence within different cultures. Just because people speak English does not mean they think alike. That no two cultures are the same is what brings richness and complexity to multinationalism. To achieve this reconciliation an organization has to make a conceptual leap. The answer lies in transnational specialization, allowing each nation to specialize in what it does best and become a source of authority and leadership within the global corporation for that particular vein of excellence. The reach is truly global but the sources of major influence are national. Leadership in particular functions shifts to whatever nations excel at those tasks. This cycle is in fact helical.

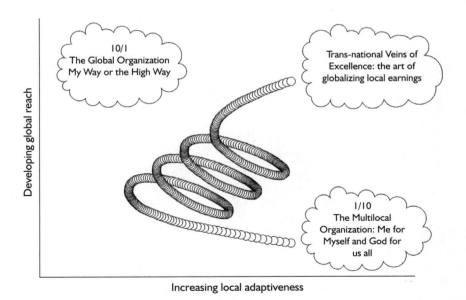

Figure 2.3 Reconciling universalism and particularism in globalization

International organizations need to look for a similar logic: it is the result of connecting particular learning efforts into a universal framework and vice versa. It is the connection between practical learning in a context of intelligent theories. In this dialectic the best integration processes are developed, disadvantages made into advantages. However, it is not easily achieved and needs the involvement of senior managers. This is known as the clockwise helix, meaning that you start at the horizontal (particular) axis and work your way to reconciliation by accommodating the vertical axis (see Figure 2.4). The alternative approach to reconciling (the anti-clockwise helix), where you begin from the vertical axis and accommodate the horizontal value, is equally valid.

When training managers across the globe, Heineken was faced with delivering their training program in the various countries in which

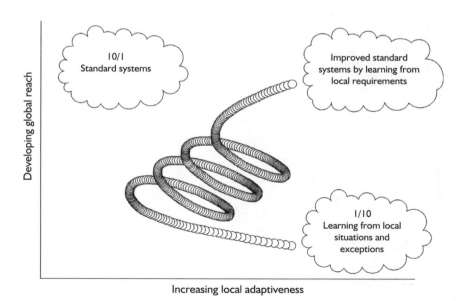

Figure 2.4   Learning from Best Practices

they had a presence. But should they deliver one standard program in each destination (universal), or a different (particular) program to meet local needs? They successfully reconciled this dilemma by continuously approaching from both extremes. They use local knowledge as an input to the design of a standard training program, but then also adapt the improved generic program to meet their local needs.

In some situations, marketing strength derives from universal world branding. Thus Coca-Cola is Coca-Cola everywhere and represents the American dream, although the list of ingredients on the can or bottle may be in a local language. Similarly, British Airways are selling safe, reliable, quintessential Englishness supported by local agents in the different destinations it serves.

There is an alternative to taking the best practices and globalizing them. When Fons was asked to give a presentation for Applied Materials in Santa Clara, California he was struck by the 57 nationalities in their top 100. American CEO Jim Morgan shared power with his co-founder, who is Israeli. We met a Japanese HR manager, a German head of technology and a French marketing VP. If what you deliver globally is developed by a multicultural team, the helix has become anti-clockwise again. You start with a global approach that is sensitive to local circumstances because of the variety in your top team.

We recognize the limitations of the earlier questionnaire that included the car accident question (see page 34). Whilst this has the advantage of forced choice, it causes the respondent to reflect on the dilemma – and how they would approach it. It enables us to place individuals along the bi-polar scale; however, it does not tell us anything about how the individual responds to the dilemma with regard to how they might reconcile the opposing choices. In order to

The car and the pedestrian

You are a passenger in a car driven by a close friend. He hits a pedestrian. You know he was going at least 35 miles per hour in an area of the city where the maximum speed allowed is 20 miles per hour. There are no witnesses. His lawyer says that if you are prepared to testify under oath that he was only driving at 20 miles per hour it may save him from serious consequences.

How would you act in this case?

1. *There is a general obligation to tell the truth as a witness. I will not perjure myself before the court. Nor should any real friend expect this from me.*

2. *There is a general obligation to tell the truth in court, and I will do so, but I owe my friend an explanation and all the social and financial support I can organize.*

3. *My friend in trouble always comes first. I am not going to desert him before a court of strangers based on some abstract principle.*

4. *My friend in trouble gets my support, whatever his testimony, yet I would urge him to find in our friendship the strength that allows us both to tell the truth.*

5. *I will testify that my friend was going a little faster than the allowed speed and say that it was difficult to read the speedometer.*

assess their personal response, we have therefore extended the original forced-choice questions to include options to reject reconciliation (answers 1 and 3), compromise (answer 5), and reconcile from the universal to the particular (answer 2) or from the particular to the universal (answer 4).

In this way we can assess both the cultural orientation of the individual in the way that they approach dilemmas (more universalistic or more particularistic) and their propensity to reconcile.

Let's stress again that the central aim of this book is to help readers to improve and develop their ability to deal with dilemmas at both the personal level (dilemmas faced when working with other people) and at the level of the organization. As we've said, the capacity to reconcile dilemmas is how we define intercultural leadership competence and is a direct measure of leadership potential relevant to the twenty-first century.

Thus the early model in which we would place a respondent along a conventional linear profiling scale:

Figure 2.5 Linear profile

is replaced by a two-dimensional assessment which shows the degree to which they choose the universalistic or particularistic approach when facing dilemmas, and the degree to which they achieve the reconciliation of these dilemmas (see Figure 2.6).

Whilst the above enables you to recognize your own orientation for how you start to approach dilemmas, you now need to consider how you "finish" in dealing with them. Do you end by rejecting other orientations (low competence) or end by successfully reconciling opposite orientations (high competence)?

Figure 2.6   Non-linear profile

By combining questions that follow the logic of the above example, we have produced scales of intercultural leadership competence for each dimension, and this is the basis of our new ILAP InterCultural Leadership Assessment Profiling instrument (see www.cultureforbusiness.com).

It is likely that the degree to which you reconcile is not the same for each cultural dimension. So consider those dimensions where your propensity to reconcile is lower. This model gives you a strategy to focus your attention on which dimensions you need to consider first to increase your effectiveness. If you can achieve this successfully, you are well on the way to a shared understanding with new business partners and a framework for developing your leadership competence.

Our research evidence from these instruments in our new reconciliation database confirms that intercultural competence, as defined by the propensity to reconcile dilemmas, correlates directly with 360° peer assessment of bottom line business performance and is a key characteristic of effective leaders. Organizations that have leaders with this competence at the individual level are effective at the corporate level in growing and surviving across the world in the global marketplace.

We can now follow this same logic through the remainder of the value dimensions.

INDIVIDUALISM VERSUS COMMUNITARIANISM

The second of our dimensions covering how people relate to others concerns the conflict between what each of us wants as an individual, and the interests of the group to which we belong. Do we relate to others by discovering what each one of us individually wants and then trying to negotiate the differences, or do we place ahead of this some shared concept of the public and collective good? The 65,000 managers who have answered the following question have revealed their response to this dilemma.

Two people were discussing ways in which one could improve the quality of life.

a: *One said, "It is obvious that if one has as much freedom as possible and the maximum opportunity to develop oneself, then the quality of one's life will improve as a result."*

b: *The other said, "If the individual continuously takes care of his fellow human beings the quality of life will improve for everyone, even if it obstructs individual freedom and individual development."*

With which of the two answers do you agree most?

Figure 2.7 shows the percentage of people who chose answer "a" (individual freedom)

We all go through these cycles, but starting from different points and conceiving of them as means or ends. The individualist culture sees the individual as the end and improvements to collective arrangements as the means to achieve it. The communitarian culture sees the group as its end and improvements to individual capacities as a

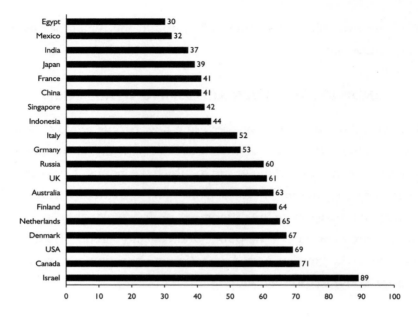

Figure 2.7 Individualism versus communitarianism (collectivism): percentage opting for individual freedom

means to that end. Yet if the relationship is truly circular the decision to label one element as an end and another as a means is arbitrary. By definition circles never end; every end is also the means to another goal.

The effective international leader or manager will recognize that individualism finds its fulfillment in service to the group, while group goals are of demonstrable value to individuals, only if those individuals are consulted and participate in the process of developing them. The reconciliation is not easy, but it is possible.

INDIVIDUALISM AND COMMUNITARIANISM
BY RELIGION

As can be observed there are major differences around the globe. Data mining shows that country is again the most discriminating variable.

Entropy	Individualism–Communitarianism
Lowest (most important variable)	Country
	Religion
	Industry
	Education
	Age
	Gender
	Job function
Highest (least important variable)	Corporate Climate/Culture

During our entropy analysis we found that religion was the second major variable that explained the variance of the Individualism score. Differences are not surprising, with Judaism and Protestantism scoring as the most individualistic and Hinduism and Buddhism the most communitarian. Again, the nationality of the person cannot explain all the differences (see Figure 2.8).

An alliance of the R&D activities of a large international oil company operating in the Netherlands with their Japanese counterparts led to an interesting discussion on how to implement a reward structure. The alliance involved predominantly Dutch, British, American, Germans, and Japanese who all needed to work in multicultural teams. Let's review the options.

An individual bonus scheme could be implemented which would stimulate the Americans and British to be even more competitive. The communitarian Japanese and Germans would be severely demotivated by this type of reward system. Alternatively we could design and implement a team bonus. Great for the Japanese. But would it motivate the Anglo Saxons? No way.

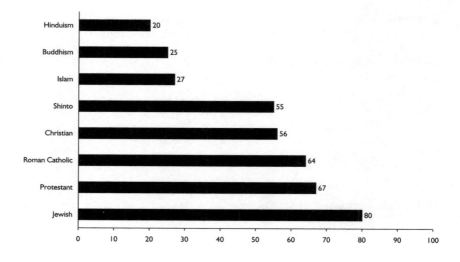

Figure 2.8 Individualism by religion: average score by religion

So why not take a compromise and have a mixed system of 50 percent variable pay based on team performance and 50 percent on individual bonus? Half of the group might still go for one end while the rest might go for the other one.

However, in this actual case, the leadership successfully sought and achieved reconciliation. For the first time in its history, the organization installed a reward structure where a mixed system of team and individual performance were included, but individuals could only get a bonus when teams voted them as the best team players. Additionally, teams were asked to make presentations on how they had nurtured individual excellence. The audience voted on the best team. This system was successfully installed and is an example of co-opetition, the art of both competing for cooperation, and cooperating for better competition.

Figure 2.9 summarizes this reconciliation.

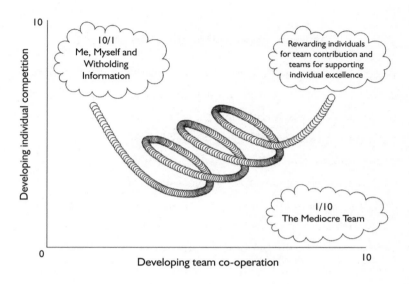

Figure 2.9 Co-opetition

On a macro-level, we have seen this philosophy of co-opetition happen at Sematech, the American Institute for Semiconductor Industries. It was originally established by the US Ministry of Defense, which was worried that South East Asian companies would become leaders in high end microchips. The institute that was formed forced the American sector to cooperate to beat the Japanese and Korean semiconductor industries. To cut a long story short, within five years Intel, AMD, and National Semiconductor almost destroyed the South East Asian semiconductor industry and yet they were originally competitors. It became possible to cooperate amongst the highly competitive organizations. Cooperation was an effective strategy in the then current conditions, in which they could later compete. The beauty of the story is that the former competitors in Asia were invited to join, which they did with great joy. An even greater example of how you can compete to cooperate.

International computer chip project

Two large companies, one American and the other Japanese, decided to work together to develop a computer memory chip 16 times more powerful than those already on the market. As the joint venture was the brainchild of the American company, it was decided that the Japanese researchers would move to the USA for the duration of the project. One of the first problems that arose was one regarding working space. While the Japanese were accustomed to working together in large, open rooms conducive to team work and the sharing of ideas, the American workspace was carved up into small individual offices. The Japanese were uncomfortable with this arrangement because they felt that the exchange of information was cut off, severely limiting the creative ideas that come from working in a group. Although they asked for an open workspace, the Americans were not very responsive and the Japanese ended up getting together in the hallways to discuss their ideas. If these two companies had been able to reconcile their value differences by combining individual work and group work, they could have learned from each other.

NEUTRAL VERSUS AFFECTIVE

In relationships between people, reason and emotion both play a role. Which of these will dominate depends on whether we are affective, i.e., display our emotions, in which case we probably get an emotional response in return, or whether we are emotionally neutral in our approach. We are still emotional, but don't reveal it to others.

Typically, reason and emotion are of course combined. In expressing ourselves we try to find confirmation of our thoughts and feelings in the response of our audience. When our own approach is highly emotional we are seeking a direct emotional response: "I have the same feelings as you on this subject." When our own approach is highly neutral we are seeking an indirect response: "Because I agree with your reasoning or proposition, I give you my support." On both occasions approval is being sought, but different paths are being used to this end. The indirect path gives us emotional support contingent upon the success of an effort of intellect. The direct path allows our feelings about a factual proposition to show through, thereby joining feelings with thoughts in a different way.

Here is an example of one of the diagnostic questions exploring this dilemma.

In my society, it is considered unprofessional to express emotions overtly.

Please select your position on the statement above:

(a)   Strongly agree

(b)   Agree

(c)   Undecided

(d)   Disagree

(e)   Strongly disagree

Figure 2.10 shows the results we got. Again, country was the single most discriminating variable.

The expression of opinions in an open and often passionate way is frequently compounded by the strong personalities of the individuals concerned into fairly fixed opinions and a sometimes adversarial communication style. It is often necessary to restate the importance of basic communication skills such as listening.

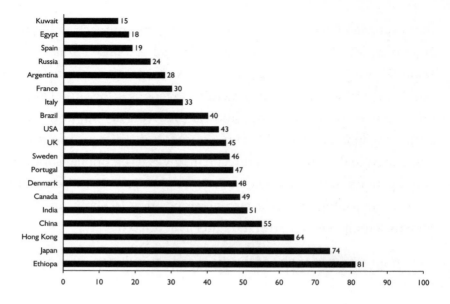

Figure 2.10 Neutral versus affective: percentage not expressing emotion overtly

This scenario reveals more than the different degrees to which different cultures display emotions. It also shows that some cultures prefer to show positive emotions or negative emotions, praise or complain, more readily.

AFFECTIVE AND NEUTRAL CULTURES ACROSS FUNCTIONS

The differences in the degree to which people express emotions correlate with job function. It is not surprising that computing and legal staff would rather have a heart attack than express their emotions. On the other hand, we find marketing, administrative, and manufacturing people most open about their emotions. Look at the large discrepancy in neutrality between admin and secretarial staff shown in Figure 2.11.

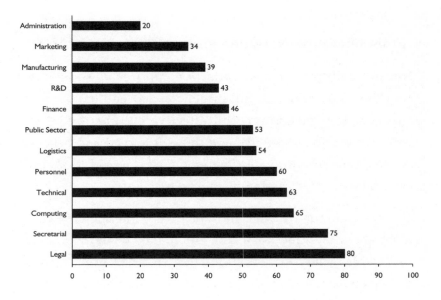

Figure 2.11 Average "neutral" score across functions

Variety in value differences

Entropy	Neutral–Affective
Lowest (most important variable)	Country
	Industry
	Job function
	Religion
	Corporate Climate/Culture
	Age
	Gender
Highest (least important variable)	Education

RECONCILING AFFECTIVE AND NEUTRAL CULTURES

Overly affective (expressive) and neutral cultures have problems in relating to each other. The more neutral person is easily accused of being ice-cold with no heart; the affective individual is seen as out of

Emotional Americans and grumpy Germans at AMD

Neutral cultures often see affective cultures as somewhat childlike and irrational, full of generalized enthusiasm and superficial sloganeering. And affective cultures often see neutral cultures as secretive and difficult to read and believe. So this difference in displaying emotions can lead to skepticism, a lack of trust, and ultimately to hostility.

Charles Hampden-Turner and Fons were interviewing Germans about the Americans with whom they would work in a new AMD facility to be built in Dresden. The Germans were feeling embarrassed by the jovial behavior that the Americans were displaying. "They tapped us on the shoulder and praised our good work. To be honest we know when our work is good. We don't need them to tell us that so frequently. At times it feels as though we are like second-hand cars."

The interviews with the Americans showed almost the opposite picture. "The Germans don't show what they feel easily, and if they do it is often so negative. They seem to like to complain a lot. And when we do good work they don't say anything as if it is normal to do so. This is not very motivating."

control and inconsistent. When such cultures meet, the first essential task for the international manager is to recognize the differences, and to refrain from making any judgments based on emotions, or the lack of them. Then the manager must respect that the other person has the right to behave the way that they do. Different cultures give different meaning to the display of emotions, which explains why there are differences between cultures.

The neutral rollercoaster in Japan

The traditional wooden rollercoaster ride has been a major attraction at funfairs for nearly a hundred years. In the last decade, promoters have sought to give even greater thrills with "white-knuckle rides." The engineering of such rides requires the design engineer to provide a series of accelerations and twists to excite with just enough respite to allow recovery immediately before the next thrill. Western joyriders scream and wave their arms to participate in the spirit of the experience.

Supported by modern electronics and safety features, this is now big business and specialist manufacturers from the US and Europe have sought to export their offerings. One such Californian company installed several of its rides in Japan. In spite of a well-proven design, Japanese riders continued to receive head injuries. Observation revealed that the Japanese were more likely to keep their heads low, leaning forward in a semi-bowed posture (thereby striking their heads on the bar designed to hold them in place) rather than adopting a more upright, arm-waving position. Expensive modifications were required that prevented head injuries – to the point where safety legislation in Japan now requires design solutions to take their relative neutrality into consideration. Their neutrality did not of course mean the were not experiencing the thrill; it's just that they were trying to control it by lowering their heads.

Kodak introduced an ad trading on "memories" which Americans love, but which the British saw as overly sentimental. Michael Porter said that Germans didn't know what marketing was about. In his American conception, marketing is about showing the qualities of your products without inhibition. Germans might see this as bragging, unacceptable unless you are selling second-hand cars. The degree to which you express positive things in Germany needs to be much subtler; a subtlety that might well have escaped Porter.

IT'S COOL TO BE EMOTIONAL

In *21 Leaders for the 21st Century,* we found some leaders to be very passionate and others to be very controlled. When we observe the expressive behavior of Richard Branson we have noticed that his colleagues praise him for having a very controlled attitude when necessary. On the contrary, colleagues of Michael Dell like to warn you about his passion, as normally he comes over as very controlled.

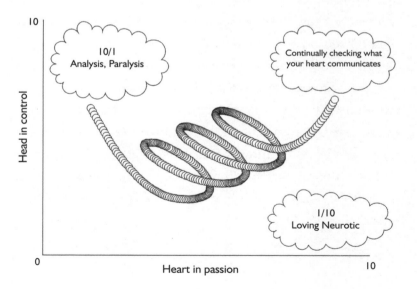

Figure 2.12　Cool to be emotional

This is a matter of reconciling through foreground or background. To be effective as an international leader, it does nor really matter what is in the foreground or in the background, as long as they are connected to each other.

CHAPTER 3

Further value dimensions

Let's look at the remainder of the value dimensions.

SPECIFIC VERSUS DIFFUSE

This cultural dimension concerns the degree of involvement in relationships. It deals with the degree to which we engage others in specific areas of life and single levels of personality, or diffusely in multiple areas of our lives and at several levels at the same time. In specific-oriented cultures, a manager segregates out the (specific) task relationship she or he has with a subordinate and isolates this from other matters. But in some cultures, every life space and every level of personality tends to permeate all others.

An example might help. If you asked someone why they had got married, they might answer "to get the best tax advantages." They would be from a specific culture, where marriage is concerned with the "specific" issue of maximizing tax allowances. If, on the other hand, they say "It was love, and the union of our two families," then they would be from a diffuse (and communitarian) culture. And it would obviously be reconciliation if they loved tax advantages too!

A specific culture is one where the majority believe in shareholder value. A diffuse culture is one where it's all about *Weltanschauung*; it's holistic. They would emphasize stakeholder value. Specific is analytic, and diffuse is holistic or synthetic.

Kurt Lewin, the famous German psychologist, said, "Americans are amazing people. They are very open. You hardly know them and they talk to you. How can the Americans be so open?" The answer is that Americans can be so open because they are specific, but they retain a privacy they keep to themselves. This is the peach model, easy to bite into, but you eventually hit the hard nut in the center.

What is public in America?

Figure 3.1   Specific versus diffuse: what is public and what is private?

Fons writes:

When I was in America, I had a friend who was a typical American and who helped me move apartments. At the end of the day we were both tired and I said "Bill, would you like a beer?" I turned around, but he was already in my refrigerator. For an American a refrigerator is a public space, for most Europeans it's private: "Don't go into my refrigerator!"

For the first three months, we didn't have a car, and, typically American, my friend would offer to lend me his whenever I wanted to borrow it. There is no way that this would have happened in Germany.

While in America, I often saw people move and leave their furniture behind; furniture is "public" (it has a specific functional meaning). This would be impossible in France. You can't get rid of furniture; it belongs to the family, its meaning is more than just a piece of furniture — it represents something about the family and its history.

According to Lewin, this leads to what we call specific relationships. If I relate to you and you relate to me, we have to give meaning to

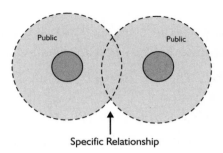

Specific Relationship

Figure 3.2 A Specific Relationship occurs between both partners interacting in their public space

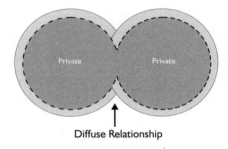

Diffuse Relationship

Figure 3.3 In a Diffuse Relationship, both partners share their public and private space

what this relationship is about. So you're not a human being; you're a human resource! This is what Kurt Lewin called the "U type." He was a German and called the diffuse orientation the "G type." In America, they will give you an academic title – "Dr" – but they only use it in the university. One step outside the university and people say "Hello Fons, Hello Peter;" inside, it's "Dr Trompenaars, Dr Woolliams". Even your title is specific to the situation. In Germany, although a better example is Austria, you are called "Doktor" everywhere: "Herr Doktor" at work, "Herr Doktor" in academia, "Herr Doktor" at the butchers. That is the opposite model.

So we can see the problems faced by Americans going to Europe or Asia and how the meaning they give to initial relationships stops at the border. In Europe and Asia, privacy is important. You are addressed as "Sie" and not "Du"; "vous" rather than "tu." But if you're in, you're in for life, and this is a diffuse relationship. "Herr Doctor" is not a specific label on a public life; "Herr Doctor" is you, defining your identity.

So what does this mean for business? Consider a meeting between Marketing and Research & Development. The R&D team have presented an idea to the marketing team, and the marketing people say "It's a lousy idea." What does that mean in the minds of the R&D team? Because R&D is a diffuse culture, the idea represents them, who they are. They don't separate their research ideas from their identity, so the marketing team have just offended R&D.

But the marketing team would never see it that way because they are very open. It's almost impossible to insult them, you can say anything about them because they won't take it personally, which is evidence of a specific culture.

What has happened here is that the marketing team have strayed into the "danger zone" of privacy by inadvertently moving into the

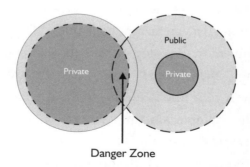

Danger Zone

Figure 3.4 Specific and Diffuse Encounters

private arena of the R&D team. For the marketing team, discussing ideas is a public matter. For R&D, it's private.

This is where the concept of "losing face" originates. Losing face is making public what is perceived as being private. And we all know how important it is to maintain face in countries like Japan and Spain.

The big problem between cultures is where a diffuse culture meets a specific one. A diffuse culture is recognized by indirect communication. This is a big difference between the British and the Americans. The Americans like to go straight to the point like the Dutch or Australians. In contrast, the English and Japanese are more subtle and indirect. If they think a proposal is bad, they might say "That's a very interesting presentation that needs more research." A Dutchman would say, directly, "This is really bad."

Here is an example of a diagnostic question that differentiates people on this dimension:

Your boss asks you to paint his house at the weekend. There are two arguments based on different value systems:

(a)   *You don't have to paint the house – that's specific, because the relationship you have with your boss is specific to the world of work, not his domestic situation.*

(b)   *"Yes, it's my boss, I have to do it." This is diffuse; your economic life and family depend on your boss, so you will help. Your relationship is more than just what you have in the office.*

With which statement do you agree?

Again, we find large variations across cultures from 91 percent who would not help the boss in Sweden to 32 percent in China (i.e., 68 percent would help their boss there). Some scores, such as that for Japan, where 71 percent said they would not help, didn't appear on the face of it to have validity, but further probing revealed that people in Japan tend not to paint their houses – they use wood treatments and other materials. This shows some of the difficulties of cross-cultural research. However, by using other diagnostic questions such as the following, we were able to again construct a database of countries along this dimension.

People have different opinions about how a job can be best done. Which way do you prefer?

(a)   The best job will be done if the people who work with you know you personally and accept you the way you are, both within and outside the organization.

(b)   The best job will be done if the people who work with you respect the work you do, even if they are not your friends.

Again the answers showed significant differences across countries.

SPECIFIC AND DIFFUSE CULTURES ACROSS AGE CATEGORIES

There are issues of convergence of cultures (what we have called, for example, "eurovergence") and differences between generations. In addition, we must allow for what simply happens as we grow older and more experienced in dealing with diversity, and presumably have traveled more, for both business and pleasure.

The overall trend from our database is that older managers and leaders become more specific. This may in part be due to our sample,

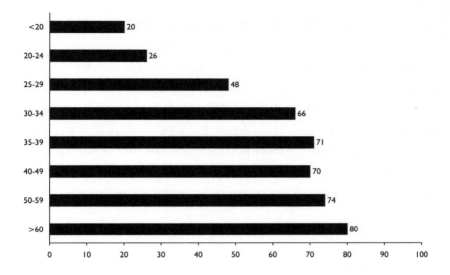

Figure 3.5 Average "Specific" score across age ranges

which is made up of business people, and may experience detachment from the family and its more diffuse dynamics.

Entropy	Specific–Diffuse
Lowest (most important variable)	Country
	Industry
	Religion
	Age
	Gender
	Education
	Job function
Highest (least important variable)	Corporate Climate/Culture

RECONCILING SPECIFIC AND
DIFFUSE CULTURES

We can observe this dimension in action in the various alliances between many of the major airlines. In our work with British Airways and American Airlines, we helped the parties recognize and respect different ways in which they define the relationship with their passengers. It is typically American to emphasize "core competencies" and "shareholder value." In contrast, British Airways emphasize service with hot breakfasts, champagne in some classes, and the like.

In this "One World" alliance the options were:

- "Serve the cattle with Coke and pretzels."
- Serve not only hot breakfasts but also add some massage, shoe polishing, and other extras and hence "go bankrupt on the flight."
- Compromise and serve hot pretzels, so it becomes certain that you will lose all the passengers.

Reconciliation here is the art of trying to define specifically those areas that provide a more personal service and deepen the relationship in the service being provided. Only this would work.

The success of the alliance will depend on this very reconciliation: the competency of the employees of the airlines to consistently choose those specific moments to deepen the relationship in the service being provided. A compromise – hot pretzels – will lead to a business disaster, and we have often seen them in alliances.

Some two years ago, Merrill Lynch (ML) was facing fierce competition from Charles Schwaab on the Internet. While ML's financial consultants were used to developing long-term and expensive relationships with their clients, Charles Schwaab decided to put its efforts into helping clients online. After a couple of years, ML saw a dramatic rise in market share go to the online traders. The specific services of the Internet were winning over the diffuse relationships, which were much more costly. After long deliberation, ML decided to introduce online trading but in a more subtle and sophisticated way than Schwaab. The sophistication lay in how they combined (reconciled) the different cultures of the Internet and the financial consultant.

First, the consultants mined their own Internet clients to identify those they could help further through more personal contact on the Internet. And conversely, regular clients were helped to install web cams allowing them to contact their consultant more quickly on the Internet; they were also able to access their own portfolios immediately online. ML created clicks that stuck. The market share has been regained with an improved fee structure.[3]

That's how the Internet can be used to deepen a relationship. Barnes and Noble sell more books online than Amazon.com, because they have bookshops. Reconciliation is the integration of both the specific and diffuse services.

ACHIEVED VERSUS ASCRIBED STATUS

All societies give certain members higher status than others, signaling that unusual attention should be focused upon such persons and their activities. Some societies accord status to people on the basis of their achievements whereas others ascribe status by virtue of age, class, gender, education, etc. The first kind we call achieved status and the second ascribed status. While achieved status refers to doing (what you do), ascribed status refers to being (who you are).

Achievement-oriented cultures will market their products and services on the basis of their performance. Performance, skill, and knowledge justify their authority.

Ascription-oriented cultures often ascribe status to products and services. In particular in Asia, status is attributed to those things which "naturally" evoke admiration from others, i.e., highly qualified technologies or projects deemed to be of national importance. The status is generally independent of task, specific function, or technical performance.

There are more implications in terms of the values given to authority and accountability. In achievement-oriented cultures, it is assumed that people in positions of authority will feel a sense of accountability for the accomplishments of an organization. This is based on the rationale that if someone is the boss, they must be there because they've earned the title and position. But in many cultures, positions of authority are natural consequences of who your family are, of having gone to the right school, having been born into the right class, or gender, or having seniority. So the fact that someone is in a position of authority doesn't necessarily mean that they will need to achieve, or be motivated to achieve the objectives of the organization to remain worthy of the position.

You can imagine how this can impact on personnel planning and career development if you are relying on managers in remote locations to prepare the groundwork for your efforts and to follow-up after training is delivered. In some ascribed cultures, this just won't work because the managers are not in their positions based on their achievements (as we define them in Western Society) and you can't simply replace them by managers who achieve results. Any such new management would be viewed by employees with ascribed status as having no status at all, no standing within the organization, and no credible authority.

This dilemma is obviously a great challenge when business partners have different traditions for how people move up the ladder in the organization. In achievement-oriented cultures, your position is best secured by what you deliver. In the worst case, you are only as good as your last performance. In ascribed cultures, seniority and long-term loyalty are very much more important.

We asked our 65,000 participants to give their opinion about the following statement:

The most important thing in life is to think and act in a manner that best suits the way you really are, even if you do not get things done.

The results are shown in Figure 3.6.

The issue therefore is how can one ever respect the status attributed to people whose whole society and history has been built on avoid-

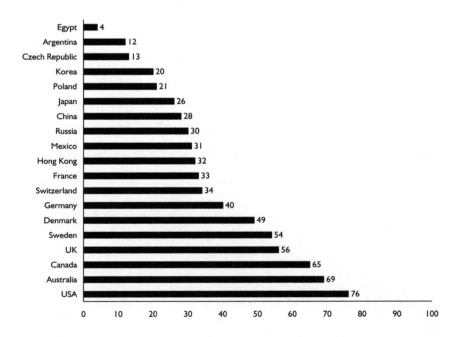

Figure 3.6 Percentage not agreeing with "acting as you really are"

ing these issues? We should not forget that large parts of "new" countries like Canada, the US, and Australia were built on people who left Europe (voluntarily or not) to avoid being judged on where they were coming from, their parentage, and social background.

In these countries, we ask people what are their own areas in which status is given to people (ascribed), rather than earned. One area that is very much shared by all cultures is that of being a parent. Children cannot easily fire you regardless of whether or not you do a good job! Most parents know that, and they would rather do well despite it; otherwise their children would be stuck with a mediocre environment. So we find in some cultures that attributed status gives you even more responsibility.

ACHIEVEMENT AND ASCRIPTION ACROSS HIERARCHICAL LEVELS

When we review our database across hierarchical levels, we can see that achievement orientation increases with seniority. Perhaps juniors or staff lower down the hierarchy see their seniors in terms of their status because they control (manage) them, and not just because of their pay; they may not be aware of what their seniors actually do or achieve. Whilst this is not surprising, the consistency is very high.

Entropy	Achievement–Ascription
Lowest (most important variable)	Country
	Industry
	Religion
	Job function
	Age
	Education
	Corporate Climate/Culture
Highest (least important variable)	Gender

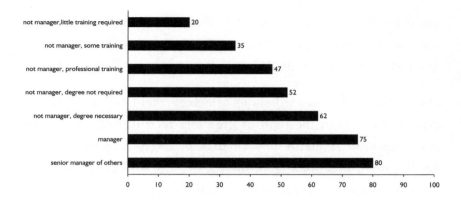

Figure 3.7 Mean score on "achievement orientation" across managerial hierarchical level

TOWARDS RECONCILIATION OF ACHIEVEMENT AND ASCRIPTION ORIENTATIONS

Despite far greater emphasis on either ascription or achievement in most cultures, the two usually develop together. Those who start by ascribing usually exploit their status to get things done and achieve results. Those who start by achieving usually begin to ascribe importance and priority to the persons and projects that have been successful. Hence all societies ascribe and all achieve after a fashion. It is once again a question of where a cycle starts. The international manager rides the wave of this dilemma.

We can see this particular dilemma – between the achieved and ascribed status – in action in the profit-oriented versus non-profit status of BUPA, reconciled successfully by Val Gooding. Should she set a goal of a 25 percent profit to shareholders to compete on the stock exchange, or make enough return to serve the sick and the weak? To care about the people you serve is a precursor to success and you must ascribe status to them. The provident status of BUPA reconciles the need to achieve business growth with providing primary health care. Care for your employees through a strong successful business base and they will pass that care on to the clients (patients, in the case of BUPA).

One of the classic reconciliations of achievement and ascription in organizations is in the field of graduate recruitment. We ascribe graduates with the status of "soon to be managers," rotate them into development positions, give them exposure and challenges and (unsurprisingly) see many of them attain the status and success they were intended to achieve. Critics call this a self-fulfilling prophecy, but there are many examples in education, business and sport where ascribing people with the probability of success helps them to achieve it.

Another example comes from Motorola. After working ten years for the company, one could not be fired unless the CEO put it in writing. Working that successfully at Motorola indicates great achievement. What happened to those people who got "tenure"? They worked even harder and demonstrated tremendous loyalty. It is perhaps because Motorola is traditionally a family company; families know that the best way to get achievement is to ascribe status to people.

The reconciliation is also captured in Robert K. Greenleaf's bestseller *On Becoming a Servant-Leader*. He explains that leaders who are open to discussing every action democratically run the risk of loosing their authority because every move has to be taken into consideration. This becomes "lost democratic leadership." On the other hand, once leaders insist on leading without being open to any input, blind followers become lemmings and all drop off the cliff together.

"Servant Leaders" will continuously gain authority by crafting decisions between their own viewpoints and the inputs emerging from

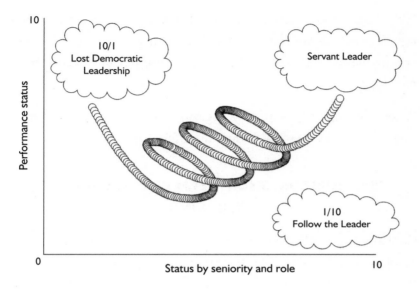

Figure 3.8 The servant leader

others. This type of leader leads through connecting great ascribed vision with the emerging viewpoints of their followers.

TIME ORIENTATION AND SEQUENTIAL VERSUS SYNCHRONOUS CULTURES

If only because managers need to coordinate their business activities, they require some kind of shared expectations about time. Just as different cultures have different assumptions about how people relate to one another, so they approach time differently. This orientation is about the relative meaning, and thereby importance, cultures give to a number of facets of time. These include how they give meaning to the past, present, and future and to the long- versus short-term. How we think of time has its own consequences. Especially important is whether our view of time is sequential, a series of passing events, or whether it is synchronic, with past, present, and future all interrelated so that ideas about the future and memories of the past both shape present action. Are you driven by the clock and arrive at the office at 8.30 a.m., because that is the start of the routine day, or do you arrive in sufficient time for the first important event, the first meeting?

When looking at how people organize time differently across cultures, we observe a wide variety of differences.

TIME HORIZON: SHORT-TERM VERSUS LONG-TERM THINKING

Consider this well-known joke. A Russian and a Spaniard are in discussion. The Russian asks the Spaniard about the typical Spanish trait, and the Spaniard explains the infamous *mañana* concept. The Spaniard is surprised by the resulting enthusiastic response and asks "Don't you have something like *mañana* in Russia?" The Russian replies, "Yes we do, but none of our expressions conveys that sense of urgency so well."

This little joke clearly shows very different senses of time. Indeed in some cultures, a sense of urgency seems to be replaced by a sense that all will fall into place if you're patient. Other cultures, on the contrary, believe that immediate action is called for.

Just reflect on what time sense you have when emphasizing shareholder value. Your time sense becomes shorter because performance is judged every quarter. The cutting judgment of short-term cycles determines how much you have contributed to the creation of value for shareholders – people who never share. Once stakeholder value is dominant in your thinking, your time horizon needs to widen.

The same influence can be seen across industries. If you work in high tech, where you know that your products are outdated before they hit the market, you develop a short time horizon. Compare this

The older the company, the better

A new European company was formed when two older companies merged in 1970, and that year was mentioned in their company brochure as the year the company was founded. When the organization started looking into the possibility of doing business in China, they had their brochure translated into Chinese and handed it out during every interaction with their Chinese contacts.

At a certain point, they learned that one of their potential joint venture partners was comparing them with their major competitor, who was also active in China. The Chinese counterpart commented that the competitor was almost twice as old and hence had much more experience. In actual fact, one of the ancestor companies of our company had been founded two decades earlier than the competitor and was also the inventor of the technology concerned. However, because the date of the merger was taken as the date that the present company had been founded, that part of the company history had not been included in the brochure. This kind of mistake can make the difference between success and failure for a company in China, so the company quickly produced a new brochure in Chinese .

with a finance manager of an oil company who has a 20-year depreciation schedule for the newly developed cat-cracker from an investment of US$1 billion.

In order to assess whether cultures are rather short- or long-term oriented, we asked the people on our database the following question:

Consider the relative significance of the past, present, and future. Indicate your relative time horizons for the past, present, and future:

7 =   *Years*

6 =   *Months*

5 =   *Weeks*

4 =   *Days*

3 =   *Hours*

2 =   *Minutes*

1 =   *Seconds*

My past started ☐ *ago, and ended* ☐ *ago.*

My present started ☐ *ago, and ends* ☐ *from now.*

My future starts ☐ *from now, and ends* ☐ *from now*

Among the respondents from our database, we found that Swedes and Finns are in the top quartile of long-termism. It may not be surprising that societies which have been dependent on their trees for so long have developed a long-term commitment to nature. It takes approximately 35 years for a tree to grow until it is ready for lumbering. In sharp contrast, in most cultures around the equator you chop a tree or pluck a fruit and it is replaced very quickly. Why worry about long-term planning? With a shorter-term horizon, we find many African and South American countries (where harvests are abundant in optimal conditions) next to North American cultures and Australia.

TOWARDS RECONCILIATION

One of the frequently recurring dilemmas we identified across cultures is that between a culture with a predominantly shareholder view of life versus one that believes in longer-term stakeholder value. For example, the Dutch-based company CSM had the temerity to declare stakeholder value in their core principles. This is understandable when one considers the cooperative culture stemming from their origin in the sugar industry. But one division was not at ease with this because they were the cash cow of the company producing most of its profit. The reconciliation CSM found in one of our workshops was as brilliant as it was simple and is shown in Figure 3.9

PAST, PRESENT AND FUTURE ORIENTATIONS

Cultures also differ in the way they give meaning to the past, present, and future. We adapted the following exercise from Cottle (1967), which we implemented in software on our web-based and interactive CD-ROM questionnaires.

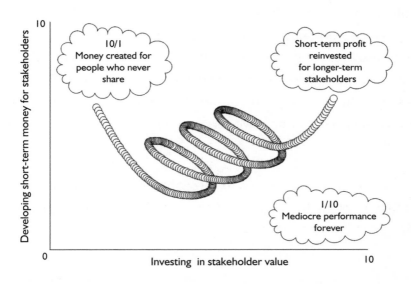

Figure 3.9 Short and long term – shareholders and stakeholders

Please consider the following question:

Think of the past, present, and future as being in the shape of circles.
Please draw three circles representing past, present, and future.
Arrange these circles in any way you want that best shows how you
feel about the relationship of the past, present and the future. You
may use different size circles.

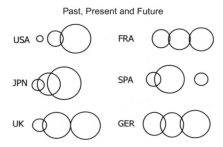

Past, Present and Future

Figure 3.10 Time orientation

This construct is based on a conceptual framework derived from St. Augustine who said "All this talk about past, present and future is nonsense because the only thing that exists is the present." But we have three "presents;" the present of the past, the present of the present, and the present of the future. The meaning we assign to the present depends on how we relate to the past, the present, or the future.

Our respondents have given us interesting insights into their views of time over the last 15 years of research. Here are some examples stemming from one meeting:

"I love this meeting because it's just like the meeting in Phoenix
back in '87. Now that was a great meeting."

"I love this meeting because I can use all the things I'm learning here just as soon as I get back to the office."

"I love this meeting because it's so enjoyable just being here, seeing old friends, meeting new people. This is the best group I know."

The meeting means different things to each person because each of them relates differently to time. We all live in the present, and however strongly we think about the past or the future, they don't exist. Of course, we all know the future doesn't exist (yet)! But many people forget that the past does not exist either. They say "Of course the past exists. Come to the middle of London and I'll show you some beautiful old buildings that have been preserved. They're a bit of the past living right now." But those buildings are actually part of the present. Why do we think those buildings are old? Because of the present state of the buildings. If this were the past they would be new.

Of course, we have moments where the present is much more affected by the future; when we're planning, for instance. And we have moments where the present is much more affected by the past. When making a presentation to clients, some cultures will emphasize the past by referring to projects they have already successfully completed as evidence of their capability. Future-orientated cultures will emphasize that the proposed project is new. For them the already-completed projects are not evidence of ability to complete the new project with its unknown problems. Rather, they would emphasize their project management control system to indicate how they would control the future and ensure the project was completed on time and within budget.

Our database shows these differences across functions (see Figure 3.11) as well as country differences (see Figure 3.10).

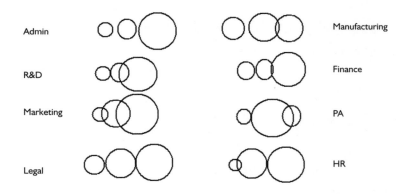

Admin

R&D

Marketing

Legal

Manufacturing

Finance

PA

HR

Figure 3.11   Past, present and future across functions

Let's consider the problems that arise when you're faced with the task of introducing strategic planning, goal setting, or management by objectives into cultures with different perceptions of time. Manufacturing or production departments might care less about planning for the future because the future has little or no bearing on their present. Any planning that they do is little more than reflecting on what might happen based on what they know from the past. They concentrate on getting the product out of the door, a very present-oriented activity. And the same is true for many sales departments; planning for anything longer than the current sales cycle is seen as waste of precious selling time.

On the other hand, consider the R&D department. R&D's only link to the present is how today's experiments will impact on the long-term expected outcomes, which always exist in the future.

Along with R&D, the marketing department is very future-oriented and spends half its time planning. And since marketing believes there will be a significant future, their planning consists of devising new paths and new possibilities.

SEQUENTIAL VERSUS SYNCHRONIC

We all recognize how different people organize their time in terms of schedules and activities and how much they do or don't keep to them. If you are in England or Switzerland, the members of a queue keep tacit watch on newcomers: if you were to sneak into the middle of a line the people queuing will indicate clearly that your turn will come in exactly the same place as it would have done had you joined the queue at the end.

And how do we keep appointments? We learn from time management courses that you should do the important and urgent things first. Deadlines are the same. But will a deadline and its urgency be treated in the same way around the globe?

The way we deal with time is often used by many to comment on cultural differences. In *Did the Pedestrian Die?*, Fons cited the French who often compare the Swiss to robots, planning all their activities by the clock, eating because it is 6.00 p.m., not because they are hungry. If you characterize the French as people who are always late, you hear other people say: "Oh, did you hear that?" These individuals do not understand that in most countries of the world it is normal to be late. It is only Northern Europeans and North Americans who characterize people with a flexible time orientation as "primitive and inefficient." A Frenchman once explained to us very clearly that the problem of being late was only a problem for people who were punctual. People who are always on time often don't know what to do when the person they are meeting arrives late. This type of person always loses time. And the French never do; they always have something else to get on with. You can never tell exactly when someone will arrive.

Edward Hall described the way the Swiss organize time as "monochrone," while the French are "polychrone." Monochronic

Appointments

Germans share a linear concept of time. This means that time is conceived of as a sequence of intervals, marked off by discrete points on a line leading from the past to the present and to the future. This requires the exact planning of dates and appointments, which are each accorded a fixed time slot. Schedules are therefore to be taken seriously and often supersede social and more personal obligations. The whole system tends to depend on each individual sticking exactly to their timetable, so that tolerance for delays and tardiness is very low.

On the other hand, if you make an appointment for 10.00 a.m., a Chinese counterpart will most likely remember that they have a meeting with you "in the morning." In this context, it is important to be aware that there may be other people who have requested a meeting in the morning. If they are Chinese, they probably won't have specified a time but will have simply scheduled an appointment "in the morning." Therefore, when you appear at 10.00 a.m., you may find your counterpart talking to a visitor who has just arrived. Depending on the status of your relationship with the counterpart, you may be asked to wait for a while or invited in to be introduced to the unknown party and take part in the conversation. Similarly, you may be lucky and find your counterpart unoccupied upon your arrival, but another appointment may walk in fifteen minutes later. This person will then be asked to wait or be invited to join you.

cultures organize time on a thin line and can only do one thing at a time. You can recognize people from these cultures when they are on the phone, because they will make gestures that you should not interrupt them. You can only do one thing in a focused way. Now look at Italy – you see Italians on the phone, having multiple conversations, sipping a cup of coffee, organizing themselves, all in parallel. Polychronic Italians are used to organizing time in a band consisting of parallel lines. That is why someone who has an appointment can arrive 30 minutes late without offering any excuse; the other party will always have something else to do. In Arabic cultures, it is important to pick the right day. Another way to recognize the difference is to look at the various eating and cooking habits. Monochronic cultures often have food that needs to be planned precisely; polychronic cultures love stews or beans (the longer they simmer the better they taste), or use almost-instant food like spaghetti.

In spite of the fact that these time differences are very familiar to us all, organizations frequently fail to recognize how they can seriously affect business across cultures, as the "Salami Case" illustrates.

"Anyone else want salami?"

In sequential cultures, customers take a number at the deli counter in the supermarket and wait their turn to be served. This is perceived as "fair" and is also efficient as customers can continue to browse while waiting, rather than just queuing.

In synchronic cultures, the assistant serves the first customer with the first item on their list (say salami) and then asks "Anyone else want salami?" The assistant thinks along the lines of "now, I have got the salami, who else can I serve at the same time?" This is also perceived as efficient. It is certainly sociable, as the people being served chatter to each other.

A global computer company, "ABC Inc.," has a successful software house based in the US, which has a long established series of systems in the area of Hotel Guest Management Systems (HGMS). These systems are based on a client server architecture with NT servers supporting client workstations. The user system provides a front end to an Oracle database server in each hotel. The existing systems are well de-bugged and have been operating successfully during the last three years for their most important client – a major hotel chain. All the existing installations are based in either the US, UK, or Northern Europe.

The hotel chain has recently taken over some 22 existing hotels in major cities in Italy and refurbished them to their corporate standards. They were advised by the local ABC dealer to purchase ABC Inc. computer hardware and the HGMS software as a turnkey solution. Although the subsequent check-out module performs according to the original specification, it is proving to be totally unsuitable in practice and the associated poor publicity and hotel guest dissatisfaction could prove damaging to the corporate image of ABC Inc. The head of small systems sales in Italy (an Italian) agrees that the system does not meet local needs and is concerned that Olivetti may steal not only this client, but future hotel business in Italy.

The problem occurs because of the way that hotel staff expect to operate the check-out system to satisfy customer needs. When checking out guest A, they ask for their room number and compile and print a list of extra charges as an invoice for the guest to verify. While guest A is studying this printed list, the hotel staff expect to be able to serve Guest B at the same time – to retrieve their record and begin some processing with record A still open.

However, the way the system is designed does not allow this. All views from the multi-access system are single on a given client, as systems transactions are based on a two-phase commit to maintain the referential integrity of the database inherent in the Oracle engine. Querying a customer account, closing the initial query, opening the next, etc., is tedious and has a slow response time. So in practice, customers can only be served sequentially. This causes frustration with local guests (Italians, etc.) but is acceptable if only American and/or Northern European guests are in the check-out queue.

TOWARDS RECONCILIATION OF TIME ORIENTATION

The international manager is often caught in the dilemma between the future and longer-term demands of the larger organization and the past experiences of the local population. The short termism that plagues Western and, particularly, American companies, is often driven by the needs of the stock markets for annual or quarterly results and profits. The risk of a strong future orientation derives from the failure to learn from past mistakes.

In Japan, we have seen the art of speeding up the sequence by synchronizing it. *Just in Time* manufacturing it is called. Again, it is the integration of opposites that guarantees the best result.

Entropy	Time (composite)
Lowest (most important variable)	Country
	Industry
	Religion
	Education
	Job function
	Age
	Gender
Highest (least important variable)	Corporate Climate/Culture

Bombarded by stimuli

This shows how the synchronic, overlapping Israeli discussion style can affect business consultants who relate to time sequentially.

An international organizational consulting company was hired by an Israeli corporation to work on a major project. They sent a four-person team to Israel. It consisted of two Germans, one Swede, and one North American. When they arrived in the country, they were joined by a fifth team member, an Israeli. Their task was to offer advice to the marketing department where a key team was experiencing serious difficulties. The consultants decided to gather preliminary data via group interviews. On the first day of the project, the five-member consulting team sat down in a conference room with seven members of the client team. They started with an open-ended question to the group. Three people answered at once and two other people interrupted them. The three people continued talking. This brought the total number speaking to five. The consultants were busy writing notes. Then a sixth team member turned to one of the German consultants with a question. Her question stimulated a second, and then a third, from two other team members. At this point, the consulting team members looked at each other and decided to call for a break.

During the break, all the non-Israeli members of the consulting team collapsed in their chairs, drinking coffee and looking stunned. One of the German consultants sat with his head in his hands and said "I can't deal with this. I have a headache. I feel overwhelmed. I can't focus. And, if three people are asking me a question at once, whom should I answer?" The second German, the Swede, and the North American agreed that they couldn't continue to gather data and organize their notes unless only one person spoke at a time.

The Israeli consultant was sympathetic but seemed surprised. He said, "I've been enjoying every minute of this group interview. I feel energized by their input. We're getting such rich data. If we just relax and listen, everything will fall into place."

INTERNAL VERSUS EXTERNAL CONTROL

The last dimension of culture in our model concerns the meaning people assign to their natural environment. Does a culture try to control or dominate nature, or submit to it?

Prior to the Renaissance, in fifteenth-century Europe, nature was seen as an organism.

People believed there was an environment and that the environment determined what human beings needed to do. Rotter described this as a locus of external control. The environment controls us rather than the reverse.

With the Renaissance this organic view of nature turned mechanistic. If you depict nature as a machine like Leonardo da Vinci did, you begin to realize that if you push here you can cause a reaction there. The more you push here and cause reactions there, the more you depict nature as a machine. Hence the idea developed that nature could be controlled. This is the mechanistic idea of nature, that the environment is something out there that we can control.

In cultures in which an organic view of nature dominates, and in which the assumptions are shared that man is subjugated to nature, individuals appear to orient their actions towards others. People become "other directed" in order to survive; their focus is on the environment rather than themselves, known as external control.

Conversely, other people who have a mechanistic view of nature, in addition to believing that man can dominate nature, usually take themselves as the point of departure for determining the correct course of action. This is an "inner-directedness," and is reflected through the current fashion of customer orientation. But organizations have to be very careful with this approach because it won't work in societies which don't believe in, or allow for, internal control. We have to remember that the external control model has a much older tradition than the newer Western mechanistic concept.

In the rest of the world, the external model is still very much in evidence. There is an illustrative story of two Russian fighter pilots who defected during the cold war. One flew his MiG fighter plane to Japan and one to the States. Now, what did the Americans do when they got that MiG? Right, they tore it apart. Within two days, no more MiG. But what did the Japanese do with theirs? They spent weeks just looking at it. They sat in the seats and they crawled into the engines to have a feel. Westerners say "Were they kidding? Why did they want to know how the engines felt?" It was to get into the nature of the machine, the soul of the machine, if you like. That's exactly how the Japanese created Kawasaki motorcycles. They looked at and rode on BMW bikes to see how they felt, then they improved on them.

Nature plays an important part in the functional departments of organizations. When one thinks of internally-controlled, mechanistic departments, one thinks of manufacturing, production, sales, and the typical US executive. These departments and individuals start by thinking that they can control the world around them, and act accordingly. But for externally-controlled departments, one thinks of R&D (especially in high technology) and many marketing departments. These take their cues from the environment outside themselves, and respond accordingly.

Although internal versus external locus of control is frequently cited, there are few existing frameworks that describe the balance or integration of internal and external control, although Deming's quality work comes closest. Deming (2000) points to the total system, not performance, as the key to quality. Inherent in this viewpoint is an acknowledgement of the "power of business" that needs to work within nature, not try to control it. This is exemplified by the post-war Japanese success in using Deming's philosophy. We get a good idea of the strength of this approach when applied in a appropriate cultural context.

We have found significant differences in locus of control between geographical areas. For this dimension, we used several forced-choice questions and asked managers to indicate the option they believed in more. Here's an example:

(a)   *What happens to me is my own doing*

(b)   *I often feel I cannot take control of the things that happen in my life*

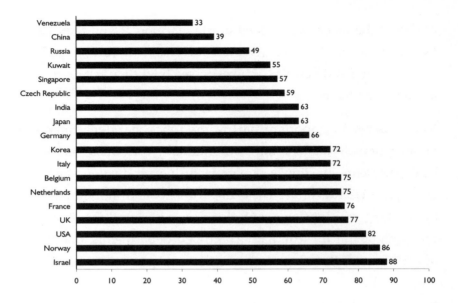

Figure 3.12 Internal versus external control: percentage selecting "what happens to me is my own doing."

Figure 3.12 shows the proportion who answered "a" (internal control).

Our database shows that Western cultures share extremely internally-controlled orientations. It is obvious that most Western managers are selected on the competence (false or not) that essentially any environment can be controlled, any market created, and any problem overcome by one's own doing. You market what we can produce, better known as technology push. Asians, who mostly come from externally-oriented cultures, are supremely equipped to be stimulated by signals from the markets. Correspondingly, they operate under the handicap of often not being the ones pushing the latest technological developments.

Thus the dilemma is between "selling what you can make" or "making what you can sell."

GENDER DIFFERENCES

The locus of control is one of the few value dimensions where men and women score with any significant difference across cultures. Both in the US as well as in Asia and Europe, males are significantly more inner-directed than females (see Figure 3.13).

Women seem to be more motivated by external stimuli while men seem to believe they are in control of their environment by superimposing their views on it.

We use a range of questions of which the following is an example to position people along this dimension:

Of the following two statements, which do you believe to be more in line with your reality?

(a)   *Becoming a great success is a matter of hard work; luck has little or nothing to do with it.*

(b)   *Becoming a great success often depends on being in the right place at the right time.*

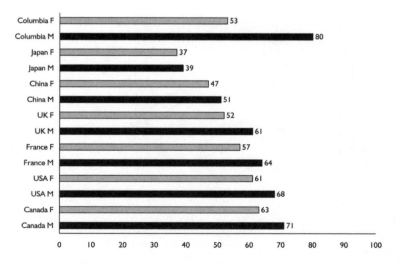

Figure 3.13   Gender differences – degree of internal control

Whilst men are equally divided, with 50 percent answering "a" and 50 percent answering "b," 58 percent of women answer "b" (more outer directed).

Entropy	Internal versus External
Lowest (most important variable)	Country
	Industry
	Job function
	Religion
	Gender
	Age
	Education
Highest (least important variable)	Corporate Climate/Culture

RECONCILING INTERNAL AND EXTERNAL CONTROL

The major issue at stake is to connect the internally-controlled culture, arising from the talent of technology push, with the externally-controlled world of market pull in order to achieve a culture of

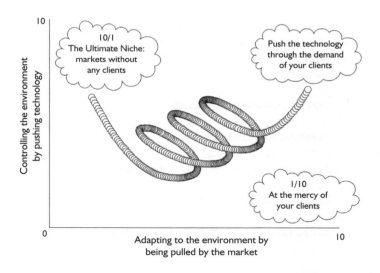

Figure 3.14 Push through pull

inventiveness. If we take a consumer electronics company like Philips, nobody will deny its great knowledge and inventiveness in its specific technologies and the quality of its marketing. The problem the company had faced was that its two major functional areas didn't seem to connect and communicate. The success of an organization is dependent on the integration of both facets. The push of technology needs to help to decide which markets you want to be pulled by. And the pull of the market needs to help you to know what technologies to push (see Figure 3.14).

YOUR OWN ORIENTATION ALONG THESE DIMENSIONS

Throughout chapters 2 and 3 we have sought to both explain each value dimension and demonstrate how these can describe cultural differences. After recognizing and respecting these differences, we can begin to reconcile them. You can usefully think about your own orientation along these dimensions and how your overseas business partners would score. Then think about where there are differences and ask yourself these questions: "What tensions do these differences produce?" and, thereby, "what dilemmas do I face because of these differences?"

You may not be aware of the differences, or maybe you and others have already been able to reconcile them. It is where these differences occur that you will be faced with dilemmas – and these you will have to reconcile. We offer our methodology as the route to the solution.

CHAPTER 4

Corporate culture

ultural factors in business derive not only from differences across national boundaries, but also from those within and between organizations. For many managers, the culture of their organization may dominate over national differences. Consider a young Japanese manager, who typifies Japanese thinking and values, working in Japan for a US company. When he gets promoted to a significant management grade, he travels the world, visiting the HQ in the US frequently. Now he spends his time working and interacting with peers, who may be of many different nationalities. It is not their country or nationality differences that dominate, but what they share in terms of the "way things are done in this organization." Their system of shared meaning is no longer from their countries of birth but from their shared way of working together, from making PowerPoint presentations to colleagues using an in-house style with corporate logos to using their own "corporate language," from talking in terms of short-term budgets (rather than longer-term Japanese thinking) to e-mail protocols and resource planning systems.

The corporate culture of the organization is now the driver. "Management of culture" is now about creating a corporate culture in which people will work together to achieve the organization's goals, reconciling dilemmas that originate from issues of corporate culture. Of course, this is not free of (national) culture. An organization in one part of the world with a society that ascribes status may choose an organization model that builds initially upon ascription rather than achievement. But what of the global company with a diverse workforce? And what is the link between corporate culture and business?

This chapter discusses how one can approach the role and assessment of organizational culture. The basic framework is to compare the current corporate culture with some idealized state as a means of eliciting the dilemmas which have to be reconciled. The ideal corporate culture is therefore discussed in the context of business goals and the dilemmas that it provokes.

DEFINING CORPORATE CULTURE

Organizational culture is an elusive concept, which has been summarized by Silvester, Anderson, and Patterson (1999). Definitions include a system of publicly and collectively accepted "meanings," which operate for a group at a particular time (Trice and Beyer, 1984); a pattern of "basic assumptions" developed as the group or organization learns to cope with its environment (Schein, 1996); and more simply as "the way we do things around here" (Deal and Kennedy, 1982). "Yet despite the numerous strategic and culture change programs that have been initiated by organizations in recent years, efforts directed at identifying specific, observable and therefore measurable features of organizational culture have met with far less success. Moreover, the transmission of cultural values also remains a neglected area in organizational psychology and whereas attempts have been made to measure culture at the team level, often called 'group climate,' there remains a dearth of research which focuses upon deeper strata of shared culture in work groups" (Silvester, Anderson, and Patterson 1999). The effect of this has been to mitigate the clarity with which organizational culture, and in particular culture change, is viewed.

Only recently have Hampden-Turner and Trompenaars (2000) revealed new generalizable frameworks based on their extensive research data that transcend these lower-order models.

THE ROLE OF CORPORATE CULTURE

Basic to understanding culture in organizations is that we can define culture as a series of rules and methods, which an organization has evolved to deal with the regular problems that it faces. Organizations face dilemmas in dealing with the tension between the existing set of values and the desired ones – or between partners of a merger or strategic alliance. While cultures differ markedly in how they approach these dilemmas, they do not differ in needing to make some kind of response. They share the destiny to face up to different challenges of existence. Once the leaders have become aware of the problem solving process, they will reconcile dilemmas more effectively and will therefore be more successful.

It is becoming more frequently recognized that organization development and business process reengineering have failed too often because they ignored aspects of (corporate) culture. However, simply "adding" the culture component does not suffice. This explains perhaps why culture is very often ignored. Values are not artifacts that can be added. They are continuously created by interactions amongst people and are not "just out there" like rocks. As such, culture is only meaningful in the context in which the members of an organization go about their daily work.

CORPORATE CULTURE IN MERGERS, ACQUISITIONS, AND STRATEGIC ALLIANCES

Globalization through mergers, acquisitions, and strategic alliances is big business – currently well over US$2,000 billion annually. They are sought after more than ever, not only for the implementation of globalization strategies but as a consequence of political, monetary, and regulatory convergence. Even so, two out of three deals don't achieve anywhere near the expected benefits that prompted the venture (Trompenaars and Woolliams, 2001).

It is common to acquire an organization with less concern for full integration simply to purchase its inherent value. Increasingly however, motives originate from a range of other expected benefits, including synergistic values (e.g. cross-selling, supply chain consolidation, and economies of scale) or more direct strategic values (to become market leaders, penetrating a ready-made customer base, etc.). The emphasis in the pre-deal and post-deal management is too often focused on seeking to exploit the new opportunities quickly under a mechanistic systems or financial due-diligence mindset (KPMG Consulting, 1999).

It is assumed that the task to deliver the benefits is to align the technical, operational, and financial systems and market approaches.

Our research reveals that the underlying failure to deliver the real benefits arises from the absence of a holistic, structured, methodological framework. Because of this, senior management does not know what to integrate or what types of decision are important in order to deliver the anticipated benefits. Whilst any integration program should be based on operational matters where the benefits are being sought, much more attention and resource needs to be given to managing the cultural differences between the new partners. Relational aspects like cultural differences and lack of trust turn out to be responsible for 70 percent of alliance failures. This is even more striking when we realise that building trust is a cultural challenge in itself. Lack of trust is often caused by different views of what constitutes a trustworthy partner. In addition, intercultural alliances involve differences in corporate cultures as well as national cultures. Problems can be due to more or less "objective" cultural differences, but also to perceptions about each other, including perceptions of corporate and national culture.

HR has a major role to play. Consideration must be given to leadership styles, management profiles, organizational structures, working practices, and a wide range of perceptions in and of the market place. In short, culture is pervasive. Even when strategists and senior managers recognise the importance of culture, frustration continues because until now they have had no means of assessing or quantifying its causes and effects, or of taking relevant effective action.

Based on our extensive experience working with client companies involved in such mergers and alliances, we have developed a new methodology that we call Cultural Due Diligence. This provides an operational framework in order that the consequences of corporate culture clash can be made explicit and thereby reconciled to ensure benefit delivery. It is again based on the three 'R's: Recognition, Respect and Reconciliation.

MAJOR TENSIONS ORIGINATING IN CORPORATE CULTURE

Much of our inductive thinking owes its origin to our portfolio of effective diagnostic and analytical tools and models, and the large and reliable database we have established. This enables either us to facilitate or let organizations themselves diagnose the tensions they are facing.

Structure is a concept that is frequently used in the analysis of organizations and many definitions and approaches are to be found. Our interest here is in examining the interpretations employees give to their relationships with each other and with the organization as a whole. Organizational culture is to the organization what personal (seven dimensions model) culture is to the individual – a hidden yet unifying theme which provides meaning, direction, and mobilization and that can exert a decisive influence on the overall ability of the organization to deal with the challenges it faces.

Just as individuals in a culture can have different personalities while sharing much in common, so too can groups and organizations. It is this pattern that is recognized as "corporate culture." Corporate culture has a profound effect on organizational effectiveness, because it influences how decisions are made, human resources are used, and how the organization responds to the environment.

We can distinguish three aspects of organizational relationships whose meaning is dependent on the larger culture in which they emerge:

1. the general relationships between employees in the organization;

2. the vertical or hierarchical relationships between employees and their superiors or subordinates;

3. the relationships of employees in the organization as a whole, such as their views of what makes it tick and what its goals are.

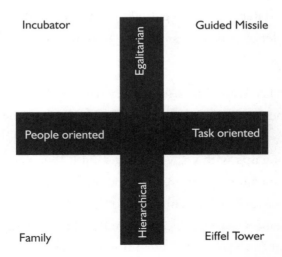

Figure 4.1   Four culture types

Our model identifies four competing organizational cultures that are derived from two related dimensions:

- Task or Person (high versus low formalization)
- Hierarchical or Egalitarian (high versus low centralization)

Combining these dimensions gives us four possible culture types, as shown in Figure 4.1.

THE EXTREME STEREOTYPES OF CORPORATE CULTURE

The Incubator

This culture is like a leaderless team. This person-oriented culture is characterized by a low degree of both centralization and formalization. In this culture, the individualization of all related individuals is one of the most important features. The organization exists only to serve the needs of its members.

An Incubator organization has no intrinsic values beyond these goals; the organization is an instrument to the specific needs of the individuals in the organization. Responsibilities and tasks within this type of organization are assigned primarily according to the member's own preference and needs. Structure is loose and flexible and control takes place through persuasion and mutual concern for the needs and values of other members.

Its main characteristics are:

- person oriented
- power of the individual

- self-realization
- commitment to oneself
- professional recognition.

The Guided Missile

This task-oriented culture has a low degree of centralization and a high degree of formalization. This rational culture is, in its ideal type, task and project oriented. "Getting the job done" with "the right person in the right place" are favorite expressions. Organizational relationships are very results oriented, based on rational/instrumental considerations and limited to the specific functional aspects of the people involved.

Achievement and effectiveness are weighed above the demands of authority, procedures, or people. Authority and responsibility are placed where the qualifications lie, and they may shift rapidly as the nature of the work changes. Everything in the Guided Missile culture is subordinated to an all-encompassing goal.

The management of the organization is predominantly seen as a continuous process of solving problems successfully. The manager is a team leader, the commander of a commando unit, in whose hands lies absolute authority. This task-oriented culture, because of its flexibility and dynamism, is highly adaptive but at the same time is difficult to manage. Decentralized control and management contribute to the shortness of channels of communication. A task-oriented culture is designed for a rapid reaction to extreme changes. Therefore matrix and project types of organizations are favorite designs for the Guided Missile.

Its main characteristics are:

- task orientation
- power of knowledge/expertise
- commitment to tasks
- Management by Objectives
- Pay for Performance.

The Family

The Family culture is characterized by a high degree of centralization and a low degree of formalization. It generally reflects a highly personalized organization and is predominantly power-oriented. Employees in the Family seem to interact around the centralized power of father or mother. Power is based on an autocratic leader who, like a spider in a web, directs the organization.

There are not many rules and thus there is little bureaucracy. Organizational members tend to be as near to the center as possible, as that is the source of power. Hence the climate inside the organization is highly manipulative and full of intrigue. In this political system, the prime logic of vertical differentiation is hierarchical differentiation of power and status.

Its main characteristics are:

- power-orientation
- personal relationships
- entrepreneurial
- affinity/trust
- power of person.

The Eiffel Tower

This role-orientated culture is characterized by a high degree of formalization together with a high degree of centralization and is symbolically represented by the Eiffel Tower. It is steep, stately and very robust. Control is exercised through systems of rules, legalistic procedures, assigned rights and responsibilities. Bureaucracy and the high degree of formalization makes this organization inflexible. Respect for authority is based on the respect for functional position and status. The desk has depersonalized authority.

In contrast with the highly personalized Family, members of the Eiffel Tower organization are continuously subordinated to universally applicable rules and procedures. Employees are very precise and meticulous. Order and predictability are highly valued in the process of managing the organization. Duty is an important concept for an employee in this role-orientated culture. It is duty one feels within oneself, rather than an obligation one feels towards a concrete individual.

Procedures for change tend to be cumbersome, and the role-orientated organization is slow to adapt to change.

Its main characteristics are:

- role-orientation
- power of position/role
- job description/evaluation
- rules and procedures
- order and predictability.

DIAGNOSING CORPORATE CULTURE WITH OUR CCAP

In the process of managing change it is of utmost importance to diagnose the current culture in which the organization operates. As Cameron and Quinn (1999) observe: "Unfortunately, people are unaware of their culture until it is challanged, until they experience a new culture, or until it is made overt and explicit through, for example, a framework or model." Measurements and assessment using our model of four corporate cultures have been based on our Corporate Culture Assessment Profile (CCAP) questionnaire; you can review examples of questions from this CCAP tool on the Culture for Business website (www.cultureforbusiness.com). The CCAP questionnaire has been constantly refined to achieve statistically significant levels of reliability and consistency, and we use this to chart both current and ideal cultures along some important managerial values. For strategic alliances and proposed mergers, we chart the corporate cultures of the aspiring partners. Our four corporate ideologies are based on well-grounded research ranging from Harrison to Handy, and Cameron and Quinn.

These enable management to appreciate the set of values in use and contrast them with the espoused or desired organizational values.

The CCAP is designed so that it measures some basic organizational processes ranging from leadership styles, decision making, business models, and the way people work in teams.

No real organization comprises exactly and completely any one of the extreme stereotypes. The profiles seek to show the relative contributions of each. In most profiles of real organizations, some contribution of all components is present to a greater or lesser degree. The interest lies in which is the most dominant or in which two quadrants dominate.

In order to triangulate our questionnaire results, key players (leaders, change agents, internal consultants) are interviewed either face-to-face or through our WebCue™ range of interactive web pages. We engage senior management in "guided fantasies" such as asking them to represent their current organization as an animal, car, or famous television personality and to state the reasons why. On the basis of these diverse inputs we assemble a picture of their dominant cultural profile(s) that is subsequently codified in a feedback report to the key players.

Research data from our 65,000 case database reveals that the dominant current, as well as ideal, state is the task-oriented Guided Missile. However after controlling for the different sizes of our samples (Dutch, US, and UK samples are the largest) we see that the distribution changes significantly.

What the current and ideal corporate culture is seems to be related to a wide range of factors. At the detailed level, there are frequently recurring differences across industries, functional areas, generations, genders, and the propensity to encourage and enable innovation.

The corporate culture model also has links with the personal seven dimensions model explained in Chapters Two and Three. Thus the relationship between employees in the Family or Incubator tends to be diffuse and in the Eiffel Tower and Guided Missile it is more specific. Status is ascribed more in Family and Eiffel Towers, while Guided Missile and Incubator organizations are more achievement oriented.

In order of increasing entropy (decreasing importance) the following tensions are found most often on our database:

Current	Ideal	
Guided Missile	Incubator	scenario 1
Eiffel Tower	Guided Missile	scenario 2
Family	Guided Missile	scenario 3
Eiffel Tower	Incubator	scenario 4
Family	Incubator	scenario 5
Incubator	Guide Missile	scenario 6

Managing organizational cultural differences is thus concerned with answering two basic questions.

1. What are the dilemmas that will derive from the tensions between the current and ideal corporate culture?

2. How can these dilemmas be reconciled?

Using our web-based interview techniques – WebCue™ – we have invited members of a large number of client organizations to elicit and delineate their dilemmas. We have collected over 7,500 such responses and find that they can be clustered into a number of recurring dilemmas. As expected, different categories of dilemmas arise for the different scenarios. We are therefore able to review these aspects of organizational culture based on what we have found with actual clients. The tensions from each scenario are generalized from

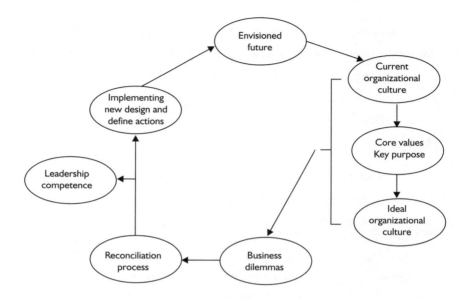

Figure 4.2 Flow of cultural change process

real client situations to avoid ethical issues and matters of confidentiality. Figure 4.2 is a representation of the process, but the entry point one chooses is culturally dependent.

Without doubt, survival of the business is ultimately the responsibility of the leadership of the organization (Schein, 1997). Not just the responsibility of the very top, but also the responsibility of all those who are able to connect actions with the survival of any particular organizational activity: it is "multiple leadership" (Pettigrew, 1985).

In some respects, the pervasive nature of implicit culture can make it difficult to manage. Even at the explicit level, traditional practices become enshrined as "sacred cows" that cannot easily be challenged. In an ideal world we would go back and challenge the implicit values behind each of these explicit constructs in order to check whether they were still the best way of delivering and reinforcing those values. When the products of culture become sacred cows they can inhibit survival, growth, and change. This is especially important when importing your sacred cows to new cultures.

As the culture of an organization is often "owned" and lived at the highest level, managers can feel they have little ability to influence the real culture of the organization in a material way without some top-down action.

We might summarize these extremes by saying that on the one hand we need to change the corporate culture to be convergent with our new business mission, while, on the other hand, we need to develop a new business mission that is compatible with our existing corporate culture.

THE ENVISIONED FUTURE

This is what the organization aspires to become, to achieve, to create – something that will require progress to attain. The more specific BHAG (Big, Hairy, Audacious Goal) is a bold mission to stimulate progress. It needs to be clear and compelling and serves as a unifying focal point of effort. It should be able to engage people by being tangible, energizing, and highly focused. A "vision-level" BHAG applies to the entire organization. Setting it 10–30 years in the future requires thinking beyond the current capabilities of the organization and the current environment. It forces an executive team to be visionary rather than just strategic or tactical. It should not be a sure bet, but the organization must believe that it can reach the goal anyway.

In our professional practice we have found that the development of a "vivid description" translates the vision into rich pictures (both vibrant and engaging), creating an image people can carry around in their heads. Once we have attained a level of passion, emotion, and conviction, we are ready to transcend the value side of the equation.

MAPPING CORPORATE CULTURE TO THE BUSINESS FUTURE

All the inputs of the envisioned future – core values and key purpose and between current and ideal corporate cultures – form the ingredients that are available to stimulate management to think about what basic dilemmas they need to resolve in seeking to manage tensions that owe their origin to issues of corporate culture.

We often invite our participants to frame the tensions they feel in actual business life and then relate them to the tensions they feel between current and ideal cultures. For example, as an actual business tension it is felt that: "Our organization is so much focused on next-quarter results, we don't have enough time to be creative and come up with our next generation of innovations." This example would translate as the current corporate culture being a Guided Missile and the dominant espoused profile, an Incubator.

We often find that an extant organizational culture has developed because the context best suited the main dilemmas their leaders were facing in business. For example, an Incubator culture is often the result of a leader who strives for a core value of entrepreneurship and innovation while having an envisoned future of becoming the most groundbreaking organization in the field of cross-cultural management thinking and consulting. A Guided Missile culture is a much better suited context for leaders who want to help clients gain the highest return on their investments in the financial services sector, holding a core value of integrity and transparency.

But business environments and challenges are changing continuously. Once an organizational culture has established itself, it creates new dilemmas (or its changing environment will) on a higher level. For example, a dominant Incubator culture can create a business environment where many innovative ideas are born but where the management and commercialization of these draws on aspects of a more market-sensitive and directed Guided Missile culture. Conversely, a dominant Guided Missile Culture can lead to an environment where employees are so much guided by their market price that it needs a Family culture to create the necessary longer-term vision and commitment.

First we capture the lists of what the key members of the organization (usually the top 25–50 leaders) want more of or want to keep of their current culture and of their ideal culture. Subsequently we ask them to select, in groups of five or six people, the three top current and ideal values, roles and/or behaviors in the light of both the envisioned future and the core values and key purpose. We ask a representative of each group to share their selections to the other groups upon which we select four or five values/behaviors on both current and ideal corporate profiles. Again we emphasize that the selection is done in the light of an envisioned future and core ideology. By doing this we assure that the selection of values and behaviors is done in a business context.

We present the results of this step in the following way:

On the one hand we want more of and/or to keep the following values and behaviors of our current organization:	On the other hand we need to develop the following values and behaviors for supporting our envisioned future and core values:
1.	1.
2.	2.
3.	3.
4.	4.
5.	5.

The lists are presented to the full group and again we split them into syndicates of five or six participants, this time with the request that they formulate two fields of tension (dilemmas) that are crucial for them to reconcile for critical success in view of the envisioned future. We make sure that the formulation of the horns of the dilemma are both equally desirable and are linked to business issues.

Here are some examples:

- "On the one hand, we need to focus on reliable technology [typical for a dominantly Eiffel Tower Culture], whilst on the other, we need to be constantly informed by our main customers [typical for one dominantly Guided Missile]."
- "On the one hand, we need to mentor and coach our young graduates for constant learning [Incubator], whilst on the other hand, we need to focus on the income of this quarter [Guided Missile]."
- "On the one hand, we need to develop and sustain a loyal workforce and thrive on rapport [Family], whilst on the other hand, we need to be able to judge their performance based on report [Guided Missile]."

It is crucial to this process that the chosen dilemmas are well formulated and support the crucial business challenges the organization is facing. Finally we ask the full set of participants to select four or five key dilemmas from which they can choose the one they want to reconcile in the next step.

Whilst this process assumes the availability and commitment of all appropriate leaders and managers, we can also accelerate this process – for example if those that need to be involved are spread across the globe. In this case we review the raw dilemmas from our web-based interviews. This enables us to identify the common features and underlying constructs that underpin them. We are therefore able to apply clustering or factor-like analysis, to reduce these to a representative set of "golden" dilemmas, which are, in effect, the tensions commonly held by the senior management team.

FREQUENTLY RECURRING DILEMMAS

All scenarios for different transformations appear in practice. Based on our research and consulting, we now list the frequently recurring dilemmas for different possible combinations. For completeness, we show all combinations, although as can be expected and as indicated above, some occur more frequently than others. We also suggest initial ideas on how each dilemma could be reconciled.

Transformation away from an Eiffel Tower (Transformations 1–3)

In many of our (organizational) culture profiles we see a shared desire to get away from the Eiffel Tower type of culture. Today, fairly highly-developed hierarchical thinking needs to become more egalitarian and formalized sets of rules need to become guidelines in which people are empowered. There's nothing wrong here, but this logic didn't seem to work in the early stages of a process where the US-based semiconductor manufacturer AMD opened a plant in Dresden in the former East Germany.

Could the Silicon Valley spirit of passion, time pressure, and doing the impossible with a limited number of people be brought to life in a region that lived for decades under the communist system? Here was a chance to put this commitment to the ultimate test. Would the formula work in this context? How would the different cultures work with each other?

A famous German (Eiffel Tower) to American (Guided Missile) dilemma is the distinction between solving problems by reasoning and logical insight on the one hand, or by empiricism and pragmatism on the other. From the German perspective, the Americans were too often, in team meetings, discussing this or that initiative. They kept changing tack and trying something new, instead of keeping to agreed avenues of inquiry. They rarely spent any time alone thinking through their problems and coming to rational conclusions.

The tension here is between the high-risk pragmatism favored by task-oriented Americans and the lower-risk rationalism favored by role-oriented Germans. From the German point of view, the Americans "shoot from the hip" without taking careful aim, whereas German engineers, coming as they do from expert cultures, like to solve problems by rational means. In extreme cases, the Americans might criticise the German engineers for "Paralysis by Analysis." You don't have forever to find solutions when problem definitions are changing quickly.

The joke about centralized planning was that it spawned local improvisation on a massive scale because the plans were so rigid. The value that the AMD Dresden team strove to endorse was that of Systematic Experimentation. The systematic part was designed to appeal to German rationality and the experimental element to American pragmatism (and improvisation). What works pragmatically is retained. What fails is discarded. Rationality remains crucial in providing insights into what works and what does not. This holds true even more for painstaking systematic experimentation, and that provides an example of how to change an Eiffel Tower into a reconciled Guided Missile culture. It enabled AMD Dresden to beat Intel – for the first time in history – when launching the 1 GHz chip.

Transformation 1

Current   **Ideal**

Eiffel Tower   Guided Missile

Typical Dilemmas

Leadership	authority ascribed to the role versus depersonalized authority by task
Reconciliation:	attribute the highest authority to those managers who have refocused their goals to the reliable application of expertise as a prime criterion
Management	expertise and reliability versus consistent goal-orientation around task
Reconciliation:	make reliable expertise and long-term commitment part of the task description
Rewards	increasing their expertise in doing a reliable job versus contribution to the bottom line
Reconciliation:	experts use their knowledge to fulfill very clearly set goals

Transformation 2

Current   **Ideal**

Eiffel Tower   Family

Typical Dilemmas

Leadership	authority is ascribed to the role versus authority is personally ascribed to the leader
Reconciliation:	leadership needs to understand the political aspects of the technical activities they manage. They become *servant leaders* of relationships.
Management	the power of expertise and reliability versus the power of politics and know-who
Reconciliation:	focus crucial systems and procedures so they support the process of management

Rewards	increasing their expertise in doing a reliable job versus rewarding long-term loyalty
Reconciliation:	members apply their expertise and fulfillment of reliable roles to the advantage of increasing the power and status of their colleagues.

Transformation 3

Current	**Ideal**
Eiffel Tower	Incubator

Typical Dilemmas

Leadership	authority is ascribed to the role versus negation of authority
Reconciliation:	to hold the experts responsible for the reliability of their innovating output
Management	the power of expertise and reliability versus the power of learning around innovation
Reconciliation:	decentralize the organization into more expert centers where roles are described in a very sharp way and aimed at learning and innovation.
Rewards	increasing their expertise in doing a reliable job versus intrinsic reward of self-development
Reconciliation:	experts use their knowledge systems and procedures to fulfill clearly described innovation outputs.

Transformation away from a Guided Missile culture (Transformations 4–6)

The challenge is to find an approach that will be effective when the surrounding culture is not compatible with this type of logic. As Fons explained in *Did the Pedestrian Die?*, we remember an American manager of Eastman Kodak who had launched a very successful program in Rochester, New York. After launching the same formula in Europe he cried on our shoulders. He complained of the inflexibility of the French and Germans, saying he had done a whole round in Europe and within each of the countries many had seemed supportive. The Germans had some problems with the process, wanting to know all the details of the procedures and how they were connected to the envisioned strategy. The French had been worried about the unions and keeping their people motivated, but he had left with the idea that all were agreed on the approach. When he came back some three months later to check how the implementation was going, nothing had been started in either France or Germany.

Anyone with a little sensitivity for cross-cultural matters could have predicted this. Germans often believe in vision, but without the proper structures, systems, and procedures that make this vision live, nothing will happen. Germans have a "push" culture. You push them in a certain direction. They are not so easily "pulled" in a particular direction compared to North Americans.

This example demonstrates that transformations from one single corporate culture to another are not linear or one way only. Transforming away from the Guided Missile to the Incubator is one step in an oscillation that may then return to the Guided Missile – to deliver results. Thus it may be better to describe the ideal culture as a "Guided Incubator" in which the two are reconciled. Such cyclical transitions are discussed further in Chapter Five.

Transformation 4

Current	Ideal
Guided Missile	Incubator

Typical Dilemmas

Leadership	depersonalized authority by task versus development of creative individuals

Reconciliation:	attribute the highest authority to those managers that have innovation and learning a prime criterion in their goals
Management	consistent goal-orientation around task versus the power of learning
Reconciliation:	make learning and innovation part of the task description
Rewards	extrinsic reward job done versus intrinsic reward self-development
Reconciliation:	describe task in terms of clearly described innovation outputs

Transformation 5

Current	**Ideal**
Guided Missile	Family

Typical Dilemmas

Leadership	depersonalized authority by task versus authority personally ascribed to the leader
Reconciliation:	attribute the highest authority to those managers that have made internalization of subtle processes a prime criterion in their goals
Management	consistent goal-orientation around task versus the power of politics and know-who
Reconciliation:	make political sensitivity part of the task description
Rewards	extrinsic reward job done versus reward long-term loyalty
Reconciliation:	describe task in terms of loosely described long-term outputs

Transformation 6

Current	**Ideal**
Guided Missile	Eiffel Tower

Typical Dilemmas

Leadership	depersonalized authority by task versus authority ascribed to the role
Reconciliation:	attribute the highest authority to those managers that have made reliable application of expertise a prime criterion in their goals
Management	consistent goal-orientation around task versus expertise and reliability
Reconciliation:	make reliable expertise and long-term commitment part of the task description
Rewards	contribution to the bottom line versus increasing their expertise in doing a reliable job
Reconciliation:	describe task in terms of expertise and reliability in its application

Transformation away from an Incubator culture (Transformations 7–9)

More than 90 percent of the world's business today originates from an informal- and person-oriented climate that the individual founder has created. Therefore the transformation from this incubator type of culture to other ones with increased formality and depersonalisation is quite relevant; when the founder of a family business takes off and grows the business, you often see two main paths taken. First the business grows through adding family members. You hear dilemmas like: "On the one hand, we need a creative environment where one is free in expression and movement, while on the other hand, there needs to be some order and respect for authority so we can build a long term future." The main dilemmas from the Incubator to the Family have to do with a respect for authority that is personalized and the loyalty that comes with it.

The second major path is from an Incubator to a Guided Missile culture. Here dilemmas unfold in the area of formalization, such as: "On the one hand, we appreciate the informal and personalized learning environment, on the other hand, we need to get our products and services to market." The Incubator is very often focused on the learning and development of its members, whilst in the Guided Missile this learning has to be applied to the increase of revenue. Another dilemma occurs around values. The corporate values of the Incubator are often held and continuously expressed by the company founder, whilst in the Guided Missile values are more often formalized and expressed in codified media such as posters and the like.

Transformation 7

Current   **Ideal**

Incubator   Guided Missile

Typical Dilemmas

Leadership	development of creative individuals versus depersonalized authority by task
Reconciliation:	attribute the highest authority to those managers that have innovation and learning a prime criterion in their goals
Management	job enrichment and personal development versus consistent goal-orientation around task
Reconciliation:	make learning and innovation part of the task description
Rewards	intrinsic reward self development versus extrinsic reward job done
Reconciliation:	describe task in terms of clearly described innovation outputs

Transformation 8

Current   **Ideal**

Incubator   Family

Typical Dilemmas

Leadership	negation of authority versus authority is personally ascribed to the leader
Reconciliation:	get the support of the leaders so they underline themselves the importance of learning and creativity. They become *servant leaders* of learning
Management	the power of learning around innovation versus the power of politics and know-who
Reconciliation:	celebrate the achievements of the present learning environment, to take the best practices from them, personalize them and make them historical events
Rewards	intrinsic reward self development versus reward long-term loyalty
Reconciliation:	members are personally held accountable for the long term commitment to the company

Transformation 9

Current	Ideal
Incubator	Eiffel Tower

Typical Dilemmas

Leadership	negation of authority versus authority is ascribed to the role
Reconciliation:	to hold the innovators responsible for the reliability of their output
Management	the power of learning around innovation versus power of expertise and reliability
Reconciliation:	decentralize the organization into more learning centers where roles are described in a very sharp way and aimed at learning and innovation
Rewards	intrinsic reward self development versus increasing their expertise in doing a reliable job
Reconciliation:	use creativity and knowledge to build reliable systems and procedures enabling them to become even better in their creations

Transformation away from a Family culture (Transformations 10–12)

This is a situation we have observed frequently where dilemmas arise for Western organizations in their effort to globalize their activities. Consider an American organization that thinks its Singaporean management takes too long to make a decision. All that consensus is fine, but it doesn't serve well in times of urgency. On the other hand, the Singaporeans think that the Americans make decisions too fast and with insufficient thought, which therefore – no wonder – leads to problems during implementation, partly because too few people have been consulted.

In contrast, we can all recognize the "quick-on-their-feet managers" who induce a "follow me, follow me" attitude. On the other extreme, we have observed Asians spending far too much of their time involving all kinds of ranks to gain consensus.

The organization culture paradigm that reconciles these extremes is best described by the notion of the servant leader, as previously described. In this person you would find the parent figure that is so popular in both Latin and Asian cultures. He (stereotypically a "he") acquires his authority from the way he serves his team through formulating and specifying the tasks of his colleagues with rigor and clarity.

Transformation 10

Current   **Ideal**

Family   Incubator

Typical Dilemmas

Leadership   authority is personally ascribed to leader versus
                          development of creative individuals

Reconciliation:	to get the support of the leaders so they underline themselves the importance of learning and creativity. They become servant leaders of learning
Management	the power of politics and know-who versus the power of learning
Reconciliation:	take the best practices from the past, codify them, and apply them to the present learning environment
Rewards	long-term loyalty versus intrinsic reward self-development
Reconciliation:	members are personally held accountable to motivate creative individuals and creating learning environments

Transformation 11

Current   **Ideal**

Family   Guided Missile

Typical Dilemmas

Leadership	authority is personally ascribed to the leader versus depersonalized authority by task
Reconciliation:	attribute the highest authority to those managers that have made internalization of subtle processes a prime criterion in their goals
Management	the power of politics and know-who versus consistent goal-orientation around task
Reconciliation:	make political sensitivity part of the task description
Rewards	reward long-term loyalty versus extrinsic reward job done
Reconciliation:	describe task in terms of loosely described long-term outputs

Transformation 12

Current   **Ideal**

Family   Eiffel Tower

Typical Dilemmas

Leadership	authority is personally ascribed to the leader versus authority ascribed to the role
Reconciliation:	management needs to understand the technical aspects of the activities they manage. They become servant leaders of experts
Management	the power of politics and know-who versus of expertise and reliability
Reconciliation:	get the support of management for the implementation of crucial systems and procedures
Rewards	reward long-term loyalty versus increasing their expertise in doing a reliable job
Reconciliation:	members apply their power to the advantage of increasing the expertise of their colleagues

Example: current corporate culture: Guided Missile; ideal corporate culture: Family

This is a commonly-desired corporate change and we have included two examples here. In the first, a US-based company – "Conflux" – we assembled the following profile of their senior management:

Amongst several dilemmas, the organization had particularly identified the need to reconcile the following:

• Every business group was out for itself, making profit that credited their leader, versus every business group contributing to Conflux's overall success and helping all customers

• Striving to make incremental progress in terms of market share and profitability for the next quarter, versus needing a holistic and sustainable vision that can be shared with customers for an overall sense of identity

• Preparing products for internal review to achieve internal budgets, versus aligning product developments to meet customers' needs

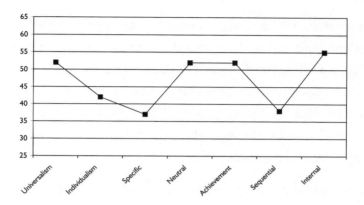

Figure 4.3 Propensity to reconcile: variation across seven dimensions model

Conflux saw itself as a Guided Missile focused on short-term quarterly results but with much internal competition. It desired to have more characteristics of a Family culture with increased loyalty to its customers and cooperation between its business groups.

The reconciliation of the first dilemma called for an integration between individualism and communitarianism, and yet we can see from the profile analysis graphic that the management team scored below average on their propensity to reconcile in this aspect. In addition, we found that the management team had a significantly below average score on reconciling specific and diffuse orientations, which was not going to help them be able to reconcile the second dilemma.

We were able to take advantage of their naturally higher propensity to reconcile in the area of internal/external control which boosted self-confidence. With minimal guidance they themselves were able to reconcile the third dilemma for which internal/external control was the underlying construct.

Obviously the coaching of individuals and groups needs to be based on more than over-reliance on profiling tools and simply showing charts and data. But we have found it opens a very powerful mechanism for revealing the origins of the lack of any tendency to reconcile and strategies to improve the skills – especially in those areas that seem crucial for the change process. Having our sound, transferable, conceptual framework available to us provides an input to the design of the intervention.

Once the leader or groups of relevant leaders agree upon the dilemmas that need to reconciled – and once that they understand their own strengths and weaknesses in different approaches – the action points to be taken tend to arise naturally. Very often it is crucial to identify the typical levers that need to be pulled in an organization in order to increase the effectiveness of the actions that are to be taken. Again, this is very often dependent on the current organizational culture.

In Family-oriented cultures HR often plays a crucial role, while marketing and finance dominate in Guided Missile cultures. The best levers to be pulled in the Incubator are often related to learning systems and intrinsic rewards, while in Eiffel Towers, committee procedures and systems often play a more central role.

The following provides general initial guidance for action points to be taken for the three dilemmas we have been considering:

Dilemma I

- **The Market** (think about what you could do in areas of customers, time-to-market response, flow of information from and to customers)

- **Human Resources** (consider areas such as management development, staff planning, appraisal and rewards)
- **Business Systems** (what can be done in the areas of IT systems, knowledge management, manafucturing information, quality systems, etc.)
- **Structure and design** (consider what can be done in areas of the design of the organization both formally and informally, basic flows of materials and information)
- **Strategy and Envisioned Future** (review the leaders' vision, mission statements, goals, objectives, business plans, and the like)
- **Core Values** (think about action points that could enhance the clarity of values, how to better translate them into behavior and action etc.)

Dilemma 2

Who is taking action and carries responsibility (consider who is responsible for the outcome on each of the possible action points)?

1.

2.

3.

4.

5.

Dilemma 3

How the change process should be monitored (consider milestones and qualitative and quantitative measures of genuine change).

1.

2.

3.

4.

5.

We use many techniques to get the BHAG on the table. As mentioned, these include guided fantasies where we ask participants to picture a car or animal that best represented the state of the ideal organization. Animal ideas at Conflux ranged from an octopus (connecting many parts of the body) to a fox (indicating quickness and smartness combined). These types of exercise can be very helpful since people are forced to use creative parts of their brains, and even more importantly, disconnect from the present, deeply-engraved, images of the organization.

We found that the best way to reconcile these contrasting leadership styles is to attribute the highest authority to those task-oriented managers who have made profitable innovation and learning a prime criterion in their goals. This works because it combines the task-drivenness of current managers with the need for innovations that were so fast to market that good profits could be made in the relatively short term.

Example: current corporate culture: Guided Missile; ideal corporate culture: Family

For our second example of the change from Guided Missile to Family culture, we'll look at a US-based company operating in Korea.

Corporate Culture in South Korea

An American electronics company has been manufacturing goods in South Korea since 1990. When competition from other South East Asian countries endangered the plant's margins, the company summoned experienced US managers to figure out why their Korean counterparts were not performing. As part of an improvement program, the Korean managers were warned to get their act together within six months – they had to work harder and correct previous mistakes. American managers promised them significant monetary bonuses in reward for achieving measurable benchmarks for profitability and quality. After six months, the results are still very disappointing. Another US manager is flown in, but his similar approach is proving just as ineffective.

A final try is given to John Paulson. He is informed that if he doesn't succeed the plant will have to be closed.

What do you consider the best course of action in view of the differences in interpretations of corporate culture between US and Korea?

Paulson will face some challenging dilemmas. A typical one concerns leadership. Authority in the Family culture is personally ascribed to the leader, making him into a father figure. In the Guided Missile the authority is depersonalized; the power of the task dominates the game. To reconcile this dilemma effectively, one needs first to get the support of the leaders so that they themselves underline the importance of the tasks. They become servant leaders of tasks (in an Eiffel Tower they would have become servant leaders of roles).

A second dilemma is concerned with the integration of the importance of the history of the organization in the Family and the focus on short-term results that characterizes the Guided Missile. One way of fulfilling the reconciliation is to take the best practices from the past, codify them, and apply them as role models for future results.

A third dilemma deals with the rewards individuals strive for. In the Family people tend to strive for an accumulation of status. In the Guided Missile, they tend to feel rewarded by getting the job done and achieve status from how well they contribute to the bottom line. Reconciliation is best achieved when Family members apply their power to the advantage of getting the task done.

Managers prior to Paulson's arrival had selected an achievement-oriented solution typical of the Guided Missile, but rejected the more ascription-oriented nature of the Family-oriented Koreans. They assumed that purely achieving goals and receiving more money would motivate their Korean colleagues. They also failed to understand that Koreans respond more positively to orders given by those with a prominent status in their company hierarchy.

In this case, Paulson requested the support of his Korean colleagues, asking them to help him out. He started by praising the organization for its past achievements but noted that increased competition had made profits vanish and quality deteriorate. He took the management aside and informally praised their loyalty and capability. "Together we can do it. Let's show Chicago that we're one of them,"

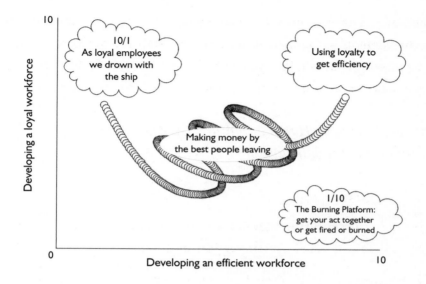

Figure 4.4 The loyalty–efficiency dilemma

he said. By doing this he attributed status to the Korean organization and thus chose the ascription-oriented solution that reconciled the achievement-orientation of the American company he worked for. Supporting the most respected managers in their efforts to improve operations showed his understanding of the Korean emphasis on status, so normal in the Family. The Koreans do respond to pressure, but only when those with status in the hierarchy apply it.

In this process Paulson took a personal risk. When communicating the importance of the survival process to the Korean staff he gave the organization one year, while he knew HQ would seriously consider closing the plant within six months if no significant improvements had been made. By asking the Koreans to help him rebuild the company on the basis of trust and respect (for which one year is the bare minimum), he stimulated them to get the first significant improvements within six months. His ascribed status as CEO helped in ascribing status to the Koreans who saw it as a platform to achieve. The previous US managers were just hammering on achievements without attributing enough status to the Korean organization and its staff. Five years later, this subsidiary is still there and is one of the prize-winning showcases of the US-based company.

Example: current corporate culture: Guided Missile; ideal corporate culture: Incubator

A traditional bank and its private wealth management

The volatility of markets in the early years of this century has made major banks reconsider their strategies. Both stratification and internationalization strategies have put their traditional structures under some pressure. John Hodgkin, a typical British banker and CEO of one of the oldest British Banks – "SUL" – invited us for a talk. We were hardly in before he said:

"It's amazing, gentlemen, how much this organization is in need of change. My major worry is our private wealth management side. In more than 150 years of existence the bank has not encountered so many changes in such a short period of time. First of all, while 90 percent of our clients were British, or rather English, now they only account for 55 percent. Internationalization of markets is the main cause, together with the integration of Europe. Secondly, our clients are demanding more short-term action. So much new money was made in the late nineties that the majority of our clients want us to make money for them in our private wealth sector just as they've made their own money. This type of trading is not what we are used to. Just look at how our clients are dressed; we can't match their casual clothing… we express in every detail what we are about or rather what we were about: reliability with a long-term view. Check and double check.

"Knowing this we bought a private wealth management bank from the USA. We had a head start because we could find many synergies upfront, but we seem to run into the same problems with them as we do with our clients. This new company – "PWEALTH" – doesn't seem to gel with our more traditional people. But, gentlemen, I asked you in because recently we've begun to lose many of our wealthy clients. They complain that they don't feel at home in our bank with its traditional values. Our decision lines are too long and we don't have enough synergies between our silos of wholesale, retail, etc. In short, our corporate culture is not appropriate for the new international environments in which we are working. How can you help us?"

This type of case will not be unfamiliar. An organization tries to solve a market issue by an acquisition. Initially at first values are added, but in a few months it becomes clear that two corporate cultures are clashing. To assimilate the new entity in the larger one is the worst you can do. That's not why you bought the company in the first place. But how often does it happen? It is possible to manage the integration in such a way that values synergize rather than clash.

We didn't need to develop an envisioned future because both SUL and PWEALTH were quite pleased with what they already had. This could be summarized as follows:

SUL's envisioned future

SUL is an ambitious institution in transition. We are committed to continuous improvement in everything we do to meet the increasing demands of our clients and other audiences through our own aspirations for excellence. Our success depends on excellent performance and a solid reputation. We aim to shift horizons beyond short-term profit to long-term value creation through sustainable development. Long-term shareholder value is the ultimate measure of that success.

By emphasising our Values, articulating our Business Principles and stimulating dialogue and transparency, we will contribute to sustainable and mutually beneficial relationships with our audiences, not least our shareholders.

PWEALTH's envisioned future

We aim for sustainable relationships with our clients through top performance and passion in the delivery of specialized services in the area of managing wealth.

From this it is clear that PWEALTH needs less words for its mission. It is perhaps the first indication of the cultural differences between a British general bank and a US specialized financial institution. This is also clearly indicated when we compare both institutions' core values. Again both companies were quite pleased with what they had developed.

SUL's core values

Four corporate values underlie our Business Principles and activities:

- **Integrity**: Above all, we are committed to integrity in all that we do, worldwide.
- **Teamwork**: We share global skills and resources for our clients' benefit.
- **Respect**: We respect each individual and draw strength from equal opportunity and diversity.
- **Professionalism**: We are committed to the highest standards of professionalism and to delivering outstanding quality.

PWEALTH's core values

We strive for the following values. They guide our behavior at any time:

- **Transparency**: We are open and honest in all the things we communicate.
- **Positive Dissent**: We like our people to challenge the status quo. We stimulate dissent but once a decision has been taken we commit to it.

- **Acting Innovatively**: We appreciate creative thinking and stimulate the development of new services. We learn from the mistakes we make.
- **Entrepreneurship**: In developing relationships with our stakeholders we stimulate new approaches and entrepreneurial behavior.
- **Delivering commercial top performances**: We strive for the highest level of commercialism in both business and human developments.

Now let's look at what both organizations produced in the light of their corporate cultures.

SUL – The Eiffel Tower

Essence: high degree of formalization, together with a high degree of centralization. This type of culture is steep, stately and very robust. Control is exercised through systems of rules, legalistic procedures, responsibilities, and assigned rights. Bureaucracy makes this organization quite inflexible. Respect for authority is based on the respect for functional position and status. Expertise and related formal titles are very much appreciated.

We want more of:
- economies of scale
- professionalism

We want to keep:
- loyalty to profession

- expertise in broad range of activities

We want less of:
- bureaucratic atmosphere and long-winded procedures
- titles
- ineffective decisions made too late
- long careers

PWEALTH – The Incubator

Essence: leaderless team in which people aim for personal growth. This person-oriented culture is characterized by a low degree of both centralization and formalization. In this culture, the individualization of all related individuals is one of the most important features. The organization exists only to serve the needs of its members, who are motivated by learning on the job and personal development.

We want more of:
- quick decision making
- autonomous teams
- working across silos

We want to keep:
- possibilities of dissent
- creative and entrepreneurial attitudes
- continuous learning

We want less of:

- disorganization and lack of consistency in policies
- not knowing what colleagues are doing
- hero type of behavior

We discussed the main tensions between both organizations and gave presentations on the most crucial ones. We then worked with teams of senior participants to frame these tensions as a series of principal dilemmas:

On the one hand we want more of and/or to keep the following values and behaviors of our current organization:	On the other hand we need to develop the following values and behaviors for supporting our envisioned future and core values:
On the one hand...	*On the other hand...*
1. we need to commit to integrity	1. we need to be effective in all cultures in which we work
2. we need to work in teams	2. we need to exchange information across teams in other divisions
3. we need to be entrepreneurial	3. we need to develop economies of scale
4. we need to be able to dissent	4. we need to be loyal to our organization
5. we need to develop solid products and services	5. we need to be driven by the needs of the clients

Through looking at the tensions developed through the core values of both organizations we had captured at least five of the key strategic dilemmas the organization as a whole was facing. Our next step in supporting this client was to conceptualize a renewed mission statement and set of core values. Our dilemma reconciliation methodology resulted in the following set of integrated values.

1.   Integrity through knowledge and respect for other cultures

2.   Professionalism through client needs

3.   Teamwork through exchanging information across businesses

4.   Dissenting views through being loyal to the organization

5.   Entrepreneurialism through developing the efficiency and effectiveness of the organization

Example: current corporate culture: Family; ideal corporate culture: Incubator

In a family-owned Spanish department store, we found our methodology very effective in helping reconcile the dilemmas between retaining the existing Family culture and supporting individual freedom so that neither the respect for traditional values nor the loyalty of the 700 staff were lost.

Reinventing a department store

In 1972 Juan Valdez opened his first department store in Barcelona. His customers consisted of the elite of Barcelona in search of the latest quality gifts. Juan traveled twice a year to the USA in order to develop new ideas in this very quickly changing and innovative market sector. These trips were followed by two trips to Asia where he found relatively cheap manufacturers who could produce the many articles he wanted to launch in Spain. Sometimes he combined his manufacturing efforts – ranging from natural stone gadgets to silk scarves – with the dominant department stores in Europe such as Galleries Lafayette.

Within five years six new department stores were opened in major Spanish cities. Juan's creative mind found very good outlets in the variety of stores, and economies of scale resulted in solid profits. In the late eighties the major stores in Barcelona, Madrid, Valencia and Seville were managed by his wife and three of his sons. The twenty smaller outlets were managed by the best sales people from the four largest stores, with at least five years of experience. Within 20 years Juan had built an empire of 700 people and six large department stores that included products like fragrances, men's and women's gifts and the latest fashion items in a variety of fields, including clothes. The 15 smaller outlets were focused on the original gift market. Juan, his eldest son Junior, and his wife Maria made up the management team. Juan was responsible for purchasing, Junior was CFO and Maria was responsible for sales. They were known as "the golden trio" in the Barcelona jet set – until Juan was killed in a plane crash while on business in Asia.

The new management team was extended with Juan and Maria's two youngest sons. Although the shops were still very profitable they were increasingly coming under serious competition from the larger department stores in Spain and lost market share quite quickly. With the passing away of the creative and egalitarian Juan, more and more politics was introduced by the family. Although they were very good to their staff, and lifetime employment had been the rule, more turnover of staff resulted. Exit interviews all pointed to the lack of perceived new challenges and products and to the increasingly patriarchal attitude of the management team. Junior was concerned with this feedback and asked us to look at the situation.

He told us about his personal worries. "I think our organization is going through a cultural crisis after my father's fatal
accident. Our turnover and profitability in business is quite
OK, although we are losing market share. Turnover of personnel worries me, since we think we know the reason. Our family
traditions have brought us great fortune with the combination
of people's loyalty and my father's refreshing views and products. He brought in the new ideas and our people could sell
them as a natural thing. Now we seem to just ride on the waves
of tradition, but in this business we need renewal. Can you
help us?"

Our analysis revealed a sound but deteriorating financial structure.
Managers at the level of the department stores were stretched since
they were held responsible for all activities except purchasing,
which was traditionally done centrally. They felt limited in their
autonomy because "Barcelona" was pulling the strings despite
regional differences in taste. Moreover, consistent complaints were
voiced about the lack of visibility of the Valdez family. In contrast
with their father, it seemed the sons were watching computers more
than people. Everyone agreed that the main problem was one deriving from issues of corporate culture.

Again we followed our approach of eliciting dilemmas from our
web-based tools. We asked participants to list the positives and negatives for both current and ideal organizational cultures. It was quite
clear that they had a balanced view for both organizational
typologies.

Family		Incubator	
positive	negative	positive	negative
loyalty	slow decisions	fast decisions	lack of long-term commitment
lifetime employment	autocracy	autonomy	neurotic
knowing people	centralized	risk-taking	carelessness
long-term vision	"old boy" network	visible leadership	broad knowledge

With our help, they formulated the following dilemmas:

On the one hand...	On the other hand...
1. we have an organization where we can trust the management	1. we are not given enough autonomy to make decisions quickly
2. management is educated broadly and have an overview of the business	2. we are in a type of business where we need to react quickly to the client's specialized and segmented needs
3. seniority is rewarded	3. we need people who want to take risks
4. we need to be innovative in our product choice	4. we need to be consistent in our image

One area was related to leadership style. On the one hand leaders were seen as visionary long-term thinkers, but detached. On the other hand, the product range and this type of business asked for quick decisions and a hands-on type of leader. Again, these types of dilemmas are best reconciled under the servant leader model.

The main business dilemma was the need for autonomy and specialisation around the variety of businesses and the need for synergy between them. This type of department store asked for innovative and trend-setting behavior in their broad product portfolio, ranging from gifts, fragrances, fashion, shoes, and other fashionable accessories. They felt that the dominating Family culture had many great characteristics, but it was not supporting a "quick-on-the-feet," risk-taking attitude so crucial for the innovating part of the business. Furthermore, it was felt that the loyal clientele was very much attracted to the elite name of the department stores but then went on to buy the things they had seen in the smaller, more specialized shops that surrounded most Valdez dynasty department stores.

What was the origin of this? The Family tradition had created department stores that attracted many people. However, increasingly these were used as "museums" where people were inspired to actually buy the products in smaller shops carrying particular brand names like Giorgio Armani, Krups, Ferrari, etc. In fact this sparked off an idea from the group to combine the strengths of both Family and Incubator culture: the development of a "shop in a shop" concept. The department store was reshaped into many small shops each responsible for a brand.

The company was reorganised into profit centers around the "families of incubators." After two years Valdez was voted the department store of the year in Spain. This was only possible because much attention had been given to the individual behavior of the managers.

Example: current corporate culture: Incubator; ideal corporate culture: Guided Missile

The continuous growth of a young and innovative company often means that an Incubator culture has tensions leading to the need for a Guided Missile component. We have found it in companies that sponsored their own growth like Apple Computer. But we often encounter this tension when a smaller entrepreneurial firm is taken over by a larger company. We have often seen this happen in larger firms that try to "buy their innovations" by acquiring small creative businesses, making their owners financially independent in the process.

Managing integration

Barry Haskell wondered whether he had done the right thing two years ago. He became frustrated with managing professionals while earning the bulk of the money for the consulting firm that he set up some 10 years before. His colleagues were professional in almost everything, including complaining about their salaries. When Barry's organization grew to over 20 people he felt he needed assistance. In his niche international consulting business, he found that he lacked the international network as well as enough consultants and the knowledge to do the implementation. So he went to one of the big five consulting firms and sold his company. Although he negotiated fiercely for independence, after two years he felt he had been gradually swallowed. Two of his best consultants resigned because they felt that "writing hours" had become more important than developing the field. Furthermore, the idea of working in a larger firm, driven by profitability, didn't appeal to them.

Barry faced many dilemmas in trying to achieve his goals of internationalization and reducing the burden of managing professionals.

Once again a major dilemma concerns leadership issues. In the Incubator, the authority of others is more or less denied, or it was at least based on the creativity of its leaders' minds. The power of learning and innovation dominate the game here. In the Guided Missile authority is depersonalized. The power of the task dominates; the people writing most of the hours and contributing most to the financial end result are respected most. The best way to reconcile these contrasting leadership styles is to make innovation and learning a prime criterion in the goals of the task-oriented managers.

A second dilemma is concerned with the development of market orientation in the Guided Missile, while an Incubator culture is aimed more at the development of creative individuals and ideas, regardless of whether there is a market for these. The bottom line is often not such an issue. One way of fulfilling the reconciliation is to make learning and innovation part of the task description to which one is firmly held.

A third dilemma deals with the rewards individuals strive for. In the Incubator people try to develop themselves through creative experiments and learning from the results. Financial rewards are almost seen as a (monthly) insult. In the Guided Missile people tend to strive to get the job done. The market determines the price. Reconciliation is best achieved when managers describe their task in terms of clearly described innovation outputs for which they are rewarded.

Following our logic and by now familiar methodology, all of the dilemmas were reconciled. The overarching dilemma is shown in Figure 4.5.

The power of the approach described in this chapter is that it focuses not on transformation, not on change per se, not on throwing away the current situation. Our methodology is heavily biased towards eliciting the dilemmas inherent in the tensions between the need for different corporate cultures to coexist or shift, and then reconciling these dilemmas. What is ideal becomes the achievement of the rec-

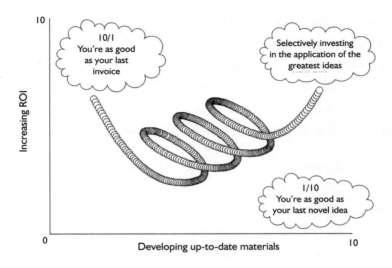

Figure 4.5 The profitability–innovation dilemma

onciliation of seemingly opposed values, not simply seeking to force a change to some new, single corporate culture.

CHAPTER 5

Managing change and continuity across cultures

n order to apply the ongoing rationale that is embedded through-out this book to change management, a complete change of mindset from conventional wisdom is required. Traditional change processes often inquire about how we can transform the current unsatisfactory situation into a new future. But once we can start thinking in a way based on our new logic, the creative juices that flow from the integration of seemingly opposing values is astonishing. And who would have dared to suggest that management hadn't failed if the organization changed back to where it was previously?

Throughout the extensive literature on change management per se, many authors have attempted to identify and categorize approaches to change, some from human systems perspectives, some from organization theory and some from a general systems view.

Goodstein and Burke (1994) describe change in terms of levels of change, strategies of change, and models and methods of change. Change can be on the level of a fundamental, large-scale change or a series of small changes for the purpose of fine tuning the larger changes. The types of strategies for change include individual change strategies, technostructural strategies, organization development strategies, and coercive strategies. Collins and Hill (cited in Hord, 1999) adopt a more assertive approach.

Many such summaries (such as the otherwise excellent critical review by SEDL, 1992) appear to have ignored the earlier categorical and analytical frameworks for change. Broadly these were:

- fix the parts,
- fix the people

or

- fix the organization.

The basic assumption underlying the empirical–rational model is that individuals are rational and will follow their rational self-interest. Thus, if a "good" change is suggested, people of good intention will adopt it.

The power-coercive approach relies on influencing individuals and systems to change through legislation and external leverage where power of various types is the dominant factor. Power-coercive strategies emphasize political, economic and moral sanctions, with the focus on using power of some type to "force" individuals to adopt the change. One strategy is nonviolent protest and demonstration. A second strategy is the use of political institutions to achieve change – for example, changing educational policies through state-level legislation.

(Southwest Educational Development Lab, 1992)

SEDL continue that in the normative-reeducative approach, the individual is seen as actively in search of satisfying needs and interests. The individual does not passively accept what comes, but takes action to advance his/her goals. Further, changes are not just rational responses to new information but occur at the more personal level of values and habits. Additionally, the individual is guided by social and institutional norms. The overarching principle of this model is that individuals must take part in their own (re-education) change if it is to occur. Sashkin and Egermeier (cited in Hord, 1999) conclude that, in a fix-the-parts approach, the "more personal assistance and continuing support from a skilled and knowledgeable local agent, the more likely that the innovation will be used for a long duration." In the fix-the-people approach that links to House's political perspective (also cited in Hord, 1999), the focus is on improving the knowledge and skills of employees, thus enabling them to perform their roles. Fixing the organization addresses the transition from the current corporate culture to the ideal corporate culture. It is to be noted that Sashkin and Egermeier themselves conclude that none of the three approaches has achieved long-term success in their studies.

BUT WHAT ABOUT CULTURE?

Many of the prescriptions for such different approaches to change are often ethnocentric and may only be appropriate in the cultures where they were researched, developed, and validated. Whilst Harrison (cited in Hord, 1999) claims success for a methodology led by HR and based on early involvement to overcome assumed resistance, it may work in his stereotypical (national) culture, but is unlikely to be generalizable to different industries – let alone across the globe.

It appears more difficult to delineate and explain business failures that owe their origin to badly managed change initiatives. Bennis (1999) observed that two most common explanations of the failure of change programs derived from a lack of senior management commitment and a failure to address the "softer" issues related to reengineering's impact on people and corporate cultures. His view is that there is a more fundamental reason for many failed change transformation efforts: in particular, that the basic vision that guides many change experts is flawed. Their "unconstrained vision," or view that mankind is infinitely perfectible, drives their change initiatives to solutions that break down in implementation, either because these solutions cannot cope with the complexities of the real world or because they encounter overwhelming organizational resistance. Even gurus who have studied change management and published their findings and frameworks extensively, have failed when they tried to apply their dictats to their own situation. Covey may have sold 13 million copies of his *7 Habits of Highly Effective People* but failed with his attempt to transform a juggernaut of efficiency training.

Kohler (2000) identifies a concern that globalization, whilst often unsuccessful in realizing business objectives, may also have pronounced effects on people and their societies due to an increased unbalancing of resource and materials consumption and beneficiaries.

Based on the many models and analysis papers in the existing literature, several authors have concluded that:

1.   change may be planned or unplanned, evolutionary or revolutionary

2.   most change will continue to be brought about by influences in the corporation's external environment

3.   in order to survive and prosper, organizations must change and adapt – as least as fast as their environment is changing

4.   change itself is inevitable – and the real issue becomes Change Management

5.   the Change Management processes are critical to organizational success because they act as agents that influence every other organizational process.

6.   badly managed change can result in:
     - Negative organizational memory about change and how change is managed
     - A retarded ability to undertake any change programs in the future

- Negative impacts on organizational performance and morale
- Negative bottom-line impact
- Accelerated onset of crises

7. Existing approaches to managing change include:
   - Change of executive leadership
   - Change in mid-management leadership roles
   - Management development programs
   - Survey/feedback programs
   - Quality circles/TQM
   - Business process reengineering (BPR)

8. While the world and organizations are changing, many fundamental assumptions about any one industry, competitors, people and technology tend to go unnoticed and unchallenged.

In preparing our organizations for the twenty-first century, new change management processes must provide a mechanism for surfacing and rethinking our deeply held assumptions; otherwise meaningful change is not possible.

THE "HOW", "WHY," AND "WHAT" OF CHANGE

Conventional approaches frame the change problem in one or other of these extremes. To focus solely on "why" may not translate effectively to "what" and/or "how." "How" questions place the effort on means where diagnosis is assumed or not even undertaken at all and therefore the ends sought are not considered. To focus on ends requires the posing of "what" questions. What are we trying to accomplish? And what needs to be changed? What are the critical success factors? What measures of performance are we trying to achieve? Ends and means are relative and whether something is an end or a means is only in relation to something else. Thus, often, the "true" ends of a change effort may be different to those intended. In this regard, the "why" question is claimed to be useful.

According to Lewin's well-known force-field theory, organizations are in dynamic tension between forces pushing for change and forces resistant to change. Established change management practice has interpreted this on the basis that it is management's task to reduce the resistance to change and increase the forces for change. But under our Dilemma Theory approach, this is only a compromise solution. It ignores that fact that increasing the force for change may increase people's resistance, for example.

THE FUTILITY OF STATIC BUSINESS TRANSFORMATION

We believe it is all too simple to begin to address these factors as either/or questions or as "what" or "why" questions because they ignore the tensions across cultural differences.

We would claim that our methodology (described in the previous chapter) for eliciting dilemmas that arise from organization cultural tensions is a proven framework for managing organization culture. However, we must now emphasize that our philosophy for change management is not about trying to change an organization's culture. This is a contradiction in terms because cultures act to preserve themselves, to protect their own living existence. Cultures have a sense of equilibrium and stability. If you try to upset that equilibrium it will swing back at you. Cultures, in short, are living systems with their own sense of purpose and proportion. You may wish them to behave differently but they have minds of their own with a tendency to persist in current patterns of behavior.

Businesses deal with so many malleable objects, which they shape to their own desires and then sell to customers, that there is a tendency to think of corporate culture as one more malleable object. But culture is not an object or a thing, nor is it malleable. It is a value difference, a living system different from ourselves.

Treating living systems as if they were malleable objects leads to some very absurd situations. Perhaps the best known is the famous game of croquet in *Alice in Wonderland*. Alice was invited to join a game in which the croquet hoops were footmen bending over, the balls were curled-up hedgehogs and the mallets were flamingos. Alice found, to her frustration, that the footmen straightened up and strolled off, the hedgehogs crawled away, and her flamingo turned its long neck around and confronted her.

That is very much what cultures and other living systems do when we try to have our way with them. They either confront us or evade us and we are left with a game that is almost impossible to play, much less to win. The fallacy lies in treating living systems like dead things.

CHANGE AND CONTINUITY IS ONE DIFFERENCE

So rather than seeing change as a "thing" opposing continuity or preservation, we will see it as a difference on a values' continuum. We seek to change so as to preserve our company, our profitability, our market share, our core competence or whatever is chiefly precious to us. Unless we change, in certain respects, we may fail to preserve key continuities and we could lose everything.

The reason for changing in certain respects is usually to avoid changing in other respects, to go on being creative, profitable, valuable to customers. It follows that we cannot override the need for corporate cultures to preserve themselves. We have to work with those key continuities. We have to say in effect "changing in this way will help you to keep what is most important to you, in circumstances which are changing." In short, we must reconcile change with continuity in order to preserve an evolving identity. All people and all organizations seek to change while remaining the same. *Plus ça change*, as the French say.

In order to change the culture which is the current reality, we need to reconcile the real with the ideal. But the only way of moving towards this ideal is through mobilizing current realities. For example, "through the expanded sales of our staple product, we can develop new products which will, in their turn, become staples." Selling what is familiar will sustain our efforts to develop what is novel.

If culture is "the way we do things around here," as Deal and Kennedy (1982) suggest, then that "way of doing things" needs to deliver the novel achievements we are looking for. We need the realism of "the way" to deliver the idealism of the changes to which we aspire. We can think of this as a circle so:

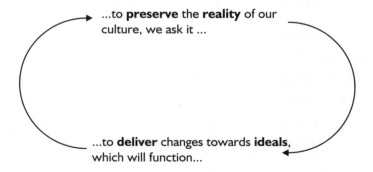

...to **preserve** the **reality** of our culture, we ask it ...

...to **deliver** changes towards **ideals**, which will function...

Such a culture preserves itself through change and realizes its ideals, so:

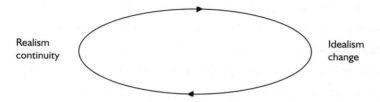

Realism
continuity

Idealism
change

CHANGING BETWEEN CULTURAL ARCHETYPES

We can now think in terms of these tensions as differences. These differences are those of Change and Continuity, Ideal and Real. In practice they interact with each other and support each other. For example, a hierarchy is ideally the result of a contest among those given equal opportunities to succeed, in which some have outperformed others. A formal system is created out of activities which were once informal, but proved so valuable that they were incorporated, formalized and repeated.

There are many reasons why companies might wish to change their profiles. The Incubator culture may have been brilliantly inventive, yet not so adept at exploiting those inventions and getting them to large numbers of customers. The Guided Missile culture may have turned novel products into valuable commodities using teams of experts to perfect these, only to face a cost squeeze; the expert team is expensive. Commodity-type products need standardization, replication, formalization to get costs down. The Eiffel Tower culture may be so set in its pecking order and its formalities that it cannot renew itself, cannot incubate ideas or turn these into accurate "missiles." A Family culture may be so comfortable, so nurturing that no one wishes to let go of this warm interior and go out on a limb.

In short, extreme Incubators, Guided Missiles, Eiffel Towers and Families tend to lack the attributes of their contrasting cultures and to suffer through this lack. If you cannot "let go" of informality or formality, equality or hierarchy, your ranges of behavior are severely limited. Persons hostile to hierarchies of excellence will cut down "tall poppies," a habit of which Australians accuse themselves. Cultures hostile to equality will hammer down the nail that stands up to participate or question authority, a trait to which the Japanese admit. Cultures hostile to formalizing and thereby exploiting inventiveness will often deplore applied science and crafts, a trait which helps explain the high number of British inventions incubated but not followed through to world-class success. Cultures hostile to informality, to nerds and geeks, may fail to benefit from inter-disciplinary inventiveness, for a lack of which some Germans reproach themselves.

All in all, every quadrant of our corporate culture map draws for its sustenance on other quadrants. To totally transform (as in business transformation processes such as BPR) from one quadrant to another needs major assistance from the quadrant in which you are currently situated, so that your ideals are propelled by what is real.

THE GENERALIZED FRAMEWORK

We can revisit the various scenarios and consider them from the perspective of both "difference" and "in constant equilibrium" between the states.

Eight Scenarios of Culture Change

We will now consider eight of the most common ways that corporate cultures seek to change as evidenced by our current research. Each of these ways is described using a scenario. This scenario reconciles the reality of the corporation's current culture with the idealization, and later realization of the culture to which that corporation aspires to move. In this process, the corporation spans two quadrants at least and uses its current reality to shape its ideals. The eight scenarios are as follows.

1   *From Incubator to Guided Missile and back*

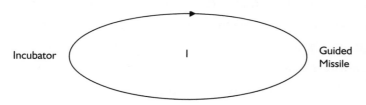

In this scenario an inventive Incubator company is facing the need to make money from its past inventions if it is to subsidise new creative initiatives. Other companies are now matching its inventiveness and are starting to exceed its level of actual innovations. It needs to find more customers for what it has invented and needs to get refined and finished products to a market becoming more demanding, if sufficient profits are to be earned. Expert teams with formal goals as to profitability, quality assurance, market share are urgently required.

Notice that the circle comes back again to the Incubator. Feedback about what customers like or do not like, what is more or less profitable, should shape the direction of research, development, and incubation. It does not hurt inventors to know where their support is coming from and may guide their search patterns to advantage.

2   *From Guided Missile to Incubator and back*

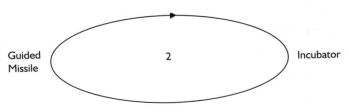

In this scenario a Guided Missile culture with teams completing projects, "guided" by rational objectives, are encountering serious questions as to how rational these objectives really are. Suppose that there were quite other ways of reaching these goals? Are the products themselves obsolescent? Are there creative contributions which the company is not measuring and has therefore lost sight of? Above all, has the time come to renew themselves?

Why not then utilize teams to point out areas where incubating new ideas could be most valuable? What do customers want which they are not getting because no one has yet solved this problem? An Incubator culture should be created out of the customer needs that the teams have identified.

Once again the circle comes back again as the new Incubator responds to the teams who gave it its mandates and who identified new opportunities for innovation.

3   *From Eiffel Tower to Guided Missile and back*

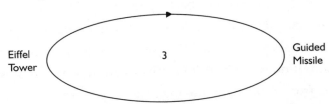

In this scenario the company has enjoyed great operational success for some years, meeting or surpassing most of the benchmarks in its industry, yet with the maturing of its markets, customers have gained more power and are demanding – and getting – from rival suppliers higher levels of personal service, along with customized products/services. Owing to a squeeze on margins much of the profit potential lies in greater customization.

The advice the company has been getting is to set up project teams that could target the special needs of key customers and begin the process of "pulling" what the company produces towards the emerging needs of the market. Some accounts are more "strategic" than others and what Customer X demands from the company today may soon become a norm for the whole industry. Project Teams are set up with cross-functional membership to see how all the functions of the corporation might better converge on what customers want. It is important that the functions be informed by such teams and be "guided" towards superior performance. What customers want can become a new benchmark as the loop feeds back to the Eiffel Tower and makes it even better.

A variation on this process puts Eiffel Tower workers and managers into Quality Circles for so many hours every week, thereby switching from an Eiffel Tower culture to a Guided Missile culture at least temporarily before taking the solutions forged in Quality Circles back to the factory floor and using these to restructure routine operations. The Quality Circle task groups concentrate on making improvements, in avoiding waste and duplication, and in re-balancing the assembly line. They take "time out" to critique their own operation, and not just their own tasks but even the overall lay-out of the shop floor may be changed at the behest of these circles.

A variation of this process occurred in the QWL groups, or Quality of Working Life. Here the team's mission is to humanize the Eiffel Tower culture so that the quality of employees' experience is improved. QWL was strong in the 70s and 80s but has now been partly displaced by Work/Life Balance which attempts to reconcile the demands of home and family with those of the work organization. This requires considerable negotiation among people in groups, including flexi-time and job sharing. Two or more employees may agree to cover a job jointly, so that A delivers both her own and B's children to school and B fetches both sets of children each afternoon.

The old T-Group, or Sensitivity Group Training, was an attempt to develop those who had to work in Eiffel Tower bureaucratic cultures, put them in a moratorium and have them develop Guided Missile group skills that were missing from their routine cultures. The T-group movement showed that teams themselves develop over time, as cultures created by their members and reflecting their priorities.

A shift from the Eiffel Tower to the Guided Missile was done accidentally in the famous Hawthorne Experiment. Several young women were removed from the factory floor and placed in a small experimental group. Here they discovered what the researchers' wanted in the form of higher productivity and proceeded to give it to them, guided by regular feedback and a common purpose. The conviviality and face-to-face relationships within the group also greatly enhanced morale.

4   *From Guided Missile to Eiffel Tower and back*

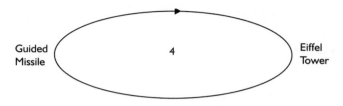

For several years a company has successfully met the growing complexity and customization of its industry via project groups, peopled by representatives of key functions, i.e., manufacturing, R&D, marketing, sales etc. This has helped it win strategic accounts and partner several key customers. But it cannot ignore the relentless commoditization of its industry, nor the high costs of the expert team, which may require only a few minutes input from highly specialized persons but might take up hours of their time.

An increasing number of orders are for routine commodities and the company will be priced out of business if it gives "Rolls Royce" service to standard requests. It must find ways of meeting these fast and cheaply, positioning itself as a low-cost supplier for this mature part of the market. It needs to belt out standard products at a profit if it is serious about survival.

Project groups are anyway better employed in newer markets making unusual requests. Once a group becomes "boring" it is time for standard products, not gilded ones. Project groups should hand over any operations that have become routine and repetitive to lower-cost processes. Their advice could be invaluable in how to cut costs and they should get feedback on the quality of such consulting.

5   *From Family Culture to Incubator and back*

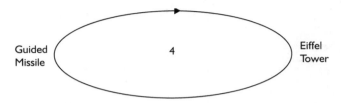

This company always had a close, fun, familiar, and intimate culture, in which the founders and their offspring had genuine concern and affection for the whole "family" of employees. The founder was a brilliant entrepreneur and his heritage has endured. His son, his nephew, and his niece all went to graduate schools and are real professionals. They are popular within the company and are very well qualified.

And yet…the founder is in his seventies. The company needs to renew itself. There have been no major innovations in fifteen years, and the business is living off the proceeds of the past. The proposal from a group of entrepreneurs is to buy up a small firm famous for its inventiveness yet lacking scale or adequate resources. The entrepreneurs want stock options which could put them at salaries larger than the founder's and much higher than anyone else earns. Nor are they very respectful of company history and traditions. "Create or die" was their message at a recent meeting.

The problem is not just their employment but the fact that their innovations, if successful, will change the whole company. It has been proposed that they share their vision of the future with the founder and he, they, and his family share it with everyone. They will decide as a group how enthused they are.

6   *From Family to Eiffel Tower and back*

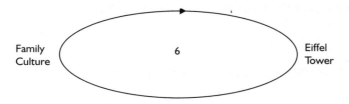

There comes a time when a company is simply too large to cohere at the level of personal relationships. Most of us can remember about a hundred names or more, but when a company gets bigger than this then informality reaches its limits. Unknown people must have a role, a task, a job description, or it becomes impossible to know whether people are doing the job they are paid to do. Bureaucracy creeps in when "the span of control" gets too wide.

Up to now no one has invented a real remedy for the "inevitable" arrival of the role or task culture, which consigns the Family culture to occasional parties. One device is to have small business units of less than one hundred, so that each "family" has "tasks" which they supervise in personal ways. Another possible remedy is to have "sculpted" or "creeping" job descriptions which are co-defined by supervisors and supervisees. Big corporations have ways of keeping family values alive; witness the Japanese tradition of the "elder brother–younger brother" mentoring relationship. Motorola still encourages the recruitment of relatives. In 1993 one employee had fifty relatives working for the company. Computer summer camps to which employees' children are invited can become an avenue for later recruitment.

Many large companies have encouraged networking among minorities and mentoring relationships across departments and functions, so that vulnerable persons have would-be champions, not in direct authority over them but ready to speak up for them.

7   *From Family to Guided Missile and back*

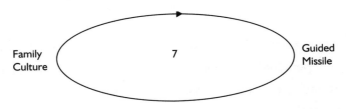

Family
Culture   7   Guided
                                     Missile

This is a good family company but it has to professionalize. The founder's sons and daughters are good people but no one seriously believes that they would have been selected on merit. Indeed, merit is not a high priority in this company nor is professionalism. Many customers have been with the company for thirty years or more and their loyalty, both to the company and to the family, is profound and touching. But the industry is changing now and there are rival technologies that need constant appraisal and expert judgement.

Three task forces have been set up, each chaired by a family member. Their mandate is to identify the professional expertise lacked and the best way to get across to such people. It is only when you set up such task forces that you realize how few experts you have! The hope is that the family members will become the main advocates of more professionalism and will allow themselves to be well advised. The company started recruiting from the country's leading engineering school only this year but most of those to whom it offered jobs turned it down.

8   *From Eiffel Tower to Incubator and back*

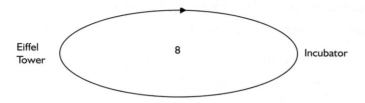

This move was relatively rare until the concept of reengineering became popular. Eiffel Tower cultures are completely dismantled by consultants, "reengineered," and then restored to Eiffel Tower status but in a new, less costly configuration. Because of the very high contrast between Eiffel Towers and Incubators this process is often traumatic and amounts to radical surgery, often costing hundreds of jobs.

The Incubator phase is temporary and rarely done by those within the Eiffel Tower culture but more usually by change agents consulting to the corporation.

A less common but more constructive alternative is the Scanlon Plan, invented by Joseph Scanlon. Routine "Eiffel Tower" operations are suspended for an hour or two each week and workers brainstorm possible changes in their work practices which will increase efficiency, lower costs, avoid waste, and innovate in general. Each work unit calculates an input–output ratio so that the pay-off for any innovations can be calculated. The general rule is that workers receive 50 percent of this pay-off, while 50 percent goes to the organization and its shareholders. For, say, 90 minutes every Friday afternoon all employees go into "incubator mode" and critique and improve their work environments.

Although such work is done in teams and is in part a guided missile operation, the stress is upon the creativity of individual workers, on working prototypes of new ideas, not on mere suggestions. Scanlon Plans almost died out in the late 70s; then the Japanese picked up on the idea and they were recreated in many US companies.

We are now in a position to place our Eight Scenarios of Culture Change upon our map, as shown in Figure 5.1.

Note that all circles which span at least two quadrants may be regarded as reconciliations of dilemmas, achieving tasks through people and developing people through tasks. We are now in a position to present our eight scenarios on six dilemma axes.

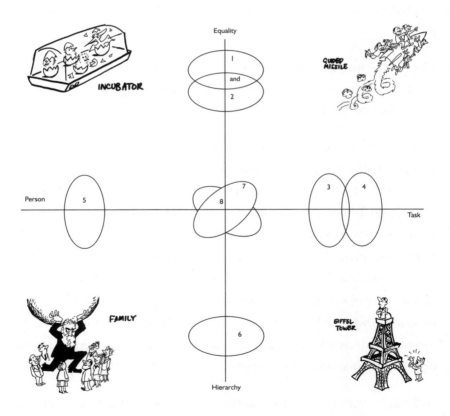

Figure 5.1 Eight scenarios of corporate culture change

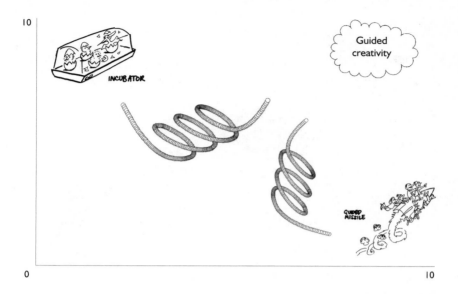

Figure 5.2 Scenarios 1 and 2

In Scenario 1 the Incubator culture (top left) takes on a sense of direction and guidance from product-oriented, customer-oriented teams, which culminates in Guided Creativity (top right).

In Scenario 2 the Guided Missile culture (bottom right) takes on the mission of innovation and creativity, monitoring its teams for originality. This also culminates in Guided Creativity (top right).

In Scenario 3 the Eiffel Tower culture (bottom right) renews itself by creating cross-functional teams oriented to projects, products, and customers, and culminating in Guided Restructuring (top right).

In Scenario 4 the Guided Missile culture (top left) needs to standardize and rationalize its more routine operations to lower costs, also culminating in Guided Restructuring (top right).

In Scenario 5 the Family culture (bottom right) needs to use its intimate relationship and informal ties to incubate new ideas and renew

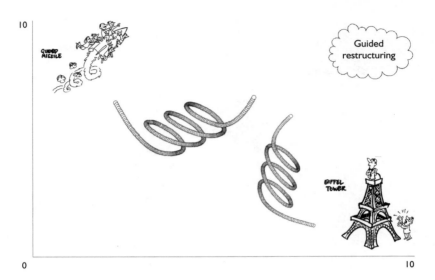

Figure 5.3   Scenarios 3 and 4

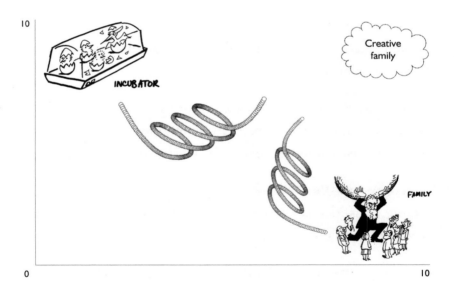

Figure 5.4   Scenario 5

its founding genius. This culminates in the Creative Family (top right).

Figure 5.5   Scenario 6

Figure 5.6   Scenario 7

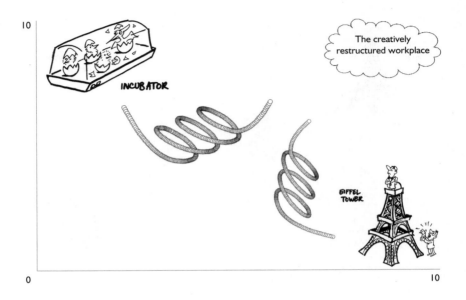

Figure 5.7 Scenario 8

In Scenario 6 the Family culture (bottom right) has outgrown its early intimacy and must allot tasks in a systematic way if it is not to lose control and direction. This culminates in the Reorganized Family (top right).

In Scenario 7 the Family culture (bottom right) decides it must professionalize and introduce external, qualified expertise. This culminates in the Professionally Guided Family using the best-qualified experts (top right).

In Scenario 8 the Eiffel Tower culture (bottom right) decides it must reorganize itself creatively, must radically rethink its structure and layout, freeing employees to assist in this process, which culminates in the Creatively Restructured Workplace (top right).

The above scenarios give us a new way of thinking about change across culture. Note particularly that these scenarios included an "and back" component, which is the essence of the dynamics. Each change scenario is more than just a single direction.

The classical French chemist Le Châtelier studied equilibrium systems and determined that a system in equilibrium will respond to stress in such a way so as to counteract that stress. This encapsulates thinking in which the parts (molecules) of the organization are constantly dancing to and fro between the extreme states. You need to have your cake and eat it.

CHAPTER 6

Marketing across cultures

Marketing professionals are becoming increasingly aware of the need to take account of culture when working in diverse markets. The issues of branding for different cultures and how to develop a marketing strategy for the global market are current fundamental questions for us all. Our methodological framework based on the recognition, respect, and reconciliation of cultural differences offers an approach to addressing these challenges.

Perhaps one could define marketing as the process of reconciling the needs and wants of the customer. All students of marketing know the story of the market researcher who went to Africa and called his boss reporting that they should call off the African launch of the shoes they were successfully selling in Europe. "Why?" asked his boss. "Because nobody wears shoes here," he was told. "Oh," said the boss, "So we must launch shoes there." "I don't understand," said the researcher, only to be told: "There is a great market out there with no competition." So many marketing professionals have told us that very often clients don't know what they want and that therefore they need to create a market (push). Others, however, say that a professional in marketing should thrive on the needs of clients and be able to listen carefully (pull). As soon as we go international we are faced even more with the imperative to reconcile needs and wants. Where internally-oriented cultures (such as the US) might start with a technology push in order to connect to the needs of clients at a later stage, the Japanese might first listen to the needs of clients and be pulled by them in order to attach to the developments of technology in a later stage.

Before we move to the central thrust of this chapter, let's first note that fundamental mistakes are too often still being made even at the most basic level of cultural differences. Many of these arise simply from language, religion, and common courtesy. Established product names in one language may have different meanings in other languages. Advertisements, symbols, or gestures in one culture (like the first finger and thumb) may have entirely opposite meanings in another. Red for danger in western cultures can send different messages about a product to a Chinese, for whom red can also represent success. Similarly, yellow as a color in marketing promotions may be offensive to Arabs when used in some contexts, yet might convey freshness and summer to western cultures. In addition, launch dates to promote new products accompanied by an extensive buffet lunch have been inappropriately scheduled during Ramadan.

More important than these overt and more obvious aspects of culture are differences that derive more subtly from the different meaning given by different cultures to apparently the same product or service. Thus people in the US may purchase a Sony Discman because it enables them to listen to their favorite music "without being disturbed by others." The Chinese may purchase the same product in order to listen to their favorite music "without disturbing others." The product may be technically identical, but the purchasing motive is different because of the different meanings and priorities given to oneself and to others' privacy.

By adopting an anti-ethnocentric approach, we can more easily recognize explicit cultural differences; however, we may not be aware of these above types of implicit cultural differences. Cultural due diligence is significantly absent from the management agenda and from many of the classic marketing models such as those of Porter. Most of classical marketing theory has been based on single culture research, especially the Anglo-Saxon studies.

Following the theme on which this book is based, our new marketing paradigm is intended to provide a robust framework for the marketer and is again based on the Three Rs : recognize, respect, and reconciliation. Thus the first step is to recognize that there are cultural differences in marketing. Different orientations about "where the customer is coming from" are not right or wrong; they are just different. It is all too easy to be judgmental about people and societies that give different meaning to their world from ours. The next step is to respect these differences and accept the customers' rights to interpret the world (and our products and marketing efforts) in the way that they choose.

Because of these different views of the world, we have two seemingly opposing views of the contrasting cultures – those of the seller and buyer. The classical approach is to focus solely on customer satisfaction: "to make what we know we can sell." But we also have to consider our own corporate knowledge: "to try to sell what we know we can make." Thus in our new approach the task of the marketer is more than abandoning our own strengths for the sake of customer satisfaction: it is to reconcile these seemingly opposing orientations.

To show how this can be achieved, we first describe some examples of products and brands that have faced fundamental dilemmas when going from local to international markets. We will follow the steps from local to global, and then on to a fully transnational brand.

Then we discuss how brands integrate the variety of value orientations into an integrated system of meaning. We explain why archetypes need to be integrated to a higher level once we go international. By following the same reconciliation paradigm, we review a variety of fundamental marketing issues that are affected by culture ranging from advertising to market research.

HOW MARKETING DEPENDS FUNDAMENTALLY ON CULTURAL DIFFERENCES

We can usefully exploit our dimensional cultural model to categorize the principal dilemmas that arise from a number of marketing perspectives.

The dilemma between the universal and the particular

In this dimension, the dominant dilemma is the global–local dichotomy. The question is whether there should be one standardized approach (identical product range and associated identical marketing support) or a local approach (different products and local based marketing in each destination). Do we think our customers are best served by becoming global and alike, or will they be more influenced by their particular national or local cultures?

This dilemma is reconciled through transnational specialization. We

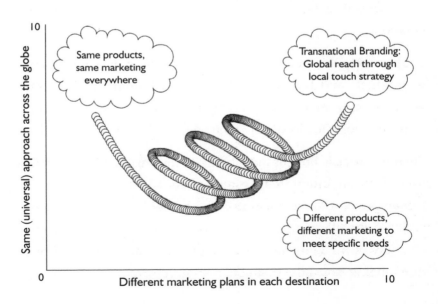

Figure 6.1 The global–local dilemma

continuously integrate best practice and satisfy customer needs by learning from the diversity of adopting, adapting, and combining the best.

We refer again to McDonalds who successfully achieve this integration by branding the Big Mac universally across the globe. The big "M" sign represents the universal corporate identity with standard furnishings and fittings in all their restaurants. Yet in the Middle East, the Big Mac is a vegiburger, and is served with rice rather than fries in Asia. Even smaller local variations are promoted, such as the 'croquet' variant in the Netherlands.

Heineken alters the temperature at which its beer is served to follow local tastes but also positions identical products differently in different markets to reflect the different meaning that drinkers ascribe to the product. In parts of Europe it is sold as "Beer as it is meant to be drunk." In the Caribbean it is positioned as being cosmopolitan. The (almost identical) TV advertisements in each island show the same shots of Paris, London and Tokyo – to represent the global branding of Heineken – but with some shots of easily recognizable, island-specific buildings or monuments to locate the global brand in the local context.

The average manager in the UK is universalistic in orientation, relying more on company-wide codes and procedures than on particular circumstances. Many managers may spend much of their time in practice dealing with the particular. However, in the UK there is a preference to start with norms and rules which apply to everyone and in all situations. This is manifest in the high priority given to the design and improvement of systems aimed at controlling the efficiency and predictability of all business processes. It is therefore common to find a great deal of emphasis on universally applicable measures and metrics both in the economic and human aspects of business. However, when we examine the functional specialism of the managers in our database (including those from the UK), we find that marketing professionals do tend to start more often from the particular perspective – that is what the customer wants – and then seek to reconcile these needs with the standard products or services they have.

Alain Giscard was giving a marketing presentation on Europe-wide trends in consumer taste. Using bar graphs, he showed that France led Europe in polysensuality (the ability to arouse the senses or appetites in multiple ways). Britain was trailing, but this trend was on the increase everywhere. The head of market research for Clorox, an American company, was having difficulties. "Surely poly-sensuality is a just a constructed concept. I mean, people don't tell your researchers 'I'm polysensual' or 'I'm feeling polysensual today'. It's a rational construct, created by your company. You believe consumers subscribe to it, but how would you recognize a polysensualist if you saw one? What would they say? The concept is not empirical!"

Alain became quite angry at this, and thumped his hand down on a whole pile of computer print-outs. "It's all here!" he shouted. "Three years of research. Very carefully verified!" The questioner shrugged his shoulders and gave up.

The problem here is that the French enjoy diffuse concepts like polysensuality and, therefore, being rationalists, not empiricists, see polysensuality as a crystal clear concept from which consumer reactions could be accurately deduced. The French do not start with "the facts" as Americans do, but with ways of perceiving and thinking; polysensuality is one of those ways. The attack was perceived as an attack not on the accuracy of the data and whether it could be checked easily, but on the rationality and mental capacity of the researcher. French market research is more interactive, with subjects reacting more to clever concepts, than the Anglo-Saxon equivalent. Data is not isolated but is interpreted based on interaction with observers.

Often, advertising from universalist companies implies that their solution is THE only possible answer to the customer's alleged question. One example of this is a zipped plastic bag, called "One Zip," which is described as THE solution to storing food and sealing in freshness. Another example can be seen in Ducal's advertisements for furniture. They describe their catalogue as "YOUR essential furniture guide." This statement is in large capitals making it stand out from the rest of the page. A fabric company calls itself the Fabric Choice Collection. Their advertisement proclaims "The finest fabric selection" and their slogan is "Always the right fabric."

The dilemma between individualism and communitarianism

This second dimension similarly gives rise to a number of key dilemmas. Is marketing concerned with satisfying individual customer needs and preferences, or is the focus on creating a trend or fashion that is adopted by the group? Individuals then purchase to show they have joined the group by following the shared trend. From the customers' perspective, do we relate to others by discovering what each one of us individually wants, or do we place ahead of this some shared concept with which we can identify and feel part of?

Thus although marketing to an individualistic culture might see the individual as an end, marketing will benefit from a collective arrangement as the means to achieve that end. Conversely, marketing to a communitarian culture sees the group as the target market yet can use feedback and suggested improvements from individuals.

The marketing relationship should be seen as circular. The decision to focus on one end is only arbitrary.

Microsoft Windows and its associated Office products offer the benefits of a group approach. Documents can be shared and exchanged, because they adhere to common file formats. Yet individuals can tailor the configuration of their system to satisfy individual preferences – such as the screen zoom level to meet their individual eyesight capabilities. Jaguar and Mercedes owners take pride in being a member of their club of fellow drivers of prestige cars. However, when they insert their key in the lock of their own car, the seats and driving mirror configure to their own preference, even though someone else may have altered these settings.

At the meta-level, we can see how Richard Branson has successfully reconciled the personalities of David and Goliath in the branding of Virgin. He successfully creates public sympathy in favor of the wronged individual confronting the collective assailant (the establishment).

The impact of the communitarian values of Chinese culture on the marketing of consumer goods is rather straightforward. Most goods are best positioned in a family or family-like collective environment. Family-like collectives frequently used in advertisements are colleagues, members of a sports team, or classmates at school. Within the collectives, the leading persons are often given some special attention or a special role.

The communitarian orientation of the Japanese has important implications for individualists doing business in Japan. When working with the Japanese, it is important to spend time working and socializing with colleagues and subordinates. In order to gain respect and be effective, one must be seen as a team player and as part of the group. As we have seen, office space is generally open so as to allow ample opportunity for teamwork, and it is common practice for the Japanese to consult with one another before taking action.

Although "self-reliance" has no translation in many languages, it has been eulogized in American literature by writers such as Ralph Waldo Emerson. Self-reliance is deeply ingrained in the average American from a very early age, and dependence is discouraged. Great emphasis is placed on personal growth and self-actualization.

Naturally, since independence and self improvement are so deeply ingrained in the average American, advertising is often designed to appeal to this aspect of the culture. There is, for example, an advertisement that shows a man facing physical as well as mental challenges and ends by saying "Be all that you can be. Join the Army." Other well-known ads are the Marlboro commercials that show a cowboy alone on his horse in the middle of the wilderness. The announcer invites the viewer to "come to Marlboro Country." The implied message is that in Marlboro Country, men are men and don't need anybody else. In more communitarian cultures this type of advertising would probably not have much appeal, but in the US it is quite effective.

The dilemma between specific and diffuse

What is the degree of involvement of the customer? Do we see customers as "punters," people from whom we can make a fast buck, or are they the basis for an ongoing series of relationships over time? Do we need a relationship first, before they can become our customers, or do we easily do business, from which a relationship may or may not follow?

Marketing through reconciliation is more than compromise. It is the craft of trying to define those specific areas to provide a more personal service and thereby deepen the relationship. Jan Carlson of SAS calls this the "moment of truth," as when during a few moments on a long haul flight the passenger interacts with the cabin crew. The experiences of these few seconds (or moments) will leave the traveler with a lasting impression that will influence their decision to fly again – or not – with the same airline and share their experience with their friends.

The role of the marketing team is therefore to identify those circumstances where specific moments can be used to deepen the relationship in the service being provided, so that it appears diffuse to the customer.

In Nordstrom, the US high-end department store, they demonstrate that they truly understand this concept. It is well known for its excellent customer service, including a "no questions asked" return policy. The company has even been known to accept returns that did not come from its store in the first place. Nordstrom actually engenders an atmosphere in which acts of exemplary service become legendary. The store even has a marketing budget for helping to create a buzz. One very well known story is that of a salesperson from their store in Chicago who helped a client buy a suitcase for his trip to Europe. After the customer left she found his passport and the ticket for his flight from New York to Europe on the counter. She couldn't find the customer so she took a flight from Chicago to NY with his passport and ticket. She was able to deliver both documents in time to the check-in counter of the departing transatlantic flight. The man promised never to buy anything from anyone other than Nordstrom again.

Obviously, these fables are extreme, but they demonstrate one thing – that this organization knows when to go the extra mile – a moment of truth.

When Fons experienced a "moment of truth"

I almost missed my flight to Ireland. It was on a Friday night around 6.00 p.m. I walked to the travel agent's desk at Schiphol Airport in Amsterdam; my flight to Kerry in Southern Ireland had a stopover in Dublin. When I asked for my ticket, the staff from the agency looked puzzled. They couldn't find it. I became a little nervous because the flight was at 6.45 and gates are often far away from the terminal. So they checked in the computer system and couldn't find a current reservation; worse, one had been cancelled some five days earlier by my office. So we rushed to the Aer Lingus desk to book a late seat. They couldn't find a free space, so they asked me for my name to book me on the next flight at 7.45 p.m. to Belfast. I would miss my connection with the last flight that night to Kerry, but what could I do? I had to speak at the Irish Management Institute on Saturday at 8.30 a.m. So I booked a seat on the later flight, arranged a hotel and a private jet from Dublin for the next morning – for a discounted price of US$3000. All with the help of wonderful Aer Lingus.

However, when I had to give my name for the bookings, the Irish lady at the desk said "Trompenaars? But we have a ticket waiting for you on the earlier flight." I realized that the IMI had organized a ticket for me, and that it was not booked through my office, but by then it was too late. So under my new itinerary I sat on the 19.45 flight to Belfast. We took off within 10 minutes, which is a record for a Friday night at Schiphol. The pilot said we got permission from air traffic control to go a bit early and that one particular passenger would be highly delighted. I realized it was me! We arrived half an hour before the scheduled arrival time, and I was able to catch the last flight to Kerry; in fact the pilot informed me that an Aer Lingus person would wait at the gate to get me on to my connection. I was driven by car to the plane waiting to go to Kerry that night; the chauffeur asked me the name of my hotel and the private jet company so they could cancel the arrangements. I made it to the conference that very evening. And I promised to tell any-body in doubt to fly Aer Lingus; I also used the case the next morning. The resulting applause was for an organization that understands moments of truth.

What is the generalization we can draw from these cases? In market-ing a brand, product or service organizations will gain significant strength when they can identify when to go deep. Obviously, if air-lines always adapt to the needs of individual passengers in the way Aer Lingus did, they would go bust. If Nordstrom employees always ran after their clients from Chicago to New York they would also go bankrupt. Let's consider the reconciliation graphic, as shown in Figure 6.2.

Due to the strong technical orientation of German management, it is often inadvisable to send only marketing or sales people into busi-ness negotiations if some technical issues may be involved. Germans do not like to discuss the broad outlines of a business proposal and leave the details to the technicians. Indeed the German side may often strongly involve its own technical personnel in making a deci-

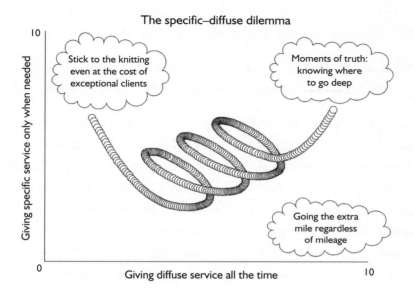

Figure 6.2 Towards "moments of truth"

sion. They are therefore more interested in the exact technical details than in seamless presentation skills. It is also important to keep in mind that generally speaking, marketing people do not enjoy particularly high status in German organizations.

In contrast, French marketing is often highly context-dependent and holistic. Turn the television on, and you may not know what is being advertised even if you understand the words and the captions. As in most high-context cultures, advertising in France often involves a context that is meant to trigger associations among French viewers. Many French advertising campaigns are elaborate and attempt to create whole environments. For example, a complete Provençal village square was created in Harrods to sell French products. L'Oréal had portraits commissioned of "Les Dames de Beauté," beautiful ladies, mostly queens and royal mistresses, who inhabited châteaux on the River Loire. The complexion of each beauty was matched to an appropriate line of cosmetics.

The dilemma between neutral and affective orientation.

What part do the display and role of emotion play, and/or is the display of emotion controlled? What shapes the purchasing decisions?

Peter Darke and his research team argue that it doesn't matter whether you're buying a new car or a new shade of lipstick; in all cases you are likely to consider both tangible factors (product features, price, etc.) as well as intangible qualities (such as how the product makes you feel). Their research demonstrates how affective (emotional) experience can be influential even when consumers are highly motivated and fully capable of making rational decisions on the basis of tangible features. Indeed, marketing research has shown the importance of affective cues (preferences based on feelings) and informational cues (preferences based on features) in the consumer decision making processes. It appears that affective cues have an impact on judgment primarily when consumers are less motivated to adopt a rational, analytic approach, especially when they perceive they have a diminished ability to judge products. Furthermore, choices made with a high affective component are often perceived as impulse purchases which consumers ultimately regret. This is the familiar "buyer's remorse" syndrome. Affectivity also explains why many women enjoy "retail therapy" even to the point of just window shopping with their friends, rather than making actual purchases.

Typically reason and emotion are linked or combined. When customers express satisfaction (or dissatisfaction!), they are trying to find confirmation in their thoughts and feelings – and trying to show they have the same response as others ("I have the same view of this product/service as you") and this is embodied in the Theory of Conspicuous Consumption (Bagwell and Bernheim, 1996). Customers, whose response is neutral, are seeking an indirect response.

The dilemma for Johnson and Johnson

What challenges arose when Johnson and Johnson wanted to launch a line of its baby products through a series of ads across different cultures?

The first series was launched in the USA where a Caucasian mother is holding her newborn first baby. The ad is filled with an atmosphere of tenderness and love. The music is a soft, typical American voice singing "the language of love." The ad was subsequently "translated" for many countries in South America, Asia and Europe. The song had local lyrics and the mother was obviously from the country where the ad was shown. Everything was different except the brand concept.

However, after some response feedback it became clear that further adaptations needed to be made. In Australia as well as in Britain, the emotional aspects were given less prominence for obvious reasons. In France and Italy, emotions played the central role.

This is a powerful example of how one can universalize the concept of maternal love and particularize the expression of emotions in the different cultures. In all markets the perceived meaning matched with the intended meaning.

As Tom Peters said in a presentation to the Shell Human Resource Management Conference in Atlanta in 1999, "It's cool to be emotional nowadays." That is reconciliation.

The dilemma between achievement and ascription

Do customers want a functional product that achieves a utilitarian purpose or are they buying status? You can tell the time from a US$1 LED digital watch as well as you can with a US$10,000 Rolex Oyster. But a Rolex Oyster is a symbolic representation of status, not simply a watch.

All societies give certain members higher status than others, signaling that unusual attention should be focused on those persons and the products they own and display and the services they consume. In achievement-oriented cultures the emphasis is on performance, reliability and functionality. In ascribed-status cultures, such as Asia, status is ascribed to products that naturally evoke admiration from others, such as high technology and jewelry. Status is less concerned with the functional capabilities of the product. Motives for acquiring ascribed status by making purchases vary across cultures.

Of course, the same product such as a Mercedes car is sold in different countries. But in Germany you will be selling reliable, quality German engineering that will get you to work down the autobahn quickly and safely. In a third world country you'll be selling status.

The dilemma between internal and external control

Are we stimulated by an inner drive, or do we adapt to external events that are beyond our control? The main issue here is to connect the internally-controlled culture of technology push (sell what we can make) with the externally-controlled world of market pull (make what we can sell).

Nobody will deny the great knowledge and inventiveness of Philips in both its technologies and the quality of its marketing. The problem was that these two major areas didn't seem to connect. The push of the technology needs to help you decide what markets you want to be pulled by, and the pull of the market needs to help you know what technologies to push.

Dilemmas arising because of the different meanings given to time

Do we view time as sequential or synchronic? Is it based on short-term or long-term interests? And do we predominantly focus on the future, the present, or the past? These are three basic elements of time that are seen differently through different cultural spectacles. With sequential cultures, time is an objective measure of passing increments. The faster you can act and get to the market, the more effective will be your competitiveness. In contrast, synchronous cultures like doing things "just in time," so that the present converges on the future. The more synchronous your timing, the more competitive you will be.

Keeping traditional products that made your name in the first place can jeopardize the creation of new ones. Karel Vuursteen of Heineken successfully integrated the (past) traditions of the Heineken family with the future needs of the company, and the traditions of the Heineken product with the need for (future) innovation – for example in the area of specialty beers. Process innovation sought new methods of creating the same result (traditional product), whilst product innovation allowed new drinks from scratch without prejudicing Heineken's premium product in the experiments.

In our research, we have elicited evidence that cultures have quite different time horizons. On the one hand we know cultures that run from quarter to quarter. Here you see the sales person dating the sale with next week's date, because they have already achieved their sales target for the current period, and so this sale can be counted towards the next period's target. Again others seem to be planning far further ahead. They are very effective in reaching far-end goals at the cost of short-term flexibility. Clotaire Rapaille has termed the first short-term approach "animal time" and the second one "founding time." The American code for time, for example, is an animal one that emphasizes short-termism and the immediate present: just do it, instant gratification, shareholder value, "greed," and the like. The long-term Japanese sense of time is best illustrated by a short anecdote. When a Japanese company wanted to become involved in the operations of Yosemite National Park in California they submitted a 250-year business plan (logical if you know the average age of a redwood tree). The Californian civil servant's reaction was something like: "Gee, that's 1000 quarterly reports!" Mainland China's approach to reunification with the Republic of China (Taiwan) is similarly long term, over several future generations.

But animal time can only work when it is integrated with founding time. At the extreme of the American time axis that focuses on the here and now, we find that the US has the oldest written constitution in the world. Other countries, including Japan and France, have changed their constitution repeatedly. In short, Americans like change, as long as fundamentals are not altered. If the foundations are stable, we are able to enjoy animal time and vice versa.

Like all these dilemmas, this basic construct applies directly to marketing. It is wonderful to see the American marketing gurus Al Ries and Jack Trout, in the introduction of their best-seller *Bottom-Up Marketing,* say "We live in an age of competition. In almost every category, today's business arena has become warlike. This change of environment has made the traditional top-down (only) approach to marketing obsolete. What good are long-term strategic plans when you cannot predict future competitive moves? How can you react to a competitor if your resources are tied up in a long-term plan?" However, Ries and Trout are very aware that you need to reconcile even though they haven't conceptualized this explicitly. They argue against the traditional theory which says that top management should first set the strategy for a marketing campaign. Then the strategy should be turned over to the middle managers who select the tactics to use to execute the strategy. They disagree and suggest the opposite: bottom-up marketing. Applied across cultures, this is an even bigger issue. We argue that the dilemma for marketing is universal. On the one hand we need a strategy that gives us a long-term context and directions for our journey, whilst on the other hand we need to be able to create different and unique ideas in our short-term needs to best serve our environment. Graphically this dilemma could be presented as shown in Figure 6.3

It is inherent from Ries and Trout that they believe that tactics in marketing will automatically create the soundest strategy. We disagree. Our evidence supports the assertion that both tactics and strategy feed into each other in a continuous crafting process. The

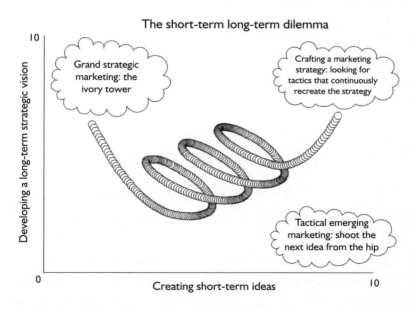

Figure 6.3 The short- versus long-term dilemma

starting point depends on your culture. Short-term cultures like to start with tactics. Conversely, long-term cultures might start with a strategy to contextualize their tactics. The winners are those who can integrate (reconcile); which direction you start from is irrelevant.

In conclusion, our new Marketing paradigm thus requires a mindset that reconciles these continuing dilemmas that can arise from all of the above cultural dimensions. Today's successful marketing is the result of linking learning effort across each dimension with the contrasting orientations and viewpoints.

THE MEANING OF BRANDS ACROSS CULTURES

Brands, products, and services are complex systems of meaning. Different issues about different meanings given to these facets pervade a variety of cultural dimensions at the same time. In this section we will combine a variety of dimensions which, in their very unique combinations, become archetypes.

Archetypical research shows that the dilemmas described above do not simply disappear but instead become more complex conjugates. Again our work shows that the internationalization of marketing creates new challenges for marketing professionals.

Unilever Japan's dilemma

A riddle puzzled the American marketing manager of Unilever Japan. He was faced with a significant decrease in sales and market share of its Sunsilk shampoo. Traditional market research failed to show any concrete reasons for this: What do you expect, was the reaction – traditional Japanese double-talk. The drastic fall in sales followed the introduction of a new commercial in which a young woman washed her hair and dried it afterwards. Slow-motion movements contributed to the ad's sensuality, her hair making a slow, undulating swing. Then suddenly her doorbell rang and a close-up showed a male hand opening the door. A pack shot then appeared on the screen.

In *Seven Secrets of Marketing in a Multicultural World* Clotaire Rapaille describes how you can decode the archetype of this product with certain "imprinting sessions." Shampoo doesn't just consist of functional characteristics, but is also part of the surrounding culture. You need to go back to the archetype of the product, and in the US this is done by linking the product with a certain sensuality.

However, this message did not get through in Japan. Japanese women were shown the commercial and asked to describe what they thought the man was going to do after he opened the door. A lot of them wrote "he takes a sword and cuts her head off" – and Unilever knew why sales had gone down. The archetypes of the brand and product may be universal; the messages are culturally determined.

In *Did the Pedestrian Die?* Fons looked at this case, and others. The Unilever example is about how messages, in the outer rim of our cultural onion, are interpreted differently. However, we also find cultural misunderstandings going to the inner levels of the onion model – to the level of basic assumptions.

A number of years ago the Japanese company NTT asked the cable division of AT&T to produce a cable on the basis of a number of technical specifications. The cables were delivered but the Americans were completely surprised when the Japanese returned them almost immediately. They had been produced exactly according to the technical standards AT&T had been given. When asked why they were returning them, NTT answered "because they are ugly." In Japan if something is ugly it cannot be good.

The Americans at AT&T now understand that today a brand is not only a collection of functional characteristics, but also a system of meaning and more deeply-held values. The understanding and use of the deepest meaning, which was once an interesting bonus for a product, is now a primary requirement for being successful in the longer term. In their works Clotaire Rapaille and authors like Margaret Mark and Carol Pearson offer a number of interesting concepts and tools in order to map the archetype, the deepest psychological structures of a product or service.

If one examines universally held models (for example, those of Jung or Maslow), it seems that humanity faces a pair of fundamental dilemmas, regardless of cultural differences.

The initial dilemma concerns the tension field in every person to find their own way as an individual and the desire to belong to a group. The second is the dilemma between the need for safety and stability contrasted with the need for challenge, excitement and the desire to change the environment. On each axis of these dilemmas we find a number of archetypes – see Figure 6.4.

In *Did the Pedestrian Die?*, Fons looked at the archetypes in detail. Let's recap.

The archetypes for the first category – independents – are the Innocent, the Explorer, and the Sage. Everyone is, in their own way,

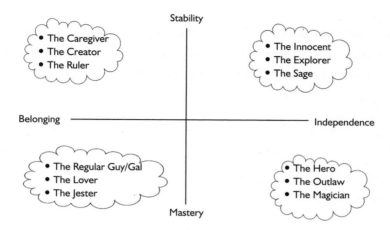

Figure 6.4 Mapping the archetypes

trying to escape from the group to which they belong. All three archetypes of this category are individualistic in nature.

Thus the *Innocent* product strives for loyalty and predictability; typical examples are Coke and McDonalds. The Innocent is universalistic, internally oriented, ascriptive and past oriented. And here you can see what happens if you deviate from an archetype, as was made clear when New Coke was introduced with a sweeter taste, to compete directly with Pepsi. Coca-Cola had to return to their roots with Classic Coke, "the real thing."

The *Explorer* brand does not exist in the tranquility of a naive paradise, but goes in search of a better world. Good examples are Timberland, Ralph Lauren, Jeep, and Starbucks. Explorer brands unite a particularistic, inner-directedness, achievement oriented and short-term future with an individualistic orientation.

Finally there is the *Sage* brand which wants to help the purchaser believe that an ideal world exists as you keep learning and growing in freedom and open-mindedness. Sage brands are universalistic, inner directed, ascriptive, beyond time, and – obviously – again very individualistic. In America the bookselling chain Barns & Noble would certainly belong to this archetype, as would TV icon Oprah Winfrey.

Successful products and people also exist in an opposite set of archetypes. This trio gives the customer the impression of "belonging," and these too can be approached in several ways. They all share a communitarian orientation.

Pearson and Mark distinguish the Regular Guy/Gal, the Lover, and the Jester as different ways of belonging to a larger group. The *Regular Guy/Gal* type assumes that all people are equal and avoids any type of elitist behavior. The orientation that is strongest here next to the sense of belonging is achievement orientation. These brands are Avis ("we try harder") rather than Hertz, VISA rather than American Express, and Volkswagen rather than BMW.

Lover brands are often present in cosmetics, fashion and travel organizations. They refer to sex appeal and beauty and belong through an affective and diffuse and external orientation. Latin brands such as Chanel, Yves St. Laurent, Gucci, and Ferrari are leading the pack.

Finally we have the *Jester* type, stimulating individuals to enjoy being with each other. Next to a group-oriented attitude they can be characterized as very affective and externally oriented. This archetype is embodied by brands such as Pepsi and Burger King, whose identity to a large part is developed by teasing their bigger brothers Coke and McDonalds.

In order to be internationally successful with a brand you need to incorporate contradictions between the archetypes on a higher level. A splendid example of this is how Barnes & Noble transformed itself to an international brand of great integrity. After Leonard Riggio acquired the well-known but financially unhealthy B&N, he immediately started a successful price war. He was therefore able to buy lots of other bookshops and chains on which he continued to stick the almost monk-like logo of Barnes & Noble. After he had preserved this quite independent and individualistic image by means of exploiting the strength of its brand, he designed bookshop after bookshop with a simple living room in which there were some comfortable chairs and in which coffee was served. Thus B&N developed into a total experience where independent "Sages" could exchange their latest brilliant ideas with similar people in a community of individualists. And B&N has grown into the largest bookshop chain in the world.

Following the same logic, the international success of Chanel can also be explained by a similar integration of archetypes. Although Chanel is a classic "Lover" brand, it is known that Chanel herself, although quite a sexy lady, was also fiercely independent. In her eyes, women could only charm men by being independent; when asked why she refused to marry one of the richest men in Europe she answered "There are a lot of Dukes of Westminster. But there is only one Chanel." And by integrating independents and lovers she gave just the right scent to successful international marketing.

The reconciliation can be mapped as shown in Figure 6.5

As above, the second category of dilemmas derives from the needs for safety and stability by riding the waves of the environment around you, and on the other the need for being in control of the environment by changing it.

The three archetypes that reflect the need to change the world could be defined as the Hero, the Outlaw, and the Magician.

Heroes are driven by the anguish of being a victim and for this reason

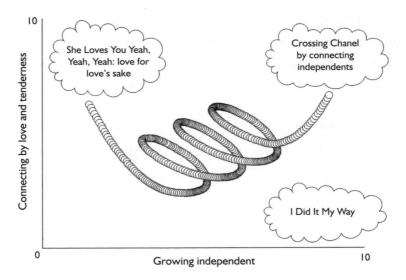

Figure 6.5 Chanel: the Lover–Hero dilemma

they admire action and decisiveness. All Heroes share an inner directed, individualistic and achievement orientation. Typical examples of Hero products are Federal Express and Nike ("Just Do It"), and, as an individual, this archetype is typified by Lance Armstrong, the American cyclist and four-time winner of the Tour de France after successfully fighting cancer. A lot of heroes are portrayed in the motorcar industry. To boast its Hero brand, Nike even went so far as to formulate its mission as: "To experience the emotion of competition, winning and crushing competitors." But you need to be careful not to go too far with this archetype. In the US there was much criticism of Nike's advertising campaign in which an athlete had to overcome all kinds of life-threatening incidents (explosions, fires) in order to finish as the winner. This was shown during the public discussion about Nike's involvement with child labor in the Far East. This shows the danger – common to all archetypes – of degenerating into a stereotype.

Decision or no decision?

An American sales representative was negotiating with some Germans from Siemens about the sale of a dozen machines for the semiconductor industry. Since his company was offering high quality at a good price, the man knew that they had no real competition. After an excellent presentation, the head of purchasing and the highest technical person, who were jointly responsible for any purchase over $10 million, were overtly impressed. They both said that they wanted to purchase the machines in approximately six months. In view of their decisive posture, the American was quite certain that this was a done deal. A week later, however, he got a written request to make a second presentation because Siemens wanted to include some of their major suppliers in the decision-making process. He was quite surprised by this because the two men from Siemens were from the highest possible decision-making level. They had agreed to the deal, but now they wanted to involve their suppliers.

The American in this case had interpreted the positive individual reactions of the two top executives at Siemens to mean that the deal had been made. What he did not take into consideration is that individuality in Germany means a strong-minded, confident personality; it does not mean that individuals have the power to make decisions without consulting the group. In this case, the German communitarian tendency can be seen in the fact that the Siemens team wanted to reach some form of consensus, even including long-term suppliers to the organization.

The archetype of the *Outlaw* has the attraction of forbidden fruit. They frequently present themselves as romantic characters, those who blow a new spirit into an organization which has suffered tyranny or oppression or which has worked too long under a dominant political party. Good examples are Richard Branson, Harley-Davidson, and Apple. Outlaws are particularistic, individualistic and achievement oriented. They cannot stand the status quo.

The third archetype is the *Magician*, the type that wants to change the world with new technologies, the Internet, biochemistry, and genetic manipulation. Splendid examples are Sony, Ritz Carlton Hotels, and the marvelous Harry Potter-like feeling that you can cross the complete world with a little bit of plastic – MasterCard. Magicians combine inner directedness with affection in the search for a new universal truth.

Unfair competition?

In 1975, AATM brought a suit against Sanyo for unfair competition. It was revealed that Sanyo had approached Sears Roebuck and had offered to supply them with "own brand" TV sets called "Sears," and priced at 15 percent below US domestic brands – a price below the cost of manufacture. A second count charged that Sears received a rebate for every hundred sets sold, equivalent to a further 10 percent price discount. Sanyo and Sears counter-argued that the discount was offered in exchange for Sanyo providing after-sales service and charging customers directly for repairs.

The AATM also complained that the after-sales service was a disguised form of direct selling with the result that customers were sold additional Sanyo appliances. The courts found in favor of AATM, but by that time, it had been dissolved. There were not enough US television manufacturers remaining.

Why were Sanyo's tactics so hard to counter? Why did Sears go along?

Sanyo was difficult to counter because businesses motivated by inner-directed self-interest can be easily picked off. Once you let the Japanese into "after-sales service" they will capture the replacement sale and the next, getting much closer to the customer. Courts are far too slow to stop these tactics even where they are illegal; you are out of business by the time the appeal is heard if not before. Sears went along because it was well paid for doing so. Outer-directed tactics can easily capture the allegiance of inner-directed profit seekers.

On the other side of the tension arc, which fulfills the need of structuring the world (or if you like, giving it safety and stability), you find the three archetypes of the Caregiver, the Creator, and the Ruler. They all share a feeling of outer and other directedness.

The *Caregiver* stands for altruism, carries the weight of the world on its shoulders and is very sensitive to the vulnerability of mankind. Caregivers are universalistic, communitarian, affective, and diffuse. This archetype is of course very popular in the health sector and in pharmaceutical, philanthropic, and welfare institutions. Brands such as Volvo, General Electric, BT, and the State Lottery therefore trade on empathy, communication, consistency, and faith – all of which are high in the standards of their messages.

The *Creator* is a reflection of the artist, the innovator, and the

Korean dilemmas

Koreans tend to be thought of as the "individualists of Asia." This is due in large part to the fact that most Asians have an external locus of control, and Koreans have more of an internal locus of control. Koreans tend to believe that they can control and influence the environment, once they understand how it works. In contrast most other Asians stress the importance of living in harmony with nature, which means accepting forces and dynamics which may be of unknown origin.

One of the dichotomies in Korean organizations is the contrast between internal control and hierarchical management styles. The Confucian view that a higher position and more experience command more respect and the militaristic Korean culture combine to yield a preference for hierarchical management systems. In a mechanistic, internally-oriented culture, the use of personal power and the occasional resulting conflicts are viewed as the normal order of things.

Korean business culture is characterized by the willingness to take risks in a highly competitive market. Korea, with a population of some 44 million people, is among the largest producers of home appliances, semiconductor chips, and ships. The fact that they have a competitive advantage in world trade may be attributed to their disciplined labor force, investment-oriented companies, aggressive managerial goals, and fierce domestic rivalry.

Part of Korea's uniqueness is its ability to fully assimilate and improve on foreign technology.

Korean companies are production oriented. Their approach has been to mass-produce standardized products, so they have been able to achieve low production costs. A unique feature of many Korean companies is their early efforts to develop their own product models and to market abroad under their own brand names. They have also been quick to establish foreign manufacturing plants. Korean companies look for aggressive growth over profitability. Volume is the key factor that leads to aggressive pricing. Having a cash flow in order to fund growth is more important than immediate profits. The *chaebol* Sankyung, for instance, states in its "Sankyung Management System" (SKMS) that "the goals of an enterprise are survival and growth."

non-conformist. Next to an outer directedness, the Creator is particularist, affective, and individualist. Splendid brands such as Sesame Street and Swatch watches have been established as such. If you can imagine it, it can also be made. But the Creator also knows that the critics will come down hard and fast. They know that they need structures to make their end product a success. If you are not careful, you can take the archetype too far into irresponsible behavior and daydreaming.

Finally, the *Ruler* archetype stands for control of what exists in order to avoid chaos. The Ruler dominates the world in the wish to help it to create wealth. Rulers are universalistic, neutral, and ascription oriented. This archetype is also clearly portrayed in commercials – American Express, Microsoft, and Procter & Gamble are good examples of Ruler brands. American Express, for example, had a successful campaign in which easily-recognized personalities used the card to be treated like royalty whether they were recognized or not.

The importance of high ascribed status in Japanese society and business is reflected in the importance of reputation, both of a person and of a company as a whole. An international company such as Unilever is known among the general public in Europe mainly by its brand names. In Japan, such a company is forced to emphasize its corporate reputation in marketing and advertising. The importance of reputation in Japan is clearly visible around lunch hour, when you will see people line up to eat at a restaurant with "reputation" even if there are plenty of other good restaurants around that have tables available.

In the same arena, cultural differences can influence effectiveness of how the archetype is communicated and received. Thus Hero brands can be very successful in internally-oriented countries as France and the United States. In more externally-controlled countries, like the Netherlands or Denmark, you have to be very careful with product comparisons in a commercial claiming that competitive products are worse than your own. Remember the time that Proctor & Gamble's detergent division was devouring OMO (of Unilever)? They launched a very tough and specific promotional campaign in Europe (and even more exposure resulted from free media attention). They showed that OMO destroyed the texture of laundry after a couple of washes. In a few weeks OMO lost significant market share, market share that was nicely re-allocated to the main detergent lines of P&G. P&G won the battle but lost the war. For a long time women in the Netherlands avoided P&G detergents because they had harmed their competitor. That's not done in externally controlled cultures, or as the English would say, "It's just not cricket."

To become successful internationally the challenge is to integrate archetypes on a higher level but avoid the pitfall of the exaggerated stereotype. For example, General Electric recognized the inherent risk of an archetype taken too far; it changed into a Hero, improving the world by innovation (and technology). Hence, GE's well-known slogan of the eighties – "living better electronically" – was changed to "GE – we bring good things to life." Text and context are thereby exchangeable. This explains the trend that can now be observed in Europe, where the accent is put on taking care of humanity. There was a recent television commercial in which an Italian football player had injured himself. Italian football fans cried and shouted in a typically overt Latin manner. The player was immediately driven from the field to a GE MRI scan and, thanks to high-tech photography, was revealed as not having a serious injury. In the next shot he scored the winning goal for Italy. Subsequently a GE operative was thanked by phone in an equally emotional scene, and the ad finished with the line "I am just doing my job."

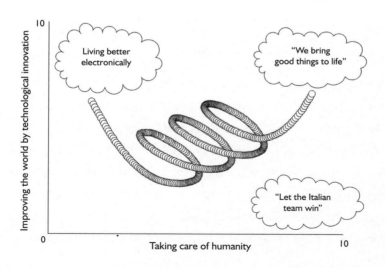

Figure 6.6   GE: the Hero–Caregiver dilemma

Sesame Street is another exemplar of an internationally successful brand. It is satisfying to observe the very subtle reconciliation of the Creator archetype within a context of the archetype, which tries to change the world as Educator. In each local version of Sesame Street around the world a creative team of artists cooperates very closely with a team of professional didactics. Creation and education and divergence and convergence are reconciled in such a manner that the show is lifted beyond culture. Mark and Pearson have noted this: "But a healthy tension between unbridled creativity and the educational work of Sesame Street is at the heart of the successes of this Creator Brand. Yet the collaboration is a happy and successful one, because, as Truglio from VP research says: 'We have a mutual respect for each other's craft'."

The reconciliation of opposite systems of meaning, or archetypes of brands, achieves success by making them less sensitive to differing cultural interpretations. The aim should be to create an integrated brand that doesn't go over the top in terms of mastering or changing the environment, or of being part of a community or of striving for

Aspro

A young couple is woken by an alarm clock at 6.30 am. The man jumps out of bed and drops a tablet into a glass of water. He walks to his partner and wakes her by upsetting the glass over her head. She demands to know what on earth it is and he replies by saying that it's an Aspro. Baffled, she informs him that she doesn't have a headache, upon which he goes back under the sheets... The ad is brilliantly finished by "ASPRO – for worse times." In any culture the Caregiver can become a Hero.

individual independence. The tension is often released through humor – such as in an advertisement for Aspro which shows how a supportive partner can become a Hero archetype.

FURTHER ASPECTS OF CULTURE AND MARKETING

This last section discusses a variety of marketing subjects that are affected by culture, ranging from advertising to market research. Space prevents us delving into all the aspects of the marketing process. We will limit ourselves to advertising and market research. But once you can follow our logic of reconciliation, you can extend the principles.

Market research

A first step in trying to ask fundamental questions about markets and customers requires market research. Many problems will be encountered, and many are very similar to the problems encountered by doing any multicultural research.

Usunier, in his impressive handbook for intercultural marketing, has devoted a whole chapter to the problems of cross-cultural market research. We restrict our discussion here to the typical dilemmas that an international market researcher will encounter and offer suggestions on how they can be reconciled.

It is unwise to extend national market research to a foreign environment without significantly reflecting on the research design. You will encounter differences in the nature of the market information, the methods of collecting that information, the validity and reliability of that information, etc. International market researchers need to go beyond their ethnocentric pre-conditioning by increasing the feedback channels. There is a need to look at formal and informal equivalence of constructs and instruments. A general guideline should be that we need to search for the meaning of products, brands, distribution, price, etc., etc. Using our language to achieve robust meaningful generalizations upon which decisions can be based, requires the reconciliation between large sample, questionnaire-like reliability with small intimate focus groups and consumer panel validity.

Functional versus holistic equivalence

The first dilemma the international researcher is likely to face is between the functional attributes of a product/service versus the holistic experience of that product.

Too many international researchers are still looking for the functional equivalence of the products that are to be launched. As a consequence many problems occur from this level. When seeking data about a car, for example, it is likely that functions of performance (speed/horsepower, aesthetics/design/color, safety, ease of use, status, reliability) are all important in any culture. Conjoint analysis can be used to assess the significant differences in the relative contribution of these functional attributes across cultures. In Sweden, aspects of safety, mileage, and reliability might have a higher significance than in Italy where aesthetics and status might score lower entropy. Obviously in gathering this information attention needs to be given to seeing whether the analysis and measurement is equivalent.

However, when trying to assess the holistic aspects of the product, we see interesting differences across cultures. As we have illustrated in our archetypal research in the preceding section, specific characteristics of a product are uniquely combined in the mind and heart of individuals of a particular culture. Therefore, when attempting research at the holistic edge of products, suddenly all functional characteristics acquire a different meaning. In some cultures for example, safety is very much linked to the color of the car, while in other cultures safety has much to do with the performance of the car and its reliability. More drivers of red cars than green cars are involved in accidents in many western cultures; this may be explained by drivers who are more "adventurous" seeking a surrogate Ferrari as the family car. The color red has meaning over and above the functional aspect of the color.

To achieve a successful international launch of a product, both the functional and holistic aspects need to be reconciled. If a product is perceived purely as an accumulation of functional characteristics in one culture while in another the feel of the whole is more dominant, international advertising becomes a nightmare. Consider a watch. In the US it needs to be functional, while in Italy it adds to or confirms the status or lifestyle of the person wearing it. And you just need to look at the tremendous success of Swatch to see that a reconciliation of both (thanks also to the introduction of quartz technology) can lead to international success. Would you have imagined that Volvo could have international success with a convertible version of its car, knowing that its status was derived only from safety? Let's represent what these have reconciled graphically (Figure 6.7)

The market researcher needs to be aware that both aspects need to be critically evaluated as a basis from which reconciliation is possible. For the more technical aspects of achieving functional and holistic aspects of market research we refer the reader to Usunier (1996) and de Mooij (1997).

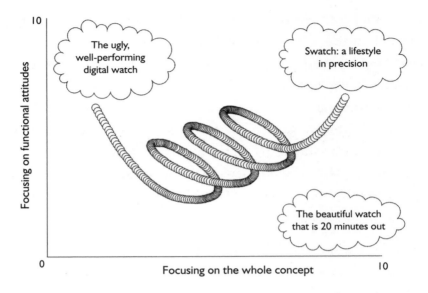

Figure 6.7 The function–whole concept dilemma

The emic–etic dilemma

This dilemma was elicited by Sapir in 1929 and refers fundamentally to the degree to which cultures are unique or not.

The "emic" approach assumes that the attitude and behavior are unique to any culture. In its extreme, it suggests that comparative research is impossible. The "etic" approach tries to look for universal similarities. These assumptions will obviously significantly influence the research design. If one assumes the uniqueness of any particular culture, then measurement instruments need to be particularized to the local environment. These instruments have the advantage of a high reliability within that culture; the disadvantage is obviously that one cannot use them in other cultures. The most obvious ones are the use of language and the researchers themselves. They are all local. But the type of instruments will also be local. So questionnaires that might be used in the low-context US are not used in Burkina Faso because face-to-face interviews reveal better information in high-context cultures. Even the use of Likert scales – ranging from strongly agree to strongly disagree – are often interpreted differently across cultures.

Again, our purpose here doesn't permit us to go into further detail so we focus on the conceptual dilemmas that researchers will face. The issue becomes one of dealing with the tension of trying to be unique in gathering data versus the need to secure robust generalizations. It is crucial for transnational marketing that these are reconciled. The launch of multi-local products doesn't provoke any field problems. You do research locally and market the product locally. Global products are no issue either; you just extend the research findings you found in the country where the product originated. However, for truly trans-national products you need market research that reconciles the emic and etic propositions.

A very fruitful approach is to take the tool developed in the home country and try to get similar results through alternative research techniques abroad. If, for example, an online questionnaire works well in the US, you might ask the same questions (etic) in another format such as face-to-face-interviewing (emic) in Burkina Faso. In the adjustment of your instruments, however, it is crucial that both functional and conceptual equivalence is reached through these different approaches. Crucial to this process is that the marketing research team consists of a mirror image of the countries involved. By discussing the dilemmas they face together, they can realize equivalence of meaning in order that the optimum research plans are executed. The dilemma appears as shown in Figure 6.8.

A good example of this reconciliation of emic and etic market research was the launch of a new Heineken advertising campaign in

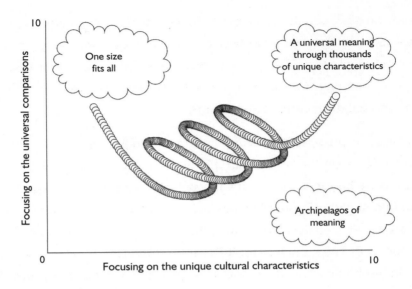

Figure 6.8 The emic–etic dilemma

Europe. Heineken uses a universal advertising message as part of its marketing strategy: a Heineken turns a stressful situation into a relaxing one. A commercial that has been particularly successful in the Netherlands shows a young woman getting ready to go out with her boyfriend. She stands in front of her wardrobe and is desperately looking for a dress to put on for a formal evening out. Her boyfriend, already dressed in a dinner jacket, is looking at her. He is obviously amused by her distress. He leaves the room and comes back dressed in casual clothing – jeans and a leather jacket. He hands her a pair of her own jeans. The pressure is off, and so is the plan for the formal evening. They go to a pub with a relaxing atmosphere – a typical Dutch *bruine kroeg* – where they can be themselves. This was interpreted as showing that the young people did not care about status, and preferred to be natural: modest, but cosmopolitan, Heineken drinkers.

This same commercial which had been so successful in the Netherlands failed when pre-tested in Greece. There it was interpreted as meaning that the young couple was unable to go to the formal event and had to settle for a less exciting way of spending the evening. Heineken was perceived in this context as being just an ordinary beer for ordinary times and ordinary people.

This difference in market perception is based on value differences. Informality and "normality" are values that are emphasized in the Netherlands, so much so that what would be considered unsophisticated and uncultured by much of the rest of the world is considered to be the ideal by the Dutch.

ADVERTISING AND PROMOTIONS ACROSS CULTURES

The use of advertising and promotions are an important part of the marketing process; that could be defined as the structured process of communication aimed at the support of sales of goods and services. Whilst "advertising" is usually used as a generic term, strictly speaking, the word itself refers to a communication where the aim is to stimulate the total market size (as in alerting the market to a new type of product that exists), and "promotion," where the aim is to differentiate your product or service from what your competitors offer. Since communication is the exchange of information and information is the carrier of meaning, advertising and promotions are significantly affected by culture.

Already we have a fundamental dilemma between seeking sales through total market growth or increased market share. Of course, this has to relate to market conditions. In one culture (or country) the market may be mature (hence the aim should be increased market share through product differentiation). In another newer or immature market (at the beginning of the product life curve), the aim might be simply to inform the customer that your product exists and is available. You may not even be concerned with branding or image. "Eat more cheese as an alternative to meat" is an advertisement to encourage people to eat more healthy foods – including your cheese product. "Eat *our* cheese because it is a new variety," in an existing cheese-consuming culture, is a promotion. Reconciling market growth and market share is of course a basic challenge to all marketers.

As with the other basic processes of the marketing activity, the development of the world economy has drastically changed the needs and competences of the advertising professionals. It is difficult to imagine today that in the early nineties we witnessed the joint launch of CNN and other telecommunications services. And it was only in the early nineties that P&G, Nike and Unilever launched their first worldwide or even European ad campaigns. The mass media has drastically changed the whole business of advertising. Mass media are seen by many as largely responsible for the globalization of business, marketing, and advertising. However, argues de Mooij, "while particular television programs may rapidly transit the globe, this is not to say that the response of those viewing within a variety of cultural contexts and practices will be anything like uniform." A wonderful piece of research by Vink (1996) on the effect of the Dallas TV soap opera in different cultures revealed that the Americans looked on it as a wonderful moment to do their vacuum cleaning, the Brazilians took it as a representation of the American dream, and for the French it was additional evidence for the vulgarity of US values. Same TV program, but what different meanings were ascribed to it!

But globalization also means that organizations face different types of competition and that economies of scale become crucial to survive. In advertising, just as in other functional activities, there are a variety of approaches possible.

The Garucci case obviously has many common points of reference with any international organization. The basic tension is a version of

---

Case Study: "Garucci"

The Italian designer: global marketing strategy or local campaigns?

The Garucci organization is well known for its designer clothing in the casual fashion business. Its range of products – jeans, blouses, and fashion T-shirts – are sold in 30 countries, mainly European, Australian, and American. It has manufacturing sites in five countries, four of which are located in Asia. It has distributors in 28 countries and two distribution organizations in Italy and the US that are in the company structure. Garucci is discussing how to relaunch its advertising strategy. The central question is: what is more beneficial – a global strategy, local campaigns in each of the countries, or some mixed format such as a regional approach?

The marketing directors of the largest 15 countries got together to discuss the following options:

- A centralized approach in which a global ad campaign would be launched through mass media
- An independent local approach where each country decides upon its own strategy
- A regional approach where each region (West and Southern Europe, US and Canada, Latin America, and Australia) decides upon its strategy independently
- A mix of the above

The firm had just introduced a set of core values which focused around integrity, innovation, avant-gardism, and social responsibility. The 66-year-old CEO and founder of the company Guilio Garucci, former designer but now businessman, emphasized the importance of those values in the ads, whatever the result of the discussion. He also emphasized the great possibilities of the Internet. An experiment of selling clothes on the Garucci site and on the Gap Inc. site showed very interesting results: seven percent of sales came through this new channel.

Here are some examples of discussion points from the meeting:

"We have always had a local responsibility for launching our products. Fashion is a very national thing and we need to continue our approach with this freedom." (Southern Europe)

"Garucci clothes are very Italian and therefore seen as very up-to-date and fashionable. We need to take advantage of that." (USA and Australia)

"The core values are lived in the product. Our ads around the globe don't consistently express this new identity." (Garucci himself)

"The budget spend for ads is getting more and more expensive. We need economies of scale and should try to centralize at least parts of the approaches."(Netherlands)

"We in Latin America don't see how we can use the US approach for our region. However, we have many things in common across Southern America." (Latin America)

"We showed the latest ad from Italy to our clients in the US. They liked it a lot but were shocked by the sensual pictures at the very end." (US)

"Our Italian and French competitors have a scattered approach. Xavier (Paris) has launched a regional campaign, while Pupi (Rome) has completely decentralized budgets again after failing miserably with a global campaign last year." (HQ, Italy)

On the basis of the above arguments what do you think would work best for Garucci's future advertising campaign?

the global–local dilemma we discussed earlier. Let's just cluster the arguments that were floating around during the meeting.

Domestic argument (by an Italian marketing professional in Milan)

"What happened to us some 10 years ago was very good. Much of our production has been exported. But the excitement should not be exaggerated. We are still selling 45 percent of our goods in Southern Europe. We are an Italian company. And in view of our core business it is very good to be an Italian company. Exports are OK, but our main focus is around the corner. Let's stick to the fact the we are Italian in our advertising campaign. What the rest are doing is their business, but it shouldn't cost HQ a penny. If there is a next step to take in, say, five years time, I think it should be carefully orchestrated from HQ."

Multi-local argument (by the head of US advertising)

"The success we had in many countries including the US and in other major markets like Australia, Japan, and the Netherlands shows that local people knew their own business. The strength of Garucci is that we are free to order everything from Milan, but the way we distribute, advertise, and sell goods are left to local organizations. If we'd taken the advertisement developed in Italy we would have irritated many of our potential buyers. The gender roles are too stereotypical and full of sexy content. Much of the subtle humor would be lost. This is also applicable to the impressive English campaign which is loaded with typical English understatements. Great for them but it would lose us clients. In our ads we focus on Italy, its culture, its creativity, but we do it in an American way. That is why we were able increase our market share dramatically last year, though partly also through online sales. We are so happy that we have our own site that the customer can pull up when they click on the US; even the language is different from the British site. And we give much more information about the quality of textures."

International argument (by Australian head of marketing)

"This could be all very true for large markets like the UK and US. We in Australia would suggest a completely different marketing and advertising strategy. Obviously we are not very densely populated, but mass media asks for lots of budget to get a message across on Australian Television. Add to that the cost of the production of the ad and we're unable to do it on our own. The Australians love the Italian-based products of Garucci and, believe me, also their ads. We would like to take advantage of the enormous investments that Milan has put into that. Even the wonderful Italian accents are appreciated because of the fact that we are selling Italy here. Obviously we have subtitled, and in some regions synchronized, the Italian language. People just love it and we pay less. On the Internet I propose that we always create two columns, like in some bi-lingual airline magazines. In the left column we will speak Italian and in the right one the language of the nationality of the reader. We keep the power of the Italian image and make it accessible in local environments. Very importantly, we need to create a feedback loop much more than ever. We need to see why some products fail in some markets so we can all learn. Or at least locally. In short, let's be an Italian company with local adaptations."

Global Argument (by the Italian Senior VP, Marketing)

"I'm listening to what you have to say. But don't forget that we have found that our main markets around the globe are either from generation X or are internationally traveled customers. They live in hotels and very often take our clothes to work. I met representatives of Canal+, CNN, and Sky last week; because of difficult world economic conditions, their prices have dropped so much that we can consider a global advertising campaign. It will put Garucci fashion products on the map for years to come. I have calculated the per country costs; you will be amazed how affordable it has become. And it gives great opportunities to make one ad where our top of the line products, for all countries, will be shown in all our main lines such as jeans, shirts, and T-shirts. We have a demo tape with us and you will see that it is done by Al Pacino in English with an Italian accent. Everyone in the world will love it and buy our products. We can't carry on locally anymore. The world has changed. Tastes have become similar in our product sectors and standardizing our ads is a logical next step.

This should also be the case with our website. We have produced one, again in English, for all our customers. It has a .org address so we can give up all the country-specific sites. It allows us great access since we are mentioning the site address in the global advertising campaign on Sky and CNN."

Transnational argument (by Guilio Garucci himself)

"Thank you for all your arguments. They all make sense to me from your individual perspectives. I see that our organization has many integrated business systems, like our recently launched IT-driven ordering system and our manufacturing processes around Asia. Also our designs are centralized in Italy with Italian professionals. Our HR and marketing approaches, however, have been kept quite local. Obviously, fashion is a business where you need local responsiveness and we largely hire local staff. We need to keep that as much as possible. What worries me is that we have not learned a lot from each other over the last five years. If I look at all the local ads and the strategies that contextualize them, I am proud to be part of Garucci and sad that I fell short in linking you together. I have also drawn some conclusions.

We are perhaps too Italian in Milan and too non-Italian abroad. So I propose the following concerning the future of the advertising strategy that binds many of us together. First of all I want to invite the seven VPs of marketing of the largest of our countries. They will manage the new Garucci marketing group from New York. We will indeed launch a series of global advertising campaigns through the mass media, and the ad will be co-produced by our international advertising task force consisting of at least five nationalities from five different regions. The advertising agency we hired is Dutch, and very much mirrors our new organization. They have many offices worldwide and many nationalities in their creative teams. Every country has to contribute a fixed percentage of their sales in order to allow this to be budgeted fairly. I have spoken to the agency and told them they had freedom within the context of our core values. We need to find a universal way to communicate integrity, innovation, avant-gardism, and community focus in the ads.

We have also hired an internet agency that will help all local companies to design their local sites in a shell of a global site, which will be available in all requested languages. Because of economies of scale, however, we will make sure that the distribution is done by a new partner – Exel – that will use its regional warehouses to ship products to all parts of the world.

A picture comes to my mind. We have been a group of separate PCs and we had a server in Milan. We need to keep the things the local PC is good at, like flexibility and voltage adaptation and then link them to a server in Milan that plays a role that is symbolized by its name. Furthermore, we will use more types of software from Milan, New York, and Tokyo, for example, so we are not stuck with one logic and so we can learn continuously from each other. I love to quote my Italian 'colleague' by saying that as such our advertising approach becomes a palette of 'united colors'."

The above extracts demonstrate that Garucci is a company that has developed from a domestic base to an international firm, through to a multi-local company and finally into a truly transnational organization. For advertising this might mean the following:

Global advertising

Essence: standardized approach aiming for economies of scale and universal concepts through functional and conceptual equivalence.

Main characteristics:
- centralized advertising
- one global product/service
- using mass media
- few cultural differences
- ethnocentrism/geocentrism.

Main Role of HQ: Controls advertising strategy with a central budget. Local activities are allowed under strict control as an extension of central approaches. HQ consists of mainly one (home) nationality. This also applies to the Marketing function.

Advertising Support: One global agency from the home country.

Examples: Coca-Cola, Nike.

Transnational advertising

Essence: standardized approach through local learning. Centralized conceptual equivalence through functional dissimilarities or vice versa.

Main characteristics:
- centralized advertising through decentralized learning
- one transnational product/service

- using mass media and local media
- respects cultural differences and goes beyond them
- geocentrism.

Main Role of HQ: Coordinates advertising strategy with a central budget. Local activities are allowed under strict control as an extension of central approaches. HQ consists of many nationalities that learn from each other. This applies to the Marketing function also.

Advertising Support: many transnational agencies across the globe.

Example: ABB.

International advertising

Essence: standardized approach aiming for economies of scale and local adaptations.

Main characteristics:
- local adaptations on a central theme
- one global product/service with adapted versions
- using mass concept and local media
- respectful of "external" cultural differences
- ethnocentrism.

Main Role of HQ: Controls advertising strategy with a central budget. Leaves local adaptations to local operations, however, under strict control as an extension of central approaches. HQ consists of mainly one (home) nationality with a few exceptions. This applies to the Marketing function also.

Advertising Support: One international agency from the home country.

Examples: Disney, P&G.

Multi-local advertising

Essence: localized approach aiming for economies of scale.

Main characteristics:
- decentralized advertising
- many product/services
- using local media
- many cultural differences
- polycentrism.

Main Role of HQ: Coordinates and consults advertising strategy with a decentralized budget. Local activities are allowed, under no control. HQ consists of mainly one (home) nationality but is small. Local activities are done by local people only; this also applies to the Marketing function.

Advertising Support: Many local agencies from the home country.

Examples: Unilever, Aegon

AN OPERATIONAL APPROACH: CCRM – CROSS CULTURAL RELATIONSHIP MARKETING

If we want to formalize such processes we can extend the ideas of CRM to a CCRM framework (Wooliams and Dickerson, 2001). In the same way that ISO9000 provides a vehicle for quality management, a CCRM approach provides a mechanism for undertaking a cultural audit in marketing strategy formulation. Management benefits from using this model to both identify the impact of cross-cultural dilemmas in their marketing strategy, as well as to provide a decision-making framework for prioritizing action and investment.

First we elicit the dilemmas and then identify from which dimension of cross culture they derive. We then obtain opinions from key players (e.g. suppliers, distributors, and customers) in the supply chain as to how each dilemma impacts on business. Measures include the effect on short-term sales, medium-term sales, costs, time delays, etc. We then combine these data using hierarchical clustering algorithms, concordance, and correspondence analysis to produce a cultural business portfolio map. In practice the parties themselves use the CCRM model and identify the relevant variables for themselves in an atmosphere of collaboration and mutual respect with their business partners.

After entering the relevant variables into the software model, a map is generated which demonstrates to a decision maker where problems with customers exist. One axis represents an index of the relative attractiveness of each subsidiary, distributor, or customer (market potential, cultural differences) and the other represents the current or evolving business position (market share, revenues). Now the strategist has a decision-making framework that gives a holistic view and serves as a basis for prioritizing strategic actions to gain competitive advantage.

For example, Motorola needs to make a decision about where to invest a limited budget to build relationships with major customers in Russia, Lithuania, and Turkey. Russia demonstrates a great potential for increased sales growth, but there also exists a major cultural difference with the supplier which will cost Motorola €500,000. The cultural difference between Motorola and the Russian customer is small (indicating that the market penetration rate may be higher and the sales budget easier to achieve) but the Lithuanian customer only distributes radio products within a small geographical territory. In contrast, a customer in Turkey is distributing products in the emerging markets with high prospects for sales growth, but the cultural differences will require an upfront Motorola investment that will cost €250,000 this year and €250,000 next year before a return is realized. How should Motorola prioritize market development?

Rather than simply seeing cultural differences as a cost, they should be seen as an investment – just like R&D. Investing this year on developing the relationship and working to reconcile the dilemmas will generate increased sales growth in the next period.

An ROR index (measuring the relative return on reconciliation of different investments) provides an objective means of evaluating market options. It is computed as the additional gross sales margin as a function of the discounted amount of investment required to reconcile the cultural differences in a given market place. This index enables the market strategist to identify where the cultural differences exist with customers today and where they might be in the future. The index also provides the shareholder with an informed analysis and rationale of management's planning, as well as being a welcomed addition to a company's corporate annual report. Senior management will now have a clear picture of where to allocate resources in each market as a means to sustain sales growth through reconciliation.

We have sought to explain and demonstrate how our logic extends to a new thinking for international marketing. The constant theme of having to reconcile dilemmas is paramount. Part of the problem is that many professionals will have to unlearn what they have held dear for many years. As world markets have become an oligopoly, the classical approach has been to identify and exaggerate differences. In the past, differentiation was thought to be king. But the evidence from our research shows that to achieve true international success, differences should be celebrated and then integrated. As trading in the global village becomes the norm, market planning that can accommodate cross culture becomes mandatory. The approach described here will be an essential component of the marketer's toolkit to trans-nationalization.

CHAPTER 7

Managing HR dilemmas
across cultures

No longer just a department hiring and firing, HR has become of strategic significance as we recognize increasingly that it is people rather than technology, processes, or products that is the ultimate differentiating resource in organizations. How things have changed. Can you imagine an HR manager advising our ancestors how to work better in teams to improve early farming practices through training programs, and motivating people more effectively or devising schemes for the division and measurement of labor? Because of these major changes and the dynamic world in which we work, HR is faced with the challenge of reconciling many dilemmas to both exercise its own function and in its support for the organization. Some dilemmas owe their origin to the past, and some to the ever-changing present.

It was not until employers began to concentrate production in mills that measuring working time became precious in the pursuit of productivity and profit. The flux of ideas emanating from the Age of Enlightenment, the French Revolution, the growth of international trade, and the rise of trade unionism, all contributed to the need for better regulation and organization of work.[4] In the late nineteenth century we find important studies by Weber, Frederick Taylor and Durkheim introducing the community to the effects of the division of labor, work study, industrial relations, and a range of increasingly sophisticated selection techniques devoted solely to the maintenance of a productive, efficient, and competent workforce. The increasingly structured class system at the beginning of the industrial revolution gave rise to personnel management along with other disciplines such as finance, marketing, and operations.

We now see a dramatic change from this nineteenth-century thinking, which was based on manufacturing where both market demand for new products and unemployment were high, so that responsiveness to customers or staff was not needed. As world markets become oligopolistic with the consumer spoilt for choice, the evolution of work has been directed to become more responsive to customers in these market-driven times. In the twenty-first century we will see that the object of management – the individual – is no longer willing to sit passively on the receiving end of managerial dictat.

But you can't simply hire a pair of hands; there is always a person on the other end. In the twentieth century, partly due to wider access to education, this changed to a situation where any subordinate came with a hierarchy of needs (and, we would add, a need for hierarchy) that demanded recognition.

Over recent decades we have witnessed the development of the autonomous and reflective individual. This is someone who has a full set of needs, internal and external to the organization. Power is diffused and shared. Management needs to reconcile the needs of the individual with the needs of the organization to get things done to achieve its strategic goals. In this new world, conflict is a normal part of life and the competence to manage the dilemmas that arise from this tension is now the new source of authority. This becomes even more apparent in the process of continuing globalization. So we must address the challenges and response of the Human Resource professionals.

Before the current century, what we would now describe as the profession of HR was unknown. Over the last hundred years, although management never reached the state of managing scientifically (Taylor's notion), the HR community turned to a "scientific approach" to develop tools for its own role – for example, for evaluating work and jobs. Many of the systems owe their origin to the needs of the American army (HAY, etc.), and wartime OR ("operational research") and later Work Study and Personnel Management.

The 1950s and 1970s shifted attention to contractual issues. In the doomed Industrial Relations Act of the 60s, the UK government tried to codify company relationships with trade unions for the benefit of HR. Compensation systems began to emerge with pay for performance and other performance measurement systems.

In the 80s, through growth, improved communication, and new technologies, the world of business took a quantum step towards becoming more oligopolistic and competitive. Even the HR division had to justify its budget, which it responded to by becoming integrated and aligned with strategy, based on the claim that in an oligopoly it is ultimately only "people" that can deliver.

In contradiction, the need for survival in the increasingly competitive marketplace, with many long established organizations and household names disappearing rapidly, resulted in one of the most over-esteemed concepts: namely shareholder value, in which employees were just replaceable resources. Hence the derivation of the title "Human Resources" (with people seen as just a resource) that replaced traditional phraseology such as "Personnel Management."

Gradually we see the evolution of the "resourceful human" at the end of the last century. To add continued value, HR was forced to become more than a partner; it had to become a player contributing to the creation of the customized workplace. And it became necessary for shareholders to think about values rather than value.

The systems and processes of HR are gradually changing to adapt to the world of dilemmas created by the customized workplace and even more by globalization. More values have to be integrated in this new paradigm.

In addition to the generic changes (especially in the Western Hemisphere), the world has also recognized another major shift due to the internalization of business. Despite this, as has been noted before, the majority of the tools and methods used by HR professionals still owe their origin to an Anglo-Saxon mindset. Typical of these are the instruments used for recruitment and selection. MBTI and JTI (Myers-Briggs and Jung Type Indicators) are the most frequently used Americanized tools applied in business to assess personality type. Over 8,000 companies use the HAY system for job evaluation worldwide. Originally developed by Colonel Hay for evaluating jobs in the American army, it later became extended into the most popular evaluation instrument for international businesses. And lately we see the enormously popular Balanced Scorecard, developed by Kaplan and Norton, that initially helped many North American firms to measure important perspectives of business beyond the simply financial.

But what have these Americanized perspectives done for (and to) non-American organizations? Obviously there was an era when globalization was taken literally. "It works in the US, so let's export it to the rest of the world," was the main principle. Generally this approach has failed. In fact, it has only worked in organizations where the corporate culture dominated the local or national cultures (the Hewlett Packard "way" and McKinsey are obvious examples), and also perhaps in organizations where the product was very dominant – such as Coca-Cola, Disney and McDonalds.

But the majority of US-based organizations faced resistance where a US logic was just too much for the local environments to bear. When an R&D culture believes that one of the three main perspectives of the HAY system (knowledge required to perform) is being given a lower weighting than another perspective (such as accountability), should we just adjust the weightings in order to keep the most talented researchers? Again, when the financial perspective in the US is seen as important compared to the customer perspective in Japan, should we assign a different weighting in the respective cultures to rebalance the scorecard? We have observed counter movements where HR practices were decentralized. Too many local (and legal) differences hindered a single, global approach. It may have worked in a multi-local environment, but when the organization becomes international or transnational, the multi-local approach fails.

WHAT ARE THE ALTERNATIVES?

We offer our thinking based on the logic of reconciliation to explain and discuss how the role of the HR manager in the twenty-first century is to reconcile major dilemmas caused by cultural differences across national boundaries and organization cultures. Some further examples and complimentary discussion are also given in *Did the Pedestrian Die?* by Fons.

THE ROLE OF HR AND CORPORATE CULTURE

In Chapter Four we described the different meanings assigned to organizational relationships. We delineated four major typologies describing different organizational logics or corporate cultures: the Family, the Eiffel Tower, the Guided Missile, and the Incubator. In the period between 1980 and today, we have observed many Western (Guided Missile) organizations that have sought to impose Western (or rather Anglo-Saxon) HR systems on organizational cultures that were based on entirely different assumptions. The result was either "corporate rain dancing" or complete ineffectiveness of the intended outcome. What do we do with a pay for performance scheme in a Family culture? And what about a formal job evaluation session in an Incubator culture? Or the encouragement of team working in a highly individualistic and achievement-oriented culture? Does HR research from US and Anglo-Saxon thinking transfer to other cultures?

We will therefore offer reasons why the effectiveness of systems might be jeopardized when crossing cultural boundaries, the dilemmas that can arise and how they can be reconciled.

RECRUITMENT AND RETENTION

Recruitment over many years has left many organizations staffed by people comfortable with the old ways of working, or old paradigms. The greater the need for global change, the greater the likelihood that new blood will be required, not simply to replace wastage and retirement, but to bring in new key skills. Selecting the right person for a post is a key decision for HR and various tools and systems have been developed to support the decision-making process. There is considerable pressure on HR to make good decisions in recruitment. On the one hand to get the right person, on the other to avoid discrimination. On the one hand so the appointee can do the current job well, on the other hand to grow the job in the future. HR faces a whole series of such dilemmas.

Similarly, organizations have to retain their best staff and prevent any brain drain or loss of key skills (and knowledge) to competitors. Do organizations invest in training, only to lose their existing staff with enhanced skills and knowledge to the employment market place?

Because attracting and retaining staff is one of the key tasks of HR professionals, it has been developed to include a wide range of methods of selection and related procedures, supported by consultants and headhunters. Surprisingly little attention has been given to

"Amadeus"

Munich-based Amadeus was faced with such a dilemma. As the organization that operates the Airline Seat Reservation management system (originally for Lufthansa but later for Air France and other major carriers), it had very important key staff trained to a high level in the particular and very specialist IT software technologies to support access to VLFADB (very large and fast access databases) – namely thousands of concurrent online reservation or booking enquiries from any travel agent or check-in desk across the world. To cope with the very high hit rate, special software and computer languages are required, not the more common Unix or Windows technologies. On the one hand these IT specialists were highly valued because of their specialist knowledge but on the other they perceived (like all IT specialists) that they were falling behind in their employability because they had no up-to-date transferable competence in IT. Most didn't even know about the fundamentals of Windows software. So on the one hand they felt secure and valued when working for Amadeus, while on the other hand theirs was the only employee in the world using the particular VLFADB software and thus they had no other place to go. Should they leave and work in the more common Unix or Windows arena – and thereby be more secure in the generic IT market place?

Amadeus reconciled their dilemma by training their IT staff in Windows and Unix even though they didn't need such skills and knowledge for their work with the company. At first sight this might have made the IT personnel immediately leave to exploit their generic knowledge, but in practice they remained even more faithful to Amadeus as the only employer they knew that would keep their skills and knowledge up to date.

a very much under-researched issue – the image of the organization to the job seeker or potential employee.

We all recognize that the old model of employment with a major corporation as a job for life is no longer true, even in Japan. Mining our database generates evidence supporting the proposition that the younger generation – from 20–30 years old – have become more outer directed, more affective (prepared to show their emotions), have a shorter time horizon and want to work more with others in teams. This is not surprising when we realize that they too have recognized that the old model of lifetime employment with one company is dead. These young, generation X, high-potential employees, and the even younger baby-boomers, have a greater self-confidence in their own individual abilities. Their preference has shifted away from the task-oriented Guided Missile to the person-oriented Incubator work environment. Their rationale for career security is based on maintaining a set of personal and transferable competencies. It is their "employability" rating, based on their contemporaneous skills profile, that drives them, not the old notion of corporate security from an employer of long-standing repute or protection by their trade union.

What might make a large organization attractive to a young, ambitious, and talented employee now? On the demand side, organizations of the old economy find it increasingly difficult to attract good candidates. There is a tension between the image of these companies and the ideals that young, talented people have in their heads. The power-oriented Family culture and the role-oriented hierarchical structures of the Eiffel Tower still dominate in both perception and reality. The big players realize this and are doing their best to respond.

The global corporate mindset appears to be bland ("it's all the same everywhere"), static and seems not to offer the freedom to develop one's own persona. As a consequence, this is not attractive to generation X. In addition, young, talented, recently graduated baby-boomers now prefer to work locally. It is clear from our consulting and research evidence that ultimately only those organizations that reconcile the dilemmas are and will be successful in the employment market.

Young graduates are attracted to organizations that have reconciled these corporate cultural opposites. These are organizations that historically have a dominant Guide Missile or Eiffel Tower culture yet still seem to attract talented staff by reconciling the tensions between free choice and deep learning opportunities, between downsizing and economies of scale, and between image and reality.

RECRUITMENT PROCESS AND CULTURE

How often does an exiting job holder, about to leave, write the job specification for his or her successor? Or how often does someone from HR write a person specification based on the present job holder?

Don't we all recognize this? Don't we all look for the same characteristics that we value ourselves, consciously or unconsciously? Indeed, recruitment is simply a sophisticated way of cloning. This is the origin of professional tools to offer objectivity in assessment. The Myers-Briggs Type Indicator (MBTI®) instrument is the most widely used personality inventory in history. HR professionals have depended on it when clients need to make important business, career, or personal decisions. Last year alone, two million people gained valuable insight about themselves and the people they interact with daily by completing the MBTI® instrument.[5]

In Myers Briggs terms, there are observable differences in personality between different countries. For example, the most predominant type in British management is ISTJ (Introverting, Sensing, Thinking, Judging), whilst in American management it is ESTJ (Extroverting, Sensing, Thinking, Judging). There is evidence from Korean MBTI research that Koreans tend to be more introverted than extroverted when the American norm is applied to interpret their score. Because introverted people are relatively pervasive in Korean society, most organizations, including educational institutions and companies, encourage their members to be more extroverted in public situations, and many evaluate an extroverted person more favorably. Therefore, there is a possibility that in assessment centers, supervisors gave higher performance ratings to the extrovert than to the introvert. Perhaps a more important question of individual differences is whether people are more similar to themselves over time and across situations than they are to other cultures, and whether the variation within a single person across time and context is less than the variation between people. But this all assumes that such instruments are based on etic constructs and not emic ones (see chapter 6) – that is, that they have the same meaning universally across cultures.

If the most frequently found manager is the ISTJ (the introverted, sensing, thinking, and judging type) is this "chicken or egg"? But what about these methodologies when the applications go beyond the environment in which they were developed? Suppose the culture likes the extroverted, sensing, intuitive, perceptive type? So, if a culture believes in judging rather than perceiving, should they just select their people accordingly? The internationalization of recruitment has clearly shown that other types are more dominant in other cultural environments. And what about trying to assess whether a person can survive in other cultures? Obviously the Myers-Briggs fans find solutions in the team and the complementarities of types, or they refer to the fact that the types are only preferences but that all is potentially within the individual. But why were the questionnaires designed on mutually exclusive values in the first place? It is because our Western way of thinking is based on Cartesian logic and forces us to say it is "either–or", not "and–and." This is in contradiction to what Carl Jung had in mind in the first place when he construed the underlying conceptual framework behind MBTI.

How can we extend MBTI by slightly adjusting the instrument and the way of thinking that forms the context of its applications and thereby make it a jewel of an tool far beyond any cultural preference? Of course certified MBTI specialists know how to best use the instrument for the purpose for which it was designed. But it is also used by many others for recruitment and the allocation of assignments.

In a situation where the culture in which people are being recruited has a slight preference for the Sensing, what could be done when one is facing an environment where Intuiting is the preference for making a successful career?

Research has sought to correlate these scales with different job cate-

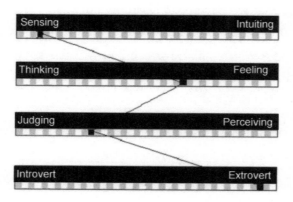

Figure 7.1   The traditional MBTI bi-polar scales

gories and functions. Thus, there is evidence to suggest which dominant type best fits a marketing role and which type is found most often amongst successful managers. However, with the internationalization of business, we are suddenly confronted with some interesting dilemmas challenging this principle.

Our fundamental concern with all instruments like the classic MBTI, 16PF and the like is that each dimension is based on the single-axis continuum. MBTI logic asks if you are Sensing *or* Intuiting. The more you identify yourself as Sensing, the less you must be of the Intuiting type. When seeking to apply the MBTI typology, or indeed any other associative model in an international context, we find that adhesion to the extremities of each scale is constraining. Although MBTI professionals do talk about combining the variety of preferences in teams and organizations, one cannot derive this approach from the MBTI instrument as it is based on forced choice bi-model questions.

We have to remember that much of this type of research owes its origin to Anglo-Saxon or, more specifically, North American thinking, even though it has been exported across the world. When we begin to incorporate other types of logic, such as Ying–yang or Taoism, we soon realize that we have been restrictive in basing the profiling on bi-modal dimensions. Let's apply this thinking and new logic to the Myers-Briggs scales. Note, however, that we are simply using MBTI to illustrate our ideas for multi-dimensional thinking, rather than seeking to criticize MBTI per se.

To test the preference for thinking or feeling the following question is asked:

When I make a decision I think it is most important:

a.   To test the opinions of others.

b.   *To be decisive.*

Thus, with a series of such questions, we are trying to place the individual along the scale, as shown in Figure 7.2.

Figure 7.2   Thinking–feeling linear scale

How the respondent answers this question gives insight when the dominant culture in which it is applied prefers decisiveness or being consulted (as in the original mode for which MBTI was conceived). But what if in a multicultural environment one finds people with different opinions? The decisive leader will agonize over the fact that many want to go for consensus. Conversely, the sensitive leader will not succeed because of an apparent lack of decisiveness. Thus we have a dilemma between the seemingly opposing orientations of Thinking *or* Feeling.

We would extend the options to include a means of evaluating the individual's propensity to reconcile this dilemma:

When I make a decision I think it is most important:

c.   *To be decisive through the continuous testing of opinions of others.*

d.   *To test the opinions of others by showing decisiveness.*

Those who answer "c" are starting from a Thinking orientation, but account for the Feeling of others. They have successfully reconciled the opposites. This process involves starting from one axis and spiraling to the top right (a 10,10 position on Figure 7.3), at which point the individual has integrated both components.

Figure 7.3   Reconciling from a thinking orientation

Similarly, those who answer "d" are starting from Feeling but spiraling towards Thinking, and again integrating the two seemingly opposite orientations (Figure 7.4).

Figure 7.4   Reconciling from a feeling orientation

In our extended prototype model of MBTI, which we call the ITI (Integrated Type Indicator), we use our own questions that represent the two extreme opposing values for each conjugate pair. However, we also add the two additional choices that represent the clockwise and anti-clockwise reconciliation between these extremes (see Figure 7.5).

By combining the answers from a series of questions in this extended format, we can compute a profile that reveals the degree to which an individual seeks to integrate the extreme dimensions.

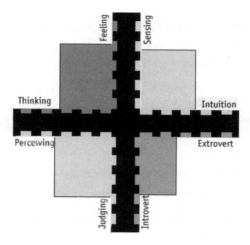

Figure 7.5 The Integrated Type Indicator profile

Each variable is scaled from 0 to 10 by combining responses to these extended questions. A typical ITI profile could then be $I^9e^3N^6s^2T^9f^1P^8j^7$ as opposed to a more normal one of simply **INTP**.

Then the overall propensity to reconcile equals

$$[(\text{Introvert} \times \text{Extrovert}) + (\text{Sensing} \times \text{Intuiting}) + (\text{Thinking} \times \text{Feeling}) + (\text{Judging} \times \text{Perceiving})] / 4 = \%$$

that is, $[(9 \times 3)+(6 \times 2) + (9 \times 1) + (8 \times 7)]/4 = 26\%$

The significance of our Integrated Type Indicator approach is that it enables us to determine the propensity for the individual to reconcile dilemmas as discussed throughout this book. In practice we use our own ILAP (InterCultural Assessment Profiler) based on our own work rather than challenge the authority or ownership of MBTI. As explained in chapter 10, this is also based on multiple choice questions, which include options that reconcile the dilemmas – and this can serve as the basis for recruitment for international leaders and managers.

DILEMMAS OF INTERNATIONAL RECRUITING

Many organizations have established assessment centers to facilitate the selection of candidates. Increasingly general attitudes are reviewed which correspond to the core values of trust, honesty, and integrity. There is no simple interview and psychological test that is able to reveal that. The goal of the assessment center is to better forecast the success of a candidate for a certain function by means of objective criteria and a standardized evaluation of behavior. It combines function-related simulations, interviews, and psychological tests. In that way the assessment center has reconciled one of the most substantial dilemmas of personnel policy, namely objectifying subjective behavior by triangulation or bringing together several viewpoints into a consistent whole.

But with each solved dilemma new fields of tension are created. In our consulting practice we have found the following common challenges faced by our clients in their process of selecting future internationally-operating managers.

Validity of the criteria measured by tests

As explained above, too many instruments are based on Anglo-Saxon and US thinking and research. But we have found that Westerners frequently appear to answer these tests differently than non-Westerners, because meaning is interpreted variously in different cultures. For example, in an Asian culture, where empathy is taken for granted, it appears that this property is not always appreciated in salesmen.

This is exactly why we have postulated the ITI (integrated type indicator) and developed our own ILAP (Intercultural Leadership Assessment Profiler). Because our database contains responses from over 50 countries, we can account for country differences as well as functional and other differences in seeking to interpret the results of measurements from our tools.

Relationship between behavior and effectiveness

The role of case studies and simulations is well established, but again problems occur if one has to deal with a multicultural group of people applying for an international job. Not all specific behavior appears to be effective across cultures for similar jobs. Let's look at a good example.

We were involved in the selection procedure for an international HR job at a large, internationally operating pharmaceutical company. In a simulation, a North American revealed himself as a serious candidate. He frequently led group discussions with intelligence and wit; we couldn't find any weaknesses in his job-related knowledge and communication skills. Up until dinner he was undoubtedly the top candidate out of five. During the meal we suddenly observed that the Chinese candidate had lost his reserve. The more informal and intimate gathering came to life with a lot of discussion, during which he communicated many unexpected opinions and insights, partly acquired during the afternoon sessions, which eventually made him the chosen person. The Western assessors were bewildered about his change of behavior.

Three possible misunderstandings can be related to this happening:

- In order to operate effectively, different behavior is frequently called for in different cultures.
- The same behavior is to be interpreted between cultures in several ways.
- Simulations and other behavioral experiments are frequently experienced differently and fulfilled in a variety of ways across cultures.

Assessment center facilitators have to be aware of these issues.

Relationship between assessor and candidate

The selection and interpretation of traits and behaviors that are obtained by tests and simulations is culturally colored. In order to minimize this problem, assessors need to be trained to account for and interpret the possible impact of culture. In observing human reality it is inter-subjectivity that comes closest to inaccessible objectivity. So-called objectivity makes an assassination center out of the assessment center.

Culture shock for expatriates

It has been shown in recent research that a minimum of 80 percent of failed expatriation was due to family circumstances. We have found that using the conceptual framework of reconciliation helps expatriates approach the tensions they face in their destination culture and also from the family–work dilemma to the point where their experiences are satisfying and thereby their work effective. This enriches their life and they no longer crave for an early termination of their overseas assignment.

DILEMMAS IN COACHING

It may not be surprising that top executives are increasingly looking for a shoulder to cry on. It is precisely during difficult periods that people learn who their real friends are. But even if it is lonely at the top, the help of a personal coach can often provide effective support and help to soften the toughness of a job. No wonder, then, that executive coaching has become an important growth industry. Currently 12,000 coaches are employed in the US compared to only 2,000 in the 1960s. In a recent Harvard Business Review article, Steven Berglas, a psychiatrist at Harvard Medical School, estimates that the number of coaches will increase to 50,000 in the next five years. It is interesting how companies see the benefits of coaches and are willing to pay top consultancy rates for their services. Unfortunately this attracts the charlatans who take advantage of the bandwagon and, as is often the case, reports of failures can dominate the more positive contributions of this noble line of work.

We first need to define the essence of this activity. In *Coaching Across Cultures*, Rosinski describes coaching as "an art to retrieve the potential from individuals or groups, in order to reach meaningful and important goals." In this process, good coaches face a number of tensions, which they help their client to reconcile professionally. In contrast, charlatans can only offer a choice between extremes.

What are these major dilemmas in this coaching arena? As with any outside facilitator, there is immediately a tension between coaching on the external (behavior), or on the internal (values and assumptions). Today the coach is thrust into the role of someone who has to change behavior quickly. This point is made by Berglas when he says that the essence of executive coaching owes much to the modern craze for easy answers. Business people in general, and Americans in particular, constantly look for new ways to change as quickly and painlessly as possible and executive coaches have stepped in to fill the gap, offering a kind of instant alternative.

The executive being coached might have a problem of assertiveness, or need to do something about the effectiveness of one of his or her teams. We know from behavioral psychology that it is too simplistic just to think about changing the way leaders function. It is important for the coach to distinguish between "the problem leader" and "the leader with a problem." This explains why tackling the problems solely as behavioral issues will be counter-productive. On the other hand, leaders with psychological problems would benefit more from the couch than the coach.

This distinction is also transferable in the coaching process across cultures. How often do cultural trainers suggest they can simply advise about correct behaviors – for example, in Italy, you need to show passion; in Japan, diplomacy, while with accountants you need to wear a gray suit. These behavioral tips don't do any harm but, as all our research shows, are totally insufficient without recognition of the deeper values they express. As we frequently say, it's like trying to impress on your first date – you'll soon be found out.

A second dilemma of coaching is whether the coach is internal or external to the organization. Of course, the internal mentor is an old established role for senior staff who – with lots of business experience and ascribed status – can provide a role model for their younger colleagues. At the other extreme we have the total outsider, not hindered by any political insight but with the risk that the subtle dynamics of the organization are ignored. The effective coach knows how to follow new paths that thrive on the political insights of the organization that they have, but with the necessary distance.

A third challenge derives from the tension between the individual executive being coached and the company who pays the bill. This is a real issue, overlooked far too often. If a coach is under the influence of those paying the fees, then he or she is simply an employee, by being an extension of the employer. Conversely, to coach the individual to the extreme is naïve and counter-productive. Lee Hecht Harrison, one of the largest suppliers of coaches in the market, has recognized this dilemma and has a guiding principle whereby the individual is given maximum focus in the coaching support but within the context of the organization's overall goals and wishes.

The dilemma between individual focus versus group focus also occurs in coaching. The challenge of the personal coach is to help the individual improve his or her role in the team, of which the individual is a part. Conversely, the role of a team coach is to help the team to make individuals excel, as is a dominant practice in Asia and in team sports.

Another dilemma is between the "rational–distance" versus the "emotional–engaged" approach. If you observe the activities of some sports coaches, such as Arsene Wenger at Arsenal, you see them frequently writing in their notebooks. In fact, Wenger is known as the encyclopedia of football, because of the number of games he has analyzed. He stands in sharp contrast to Alex Ferguson of Manchester United, who is known to release his emotions, even to the extent of kicking boots into the faces of top players. However, most successful coaches integrate distance with involvement. They distinguish themselves with different starting points.

Perhaps the ultimate reconciliation is between playing and coaching. The player-coach is a wonderful integration of both, but they are very scarce. Ruud Gullit achieved much success in England until he lost the physical ability to carry the load. Unfortunately, he lost his punch with it. Johan Cruijff was a very important coach as a player, and his successes are well known.

As a business leader, you need to devote some attention to coaching your own colleagues and staff. You should not simply wait until you are called back from retirement to play an emeritus role.

APPRAISAL AND REWARDS

The Balanced Scorecard

In order to overcome the dominant financial perspective of most measures of performance, Robert Kaplan and David Norton developed the well-regarded Balanced Scorecard.

This proposes that we view the organization from four perspectives, and develop metrics, collect data, and analyze it relative to each of these perspectives:

- The Learning and Growth Perspective – includes employee training and corporate (culture) attitudes related to both individual and corporate self-improvement.
- The Business Process Perspective – These metrics have to be carefully designed by those who know these processes most intimately.
- The Customer Perspective – based on an increasing realization of the importance of customer focus and customer satisfaction in any business.
- The Financial Perspective – retained, but not to the point where emphasis on financials leads to an "unbalanced" situation with regard to other perspectives.

The (proposed) Integrated Scorecard

In the same way that we have developed prototypes of other instruments, we would seek to extend Kaplan and Norton's ideas into an Integrated Scorecard. The fundamental challenge is to reconcile the two major cultural dilemmas that underlie the original Scorecard, i.e., the Past (Financial) and the Future Perspective (Learning and Growth) dilemma and the Internal (Business Process) and the External Perspective (Customer) dilemma.

Following the logic that pervades this book, the best support for the vision and strategy of the organization is found in how past financial performance could not be balanced with future growth but reconciled with it. An example could be that certain financial surpluses are reserved for learning budgets of the next year. We worked with the Finnish organization Partek (SISU) which achieves this consistently.

Reconciliation is more than balance. The (proposed) Integrated Scorecard would achieve synergistic increased added value from performances, rather than the simple arithmetical addition of the four components.

Extending the Appraisal Qualities ideas of Van Lennep and Muller.

For years Shell and Mars have used the "Basic Appraisal Quality" system developed by Muller and Van Lennep. When working for his PhD, Muller undertook research in Shell to assess what criteria helped people to move up the hierarchy. He found a number of qualities of leaders and selected the five most consistent. The potential of employees was reviewed annually based on these five criteria. The system is now better known as the HAIRL system:

- Helicopter quality (the power to encompass both details and the whole).
- Power of analysis (the power to cut the problem into pieces).
- Imagination (the power to use a sense of creativity).
- Sense of reality (the power to stand with both feet on the ground).
- Effective leadership (the power to lead groups of people effectively).

These criteria were defined explicitly and used at least once a year to assess the potential of graduates (junior as well as senior), and give their Currently Estimated Potential (CEP) in terms of the job level they would attain at approximately 50 years of age. It is easy to see that these competencies are culturally dependant. Research (Trompenaars and Hampden-Turner, 1997) in the late eighties confirmed this and national differences were explored. But with multivariate analysis using partial correlations we found that only three out of five categories correlated significantly with CEP. It was not very surprising that "sense of reality" and "power of analysis" correlated positively with CEP. The graduates worked in a R&D environment. But it was surprising, however, that "imagination" correlated negatively with the potential of graduates. It takes lots of research to introduce a new system which displaces established practice that has been in place for more than 25 years.

It is always easy to show the strengths and weaknesses of a system and how it supports (or contradicts) the dominant organizational culture. But once the analysis has elicited the weaknesses of a particular set of criteria, because that is a reflection of a certain culture, the question arises whether one can find a new set of criteria that can help the organization change in the desired direction.

So, assuming we should, how can we minimize the cultural factor in the assessment of people?

We replace the five single linear factors by the same five criteria but in comparison with their opposites. So for the first component, based originally on "power of analysis," we would include "power of synthesis." A scoring system was conceived that related to a revised CEP index to reflect this capacity to deal with opposites.

Under the old logic it was assumed that the higher the development the more talented the individual. We would not argue against this statement; it is a necessary quality but not a sufficient one. There is nothing against the power to analyze a larger whole into smaller pieces. In many complex situations it is very efficient to do so. However, once the smaller entity has been approached it needs to be brought back into the larger whole that, in turn, changes in quality. If the last action is taken we run the risk of getting into smaller and smaller details that are analyzed at the cost of the larger context. The pathology of the power of analysis is the crashing helicopter.

In the same way, the other original linear factors were replaced by their equivalent conjugate pairs. For example, helicopter quality was eloquently defined as "Looking at problems from a higher vantage point with simultaneous attention to relevant details. It recognizes its potential connections with other parts of the environment both within the organization and outside. It produces a detailed solution which takes full account of these wider connections, showing sensitivity to business, social, political, and technical environments." Brilliant, isn't it? It helps you to tell the trees from the forest and it can gain height and land (see Figure 7.6).

The final index was the cross-product of the ability to combine and the additional scores of both qualities of analysis and synthesis.

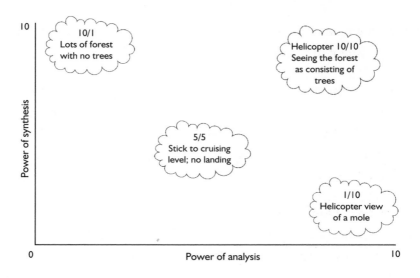

Figure 7.6 From reductionism to holistic understanding

REWARDS THAT WORK ACROSS CULTURES

Reward systems are far beyond being simple financial tools and as such they have a more substantial impact than most managers might realize. Furthermore, the link between the means and ends of such schemes (such as pay for performance) has different consequences across cultures because of the different meaning given to the components.

For convenience we can refer to Wilson's categories of reward programs:

- Regular payments like salaries and wages.
- Incentive pay such as bonuses and other variable pay related to the performance of the individual concerned.
- Benefits, which are aimed at providing financial security or services.

- Recognition programs such as certificates, public recognition or promotion.

Within these rewards you can choose either between cash and non-cash rewards on the one hand, and between all-employee and individual rewards on the other. A combination within this two by two matrix can explain how companies have sought to select the compensation program that best suits their desire to support strategy and values.

Examples of reward systems	Cash rewards	Non-cash rewards
All/teams	team bonus	social club for employees
Individuals	annual personal bonus	ascribed status – job title, or larger office

Thus HR must consider the dilemmas that arise because of people wanting or preferring to work in teams (communitarianism) or alone (individualism) and the relative importance to them in terms of cash to recognize performance or ascribed status. And further, to reconcile the global versus multi-local dilemma, namely whether the compensation system is the same across the world or different in each location – or even different in different departments or across functional disciplines.

From one of our major assignments we found that:

- Perceived motivation from variable pay was significantly higher amongst the more senior staff and those who were successful, achieving performance targets in the previous years. Furthermore staff in administrative and support roles were significantly more motivated by variable pay than their colleagues in R&D and engineering.

- The effectiveness of variable rewards was perceived to be dependent on the effectiveness of the systems surrounding them – such as the equality and equity of the ranking process, the perceived relevance of performance criteria and how much one was informed about the new approach. As when you put a new engine into an old car, all the surrounding parts come under much greater stress.

- Employees within a predominantly task-oriented corporate culture seemed to appreciate variable pay significantly more than those in a family and role-oriented culture. This was supported by evidence that people who felt they could control their environment and who were more self-oriented felt more motivated by the system than the fatalists and team-oriented individuals. Also a future orientation and a preference for controlling one's emotions were significantly related to the appreciation of the new proposed pay for performance scheme.

These conclusions might not be surprising, and might have been predictable. However, they gave rise to many dilemmas in trying to develop a trans-European policy. How does one deal with functions in manufacturing who don't believe that they can control their own output? Or with more role-oriented cultures in Germany and family-oriented cultures in France, Italy, and Spain who seem to be more motivated by other rewards, such as continuous learning, loyalty, or career perspectives (by which one can accumulate authority and thereby acquire ascribed status)?

But the benefits of these plans do not come automatically. There is a growing body of case histories that show that the success of a share plan is to a large degree dependent on the cultural context in which it is applied. The cultural dilemmas of individual–group, short and long term, directive–participative and inner and outer locus of control can be reconciled in an integrated culture.

A good example is the all-employee stock option plan at Cisco. The organizational leadership stresses that the program alone does not create an ownership culture; it is just a manifestation of it. Cisco's corporate culture stimulates teams whose individual employees are empowered to make significant decisions, linking short-term actions with long-term strategies. Moreover, employees can't be motivated by options if they don't understand them, so the company runs an education program. And there is no cultural environment where that doesn't work (Figure 7.7).

It is striking how many research findings have indicated that money is not a motivator. But Etzioni wrote about this in the nineteenth century when he said that there were three ways of controlling people: by force, by money, and through normative controls and that only the third was a motivator. Money is in fact a "dissatisfier." Employees quickly get used to the good feeling and jump to the next expectation.

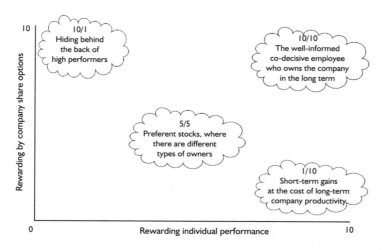

Figure 7.7 The pound in your pocket

The process of internationalization forces us to adapt much of the existing logic in management thinking. There are some options that do not work as well. You can choose a reward system stimulating team spirit. People from Japan excel at that, but it often leads to collective mediocrity. Even worst is the compromise – rewarding the small team. Both the individualist and the team player feel demotivated. The classic solution is "co-opetition," meaning cooperating in order to compete. Such reward schemes are aimed at having creative individualists molding teams that achieve beyond expectation.

THE NECESSARY ROLES OF A SUCCESSFUL TEAM

Belbin (1996) described an effective team as a group of people that aim for a shared goal through four phases: forming, storming, norming, and performing. In reality, however, the dynamic of a team is a function of the differences in the contributing team roles of individuals. It is these tensions that flow from the range of resources available to the team to different skills and thinking that have to be reconciled. But even more, the contributions from individual members are not restricted to their primary team role, but to changes and flexing to other roles as the members of the team influence and interact with each other as they try to perform. In the transitions between each of the four phases the differences between the roles become even clearer, and the reconciliation of the different orientations becomes essential.

Thus there is the potential for tension between any two primary roles. When these manifest as dilemmas and are not reconciled, the team remains in the storming phase. When the dilemmas are reconciled, the team can move to the higher levels of the "performing" mode.

Dilemmas are necessarily played out between people and it is the job of the HR professional to provide an environment in the organization in which such dilemmas can be reconciled. At the meta-level, the overall task for HR is to reconcile the tension between the organizational perspective and the individual perspective of each employee.

CHAPTER 8

Finance and accounting across cultures

n their classic work May, Mueller and Williams (1976) define accounting as a "language." If so, perhaps it is not surprising that it is afflicted by the curse of Babel. Not only do countries have their own rules, but so do industries and even individual companies. As in the other functional areas discussed in this book, this brings about a whole series of different dilemmas. As we will see, many dilemmas owe their origin to rules (universalism), which will be difficult to reconcile with company-specific needs (particularism) when we are faced with unaccommodating agencies and foreign governments.

Accounting exists to provide comparisons over time and between companies for three main purposes. The first is to provide information to the shareholders to know how and where their investment is represented, the second is for the market, and the third is so that management can manage. Whilst these purposes are different, the source information, although not its presentation, will be substantially the same.

COMPARABILITY VERSUS COMPLIANCE

We all recognize that accounting rules can be used to deliberately distort the activities of an organization and that this remains a problem. The BBC's *Money Programme* frequently asserts that "profit is just a number, it depends on the accounting policies employed." International accounting standards exist to reduce the variation between sets of accounts. Other standards exist, but are more like conventions and don't necessarily have the force of local law, let alone international law. And of course a global company has to reconcile the differences between the rules of the country where its HQ is based and its subsidiary companies in their own local setting. Management Accounts, as opposed to Financial Accounts, may be easier to reformat to provide a common basis for reporting and decision making.

Many regulations make comparability difficult. International Standard 17 recommends the capitalization of leases in line with the principle that substance should take precedence over form. German accounting rules, for example, require accounts to be prepared on a tax basis and prohibit this treatment – thus making comparability difficult unless multiple sets of accounts are prepared for different purposes. A fundamental dilemma is thus between the need for compliance versus the degree of de jure and de facto harmony (comparability). A variation of this dilemma is that the fundamental principle of fair presentation is found to compete with compliance. In the European Union, many directives have been developed to which individual nations must now comply. Difficulties can occur as a once-only problem when new rules are introduced (like a required change in liquidity following the specification of a new solvency margin that is different to previous practice), or can be ongoing.

In many ways, the origin of these problems comes from the notion of historic cost accounting because this is open to different interpretations. Thus LIFO (last in, last out) stock valuation is not common in Europe because there are no tax advantages. During inflation using LIFO, the cost of goods sold is higher and the value of stock lower than under FIFO (first in, first out). In contrast share prices rise in the US when LIFO is introduced, despite a short-term reduction in reported earnings. This is because the effect of LIFO is not to reduce the value of the company, but to increase it by reducing tax payments without changing the added value of the company's basic trading activities in any way. Some research suggests that the market place gives insufficient attention to the detail behind the accounting policies of published accounts – although of course, there are specialist analysts who study such detail carefully to provide information to stock market traders and other clients.

The question of whether it is possible to define a universal set of accounting policies has been posed may times. Demski (1976) debated this at length and concluded that accounting is necessarily "particularistic." Chambers (1976) then stated that if Demski's principle was true, we should immediately abandon the pretence that accounting is disciplined. Demski's reply to that was that it is the user's needs that differ and that each user is best served by a different (particularistic) set of accounts. However, there will always be market forces that will disclose information in the absence of regulation and it is becoming common practice to enforce contractual restraint on employees to prevent disclosure that might otherwise be to a competitor's advantage or influence the perceived value of the company in the market. The practical aspect of disclosure is determined to a large extent by accounting standards, which are embodied in the principle that those who read and use financial accounts should be aware of the basic assumptions on which they are based.

However, this approach is far too simple. We have to consider issues that derive from:

1. Objective versus subjective presentation

2. Different meanings (especially in different cultures)

3. Political will in different countries.

OBJECTIVE VERSUS SUBJECTIVE PRESENTATION

Accounting policies are the rules which companies use to determine the manner in which they prepare their accounts. They are usually based on the premise that the policy to be adopted is that judged to be the most suitable. But most suitable for whom? One area for improvement is that disclosure of accounting policy is virtually useless and it is often difficult to determine exactly what bases and assumptions have been employed. There is often considerable information but little explanation. In many situations, not only is there no single standard in place, but often no simple choice between alternatives. But recall that it is the responsibility of management to choose the optimum accounting policy for their business. It would not be surprising therefore if a manager, planning to take on a loan which required a covenant, chose accounting policies which made it easier for his company to comply with that covenant.

Often published accounts are summarized in a few pages, though they are supported by extensive supplementary information, which is often unintelligible. Even if the basis on which the accounts are prepared is stated overtly, we might still draw different conclusions from the same data.

Let's give a simple example to illustrate the point. If only one alternative is published or available, the reader may not consider that an alternative presentation could have been made.

Note that exactly the same data is used to tell two different stories.

Before the acquisition, it is projected that HQ will double its revenue from its current performance, partly because some of the customers from the new subsidiary will be included in HQ's sales. The projected revenue for the subsidiary acquired by HQ will as a consequence fall, and the total projected revenue is forecast to drop to one half of its current performance. As Figure 8.1 shows, there is a projected overall mean gain of 25 percent from the acquisition.

A year later, the past CEO of the acquired company claims that the

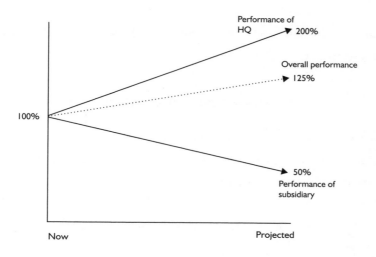

Figure 8.1   Projecting successful acquisition

acquisition was not successful. He could argue (using the identical data) that the parent company may have increased its revenue from 50 percent a year ago to where it is now but, as shown in Figure 8.2, this is offset by his subsidiary company losing half of its revenue and that therefore the total effect of the acquisition was an overall

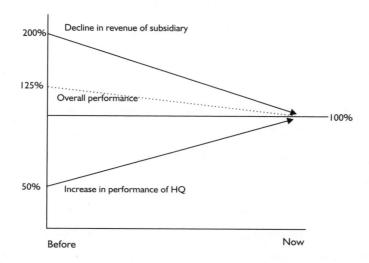

Figure 8.2   Looking back on the unsuccessful acquisition

decline by 25 percent from 125 percent of the total current level a year ago to now.

DIFFERENT MEANINGS

Solomons (1986) promulgates the benefits of objectivity to the point that accounts should be neutral rather than affective. Although all information has an effect on human behavior, accountants should seek to make it neutral. The corollary of this is that different accountants should produce the same set of accounts, yet we know this will not be the case.

In Altman's classic work (1968) on bankruptcy prediction, he did not consider the issue of takeover. Thus when Baring's was in trouble in 1995, the Bank of England worked desperately to encourage its sale to one of six international giants able to assume the losses and keep the name alive. In the United States banking industry at least, the consequence of financial failure may include takeover. But takeover can also result from financial success.

POLITICAL WILL

Some countries appear to operate with different sets of accounting philosophy so as to help their economy or dominant political parties. This can vary from governments who fail to clamp down on drug barons to those who simply operate different levels of taxation. At one time, registering your company in the Isle of Sark to reduce corporation tax was known as the "Sark Lark."

The less cooperative a country is in the fight against securities fraud, the more attractive it becomes as a locale for would-be securities law violators and the proceeds of their illegal transactions. The IMF has been actively involved in efforts, on both a country-by-country basis

Who is calling whom immoral?

As soon as we go international, we have to remember that different cultures may apply different meanings to events. Compare the following, both of which we learnt from client situations.

An American telecoms organization was supplying a telephone exchange to a regional government department of Nigeria.

A local elected politician demanded a "consultancy fee" to help "facilitate" the finalization of the contract.

The additional cost to the American company was US$20,000.

A US company agreed to purchase a large consignment of raw materials from a Nigerian mining company. Payment terms were agreed on the basis that the American company purchasing the goods would approve the invoice from the Nigerian supplier within 30 days and payment would follow immediately in their next payment cycle.

The invoice arrived on the first day of February coincident with delivery of the goods to the US. But because February has only 28 days and not 30 or 31, the approved invoice did not reach the data processing department in time for payment to be made until the next cycle, then at the end of March. The American company confirmed that it had complied to the letter of the rules of their payment terms.

The additional bank interest cost to the Nigerian supplier because of the delay was US$20,000.

and through international organizations, to encourage "non-cooperative" countries to join the international enforcement community. As a result of this international pressure, the past few years have brought about some changes in a number of secrecy havens.

Michel Camdessus, a Managing Director of the International Monetary Fund from January 1987 to February 2000, has been at the forefront of this globalization of the financial markets. Although the markets have attained a high degree of technical sophistication, the large volume of funds has made them prone to volatile movements of capital because of many shortcomings, including weak banking institutions, lack of transparency in capital movements, and an environment in which the regulation, supervision, and monitoring of financial institutions around the world has just not kept up with markets' evolution.

This, in turn, has made the recipient emerging market countries more vulnerable to periodic crisis and contagion. Second, as far as their development is concerned, too few countries can yet benefit sufficiently – or at all – from the enormous potential that globalization offers. A solution to the first problem, improving the predictability of capital flows in a more integrated global economy, would increase the opportunities for sustainable development in the world; it will of course not be enough. This illustrates the importance of reform of the international financial system and, indeed, one specific aspect of it, the soundness of the financial sector.

Camdessus further stated (to the Board of Governors of the IMF Fund Washington, D.C., on September 28, 1999) "The sound international financial system that we all desire must include sound and resilient national financial systems throughout the world, regulated and supervised according to a set of internationally consistent, transparent standards, and codes of good practice. Establishing an environment for sustainable capital flows will also require that countries wishing to attract these flows maintain the confidence of investors through establishing sound, well-run economies based on transparent policymaking."

IS UNIVERSALISM THE ONLY ANSWER?

In an endorsement and consolidation of these principles, the leaders of the largest industrial countries, the G7, unambiguously declared their support for sustained reform of the international monetary and financial system. These sentiments are also reflected in the proposals of the G22, a grouping of both industrial and emerging market economies whose work is specifically devoted to proposals on international monetary reform. The main components of such reform would necessarily include:

- internationally accepted and consistent standards and codes of good practice, based on the most successful experiences
- transparent behavior by all market participants
- strengthened national financial systems
- orderly opening of capital accounts
- a private sector that accepts the risks as well as the rewards of the emerging markets and is involved in preventing and resolving crises.

Even if there was a commitment by all governments to converge and comply, the task would be enormous. Changes required at the fundamental level will be necessary. In some countries there are regulations which require subsidiaries to have a certain year end date making year-on-year comparisons difficult. For example, US companies are required to prepare tax accounts on a calendar year basis (ending December 31). Many UK companies have their end of year in April, which is the end of the UK fiscal year.

It is not the role of agencies or governments to impose their imperialistic dictats across countries. The need is rather, through monitoring exceptions and difficulties of implementation, to continuously improve accounting standards in order to reconcile the need for a standard framework to provide a common language with a diverse range of needs across countries.

MANAGEMENT ACCOUNTING

Management Accounting, like some other areas of management control, had remained relatively consistent over several decades. More recently, management has recognized the need for new systems that would drive the pursuit towards being "world class" and co-incident with the other changes such as TQM and BPR. Roselender (1995) demanded a need for "relevant management accounting" that could provide the information necessary to achieve a competitive advantage.

In many cases, however, a priority was survival, let alone sustainable growth. Even before the Balanced Scorecard, Kaplan with Johnson (1997) had already identified the need for entirely new management accounting systems. We can cluster the problems they identified as a series of dilemmas.

- Measuring the performance of individuals (bottom up), versus measuring the performance of the organization (top down). This dilemma may be the major stumbling block to preventing change unless reconciled.
- Looking back to see what happened, versus projecting forward to next year's results. Too little planning derives from zero-based budgeting. Rather than focusing on "what has happened and why" attention needs to be focused on "what we can learn and what positive actions we can take."

- Short-term treatment of cash flows, versus longer-term strategic needs.

- External pressure from financial institutions to report short-term profits, versus internal needs for long-term investment appraisal. Long-term planning is often collapsed to short-term thinking by the use of techniques such as DCF (discounted cash flow). Much less use of these techniques is found in Japan than in the US or Europe.

- The time taken by accounting departments to achieve compliance in terms of statutory provision, shareholder powers, and institution demands, versus generating and monitoring relevant information flows.

It is interesting to note that in France the *Tableau de Bord* is relatively innovative in incorporating performance and monitoring measurements that surpass the traditional *mèthod (PRWI) des sections homogènes*.

In traditional cost accounting, there is an underlying assumption of the existence of a correlation between overhead absorption factor (used for example for direct labor hours) and the incurrence of overhead costs. However, in practice many overheads are not a linear function of production or labor hours. Thus the amount of activity and cost attributed to the purchasing department for Product A (a low-cost, high-volume product) may be similar to those for Product B (a low-volume product but with a higher gross margin). Thus it is the volume of activity that incurs the cost, not the volume of production. In spite of this, the majority of organizations still use these transitional total absorption-costing systems for internal add-value performance evaluation. As a consequence, internal decisions may be taken on an apparently rational basis, but one which is actually based on a false logic because of conflicting data in the external market place. Of course, with the pervasion of technology, labor is changing from "making or doing" (manufacturing an item on a lathe), to "controlling" (setting up and monitoring a numerically controlled machine tool that performs the manufacturing). Furthermore, indirect costs continue to shift to sales and marketing activities in our ever-oligopolistic world.

NEWER METHODS OF MANAGEMENT ACCOUNTING

Thus, even though cost accounting was never an exact science, conventional models are no longer sufficiently robust for today's business practice. We must therefore ask what dilemmas will arise in the search and application for new methods.

We will need to consider issues that result from the accounting techniques themselves as well as issues in implementation and application. Such new methods are not independent of guiding management strategies such as TQM, benchmarking, BPR, and the Balanced Scorecard.

Broadly we can summarize the new generation of approaches to include:

- *Activity Based Cost Management (ABCM).* This involves the analysis of business expenditure by reference to the specific activities required to get a product or service to an identified state or position. The aim of course is to continually improve both the value of the actions earned by the activities and the profit earned. We could consider that ABCM is a specific function, whereas BPR is the all-embracing diffuse opposite.
- *Throughput Accounting (TA).* This analysis involves continually synchronizing and adjusting the manufacturing (or service)

process around relative bottlenecks and focusing on resource capacity, time, and added value.

- *Strategic Management Accounting (SMA).* This is focused on adding value relative to competitors and the longer-term evaluation of investment, over and above working capital utilization.

Such approaches are slowly gaining ground with many organizations seriously considering such approaches, even though traditional methods are still in the majority. Generally, there has been more implementation of these new approaches in the US than in Europe. Direct labor costing is still popular in Japan which has been interpreted by Westerners as an incentive to management to monitor and minimize labor costs. From the individual employee's perspective, there is the need for them to justify their roles within the organization with decreasing job security, for which traditional budgetary control could provide such a vehicle.

EXAMPLES OF DILEMMAS DERIVING FROM MANAGEMENT ACCOUNTING

Any standard business management textbook implores that decision-making be based on decision theory – that is, that management decisions should be made on a logical analytical basis and that management accounting data should be sought to evaluate alternative courses of action. However, real business decisions are not made through such an objective analytical process. The traditional decision-making approach breaks down because of how managers apply their cultural bias to the data. Different managers in a group or team do not act consistently and consensus has to be achieved through reconciliation. The same decision is not made every time from the same scenario or base data. Even where managers think they are being objective, they may be applying a particular meaning to information that renders their view subjective or at worst ethnocentric. Increasingly, the complexity of real world problems is such that the evaluation of alternative courses of action from accounting appraisal techniques results in dilemmas in which the clear alternatives are either equally attractive or unattractive.

Authority to action versus knowledge holders

In order to implement the newer methods (ABCM, etc.), the frequently occurring dilemma is between those personnel who have the best working knowledge of existing systems and what improvements are required, versus those managers empowered to action decisions and make change happen. Communication, involvement, training, and anxiety reduction are a priori requirements for reconciling this dilemma.

Integration versus stand-alone

Many consider that ABCM systems should not be seen as an extension to the financial systems but as a total business system and not purely an accounting solution. The stand-alone approach has the advantage that it is more likely to be more manageable yet will not bring the potential benefits of a holistic or total system approach.

Inter-departmental collaboration versus loss of autonomy

Proponents of ABCM argue that it is better to break from traditional cost centers or departmental expenditure to that of cost pools. In the latter case the same cost drivers, even though they may be undertaken across departments, drive all activities. However, loss of autonomy may be interpreted as constructive dismissal by some

departmental heads, as responsibility for their own departmen-
tally-based budget disappears.

Contribution analysis versus fixed costs recovery

Using Throughput Accounting we can compute TAR values
(Throughput Accounting Ratios) for component products or individual services. Any TAR which is less than 1 signifies a product or
service that has a net revenue less than total costs. The dilemma is
between the need to rectify this position by either price increases or
cost reduction. However, this ignores the role of the contribution
made towards total cost recovery. Yet, if approval is given only on
the basis that each product or service is making a positive contribution, the total of all contributions may not be sufficient to cover the
total fixed costs of the business. The latter was the cause of the failure of many businesses in the case-making industry in the 80s,
which, during fierce competition, agreed to supply any product that
was making a contribution.

The parent dilemma: "over" versus "under" control

Each of the above can be considered as manifestations of the problem of control, which is the central basis of management accounting.
The parent dilemma is the tension between under- and over-control-
ling. The reconciliation starts from identifying those elements which
can be controlled and which should be differentiated from those that
can't (or for which it is not cost-effective to so do). The systems in
place should be designed to constantly inform management of these
variables that can be responded to and taken advantage of.

It is interesting to note that accountants use the term "reconciliation"
as part of the vocabulary of their professional practice. This generally means looking at two sources of data, such as the cost of the

same item from an invoice and secondly from a purchase ledger statement, yet which appear to be in conflict (or different), and working to find accounting errors to bring them to the same value. Therefore, accountants should already have a built-in propensity for reconciling business dilemmas. Their problem, if any, is that they believe their work is a science and not leadership, because they think that differences must be reduced to zero, rather than celebrated.

CHAPTER 9

The quest for a new paradigm of international leadership

O ver the last decade, the phenomenon of leadership has become prominent in both the academic press and professional practice. The attempt to map the personality of outstanding leaders is a quest that has challenged a diverse number of researchers. However, such existing models, explanations, and frameworks do not serve current times. CEOs seem to have fallen from their pedestals after recent financial scandals, particularly in the United States. For this reason and many others, it is clear that there is a need for a new paradigm of leadership.

We offer a framework grounded in our research and consulting, which is based on dilemma reconciliation. This conceptual approach acts as a robust framework to explain leadership in the twenty-first century both within and across cultures. But first we need to review established theories of leadership and explain why they no longer serve us in today's global market.

Over the last century a number of theories were developed which can be conveniently classified under the following three categories.

First there is *trait theory*, examining whether there is a relationship between the leaders' personal characteristics, varying from physical and social to psychological characteristics, and the success with which they perform their task. It was particularly Bennis et al. who claimed to have found a relation between the effectiveness of leaders and properties such as logical thinking (translating ideas into simple forms), persistence (learning from errors and swimming against the flow), empowerment (enabling and enthusing others), and self-control (working under high pressure and resisting intimidation).

The criticism of this work focuses particularly on the low correlation between effectiveness and personal properties. Moreover, it is frequently mentioned that such approaches fail to consider contextual factors such as the type of industry or culture. Also it seems unlikely that one can develop physical characteristics such as height, gender, and skin color... All this has been very helpful for those who say that leaders are born and not made. Furthermore, the effectiveness of many of the properties appears to be culturally dependent. For example, it is improbable that the traits of a good American leader could have the same impact in Japan or France.

A second stream of traditional thought is known as *behavioral theory*. This approach does not rely so much on the personal properties of the leader, but focuses rather on the leader's behavior, particularly that behavior which influences the performances and motivation of employees. Obviously here leadership style comes to the center of attention. It focuses on the behavior of leaders towards subordinates and the manner in which the tasks and functions of leadership are conducted. The classic study from Ohio State University, conducted in the 40s and 50s, concluded that an initiating style exists – for which performance-targeted behavior is initiated with clear super-vision, results orientation, and role clarification – as does a more "participative" consideration style, where leaders aim their behavior at cooperation and satisfaction at work.

This model is very much centered on the work of researchers such as Tannenbaum and Schmidt (1973) and Blake and Mouton (1964) who respectively distinguished autocratic versus democratic or participative styles, and task-specific versus person-oriented styles of leadership. The weakness of this approach is that it ignores the complexity of the world of the relationship between both styles. Moreover, the context (culture, for example) is not taken into consid-eration in behavior theory and evidence from our research shows this to be important.

It is not surprising therefore that the third stream of thought represents *situational theory*. If certain aspects of behavior – and trait approaches – are related to a certain context or situation, a new and promising explanation of the effectiveness of leadership evolves from this. The so called contingency theories of Fiedler (1967), House (1971), and Vroom & Yeton (1973) show that environmental variables are significant for the effectiveness of leadership. The "one best way" is buried forever. It all depends.

Fiedler, for example, hypothesizes that leadership behavior interacts with the "favorableness of a situation" to determine effectiveness. He draws the conclusion that a focused, task-oriented leadership is better in both extremely predictable and in very unforeseeable situations, whereas people-oriented leadership is better in a situation of average complexity. Vroom and others distinguish an autocratic, consultative, and group style of leadership, for which the choice would have to depend on the structure of the problem, the available information, and the required quality of the decision.

Although these three leadership frameworks describe many situations, strikingly little attention is given to the cultural context within which leadership is practiced. In fact the dilemmas that leaders are facing in the current world are hardly considered or mentioned. Our research has revealed that the most important quality of a leader is to reconcile the distant ends of a dilemma to a higher level. Both trait and behavior theory continue to stall at the dilemma when faced with culturally-bound characteristics and how they can be overcome, particularly in a globalizing world. Situational leadership would stipulate different behavior in different cultural surroundings. But how would leaders then deal effectively within multi-cultural surroundings?

A new theory of leadership is thus needed to model the manner in which leaders will deal with value dilemmas. We can infer from our research findings that successful leaders in the current epoch of rapidly changing situations and multicultural surroundings need to operate with a people-oriented style in order to accomplish their tasks. Leaders will have to be participative in order to be able to take autocratic decisions at a higher level. They will have to think logically, a logic fed by an illogical intuition. Finally a leader must be very sensitive to the situation in order to take consistent decisions regardless of that situation. Only then can one observe whether leaders are born or made. As we will see, this requires a new mindset.

A NEW THEORY FOR INTERNATIONAL LEADERSHIP

Why do leaders face dilemmas?

All organizations need stability and growth, long-term and short-term decisions, tradition and innovation, planning and laissez-faire, order and freedom. The challenge for leaders is to fuse these opposites, not to select one extreme at the expense of the other. As a leader you have to inspire as well as listen. You have to make decisions yourself but also delegate, and you need to centralize your organization around local responsibilities. You have to be hands-on and yet hands-off. As a professional, you need to master your materials and at the same time you need to be passionately at one with the mission of the whole organization. You need to apply your brilliant analytic skills in order to place these contributions in a larger context. You are supposed to have priorities and put them in a meticulous sequence, while parallel processing is in vogue. You have to develop a brilliant strategy and at the same time have all the answers to questions in case your strategy misses its goals. No wonder there are so many definitions of effective leadership.

Our framework is intended as a meta-theory of leadership that transcends culture and is based on the logic running through the whole of this book. We have found that competence in reconciling dilemmas is the most discriminating feature that differentiates successful from less successful leaders – and that this correlates with bottom line results (Trompenaars and Hampden-Turner, 2001). Leaders "manage culture" by continually addressing dilemmas. This also means, increasingly, that the culture leads the organization. The leader defines what an organization views as excellent and develops an appropriate environment in which the culture of the workforce culture is reconciled with the needs of the organization. As a result, the organization and its workforce cannot do anything other than excel.

THE INTEGRATION THEORY

The significance of the integrated approach is that it enables us to determine the propensity for the individual to reconcile dilemmas. This is a direct measure of leadership. We name this propensity to reconcile dilemmas "trans-cultural competence" and it transcends any single culture in which it may be measured and thus provides a robust generalizable model for all organizational or national cultures. Our claim is that reconciliation is the real essence of leadership.

Our approach based on a framework such as the Integrated Type Indicator (as discussed in Chapter Seven) is different because it has an underlying fundamental conceptual framework that while managers work to accomplish this or that separate objective, effective leaders deal with the dilemmas of seemingly "opposed" objectives which they continually seek to reconcile. Given the importance of reconciling opposites, we are surprised that no instrument that measures this has been previously devised (published).

Published models of leadership tend to lack any coherent underlying rationale or base pre-proposition that predicts effective leadership behaviors. These models tend to seek the same end, but differ in approach as they try to encapsulate the existing body of knowledge about what makes an effective leader. Because of the methodology adopted, these are only prescriptive lists, like a series of ingredients to a recipe (you can only guess at how the dish will turn out) and there is no underlying rationale or unifying theme that defines the holistic experience of the resulting meal.

This creates considerable confusion for today's trans-cultural leaders. Which paradigm should they fit into? Which meanings should they espouse, their own or those of the foreign culture? Since most of our management theory comes from the US and other English-speaking countries, there is a real danger of ethnocentrism. We do not know, for example, how the lists cited fare outside the US, or how diverse conceptions of leadership may be. Do different cultures necessitate different styles? Can we reasonably expect other cultures to follow a lead from outside?

Part of the difficulty in researching leadership has been that without an agreed model of what effective leaders do, it is difficult to assess the value of this participant observation. To the interpreting observer, many of the best leadership behaviors are often inexplicable and are not the stuff of science. The observations are difficult to code, classify, and regurgitate. Can we know with certainty that it would work for others?

DILEMMAS FACED BY LEADERS IN GLOBALIZING ORGANIZATIONS

University education and too much training are still failing the new generation of potential leaders and managers. This is still based on the old Cartesian logic and scientific method where problems are defined as closed systems and where the only variables that are selected are those that can be measured and controlled. Apparently, all we then have to do is to evaluate alternate courses of action and select the course that offers the lowest cost or the highest margin.

However, at Trompenaars Hampden-Turner we have derived four main propositions from our research evidence relevant to the future of globalizing organizations:

1. Knowledge and understanding is stored within corporate cultures, most especially in the relationships between people.

2. "Strategy" consists not of one infallible master plan or "grand strategy," but in hundreds of trials and tentative initiatives.

3. Learning occurs when we eliminate the less successful trials, and intensify and explore the more successful ones by continuously monitoring feedback from activities. Successful insurance is an unending inquiry into what helps customers and pays you.

4. Management of change is based on adding value rather than on throwing away the values of an old situation.

All cultures and corporations have developed habitual ways of resolving dilemmas, of being, for example, both well-centralized and highly decentralized at the same time. The job of the leader is therefore to integrate these apparent opposites. The success of a company will then depend (among other things) on both the autonomy of its parts and how well the information arising from this autonomy has been centralized and coordinated.

If the leader does not usefully centralize information, scattered operations might as well be totally independent. If the various business units are not free to act on local information, then HQ is subtracting, not adding, value. Any network only justifies itself by fine-tuning the values of decentralized action and centralized intelligence, which is then fed back to the various units.

In the last few years THT has not simply been trying to help our clients to become aware of cultural differences by mapping those differences on bar charts. We have extended our data capture, analysis, and profiling methods to chart the dilemmas that arise when you respect the differences between cultures and their value orientations.

Business leaders received these online simulated "interviews" with enormous enthusiasm. They follow a semi-structured and open question format, rather than being multiple-choice questions. Here at last business leaders can (often anonymously) formulate the real issues and concerns they have in trying to grapple with real-world problems, tensions between competing priorities, demands and values. THT's new database of these responses offers significant insights but is now so large that a more rigorous means of analysis has been required to trawl the richness of these free-text qualitative, value-laden responses.

The aim was to elicit the commonly recurring dilemmas and isolate which issues are really important and of real concern to the modern business leader. The full spectrum of software analytical tools was cast at this data. Initially we applied the more traditional KWIC analysis (Keywords in Context), followed by comprehensive Linguistic Analysis methods leading to the construction of a multi-layered unsupervised Kohonen Neural Network model.

The results of this analysis are consistent with experiences and feedback from conferences, workshops, and consulting assignments, and are that the wide spectrum of issues can be clustered into a number of categories. Of particular interest is the consistency with which leaders posed their problems as a series of extreme choices – "should we do A or B?" where A and B are either equally attractive or equally unattractive, and moreover are mutually exclusive. These are typically issues like "Should we send our young technical expert to impress the client or our most senior member of staff, even though they know little of the technology being offered?" When evaluating these extreme choices or courses of action, we find they are either equally attractive or equally unattractive but always apparently mutually exclusive.

One of our researchers found that the quality of the dilemmas correlated with seniority/leadership level (Smeaton-Webb, 2003). Thus lower-level managers were less able to elicit dilemmas. For example, they tended to give positives and negatives ("should we do or not do this," which is not a dilemma). This is further support for the construct that leaders deal with dilemmas and managers with more operational decisions. Another of our researchers (Broom, 2003) found a correlation between the capacity to elicit dilemmas and the score on the Integrated Type Indicator (see Chapter Seven).

An example of the type of response we obtain from a WebCue™ interview with a senior leader is this:

On the one hand ...	On the other hand ...
The company is aiming for global knowledge sharing in order to get consistent forecasts, plans, and expectations on likely outcomes of comparable performance	The company has decentralized sales organizations with the autonomy to fine-tune knowledge to local conditions

This WebCue™ technology is not time-consuming or over-demanding for participants; it can be anonymous, and in a very short time a very detailed view is created of the client's problems. Using list and string object software techniques, it is relatively easy to automate pre-processing, to the point where clusters of dilemmas can be reviewed by a facilitator/consultant.

This input generates so-called "raw dilemmas." These are categorized using the seven dimensions of culture model as a frame of reference, enabling us to produce a series (typically 4–8) of what we can call "principal dilemmas." We usually equate or translate each principal dilemma to a business function, like Human Resources, Strategy, Organization Structure, etc. We can thus structure our feedback to the client in terms of functional area dilemmas and value systems as appropriate. Since the beginning of 2001, Trompenaars Hampden-Turner has made extensive use of this technology resulting in the capturing of over 5000 dilemmas from a diverse client base. And this is still growing very rapidly.

A typical example for a recent client project is shown below.

Dilemma	%
Global organization interest versus Local subsidiary interest	25
Cost versus Investment	11
Individual department/person versus Total organization/unit	10
Short-term versus Long-term focus	8
Internal organization versus External focus on environment	7
Focus on specific issues versus Breadth of options	3
Other	13
Non-dilemmas	
Lack of leadership/management (complaints about the management)	10
Lack of integrity/respect (complaints about stakeholders)	8
Others	5

The dilemmas organized per business function are shown here:

Dilemma/business function	Strategy	Leadership	Knowledge Management	HR Resource	Operations	Organization /Structure
Global organization interest versus Local subsidiary interest	36%	20%	16%	8%	4%	24%
Cost versus Investment	63%	18%	9%	9%	–	–
Individual department/person versus Total organization/unit	10%	–	10%	30%	30%	20%
Short-term versus Long-term focus	75%	25%	–	–	–	–
Internal organization versus External focus on environment	28%	29%	14%	–	–	29%
Focus on specific issues versus Breadth of options	67%	–	–	–	–	33%

In many cases we triangulate the use of web-based data collection with a selected sample of face-to-face interviews and as a result of this activity, we can now consider those generic dilemmas which we find leaders face on a regular basis.

TYPICAL LEADERSHIP "GOLDEN" DILEMMAS

By clustering the frequently recurring dilemmas in our database, we observe the following generic – which might be called "golden" – dilemmas, as they were found to apply to many organizations and were admitted to by many leaders.

1. Global organization interest versus Local subsidiary interest
2. Cost versus Investment
3. Individual department/person versus Total organization/unit

4. Short-term versus Long-term focus

5. Internal organization versus External focus on environment

6. Focus on specific issues versus Breadth of options

7. Leadership versus Management

Let us take one example – the second dilemma above, cost versus investment, and how we can help leaders or senior managers from this organization to reconcile that particular dilemma. We follow a series of methodological steps in achieving this that make use of worksheet tools and grids. Here's an example of how we might follow these steps.

In discussion, we expand the dilemma to the extreme ends and ask the client to consider the following:

On the one hand...	On the other hand...
We best serve our organization by achieving a lean and mean organization and by cutting cost wherever we can.	We best serve our organization by investing in the right area for achieving long-term success.

1.   *Which of these priorities is more fulfilling to you personally?*

2.   *Judged by how it is measured and whom it promotes, which is more important to your organization?*

Refer to Figure 9.1. Suppose you could allocate 0–10 points to Priority A, "importance of cost cutting" and 0–10 points to Priority Z, "importance of investing." Where would you locate your organization currently? (Place an X in that square.) To where would you like to see it move? (Place an O there.)

3.   *What organizational measures can the firm implement to move closer to the 10/10 position?*

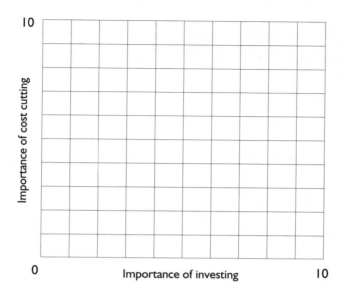

Figure 9.1   The dilemma grid of priorities

4.   *What individual steps can you as a professional take to move closer to the 10/10 position?*

5.   *Compare the answers that individual (syndicate) group members have given to the questions above.*

LEADERSHIP DILEMMAS CONCERNED WITH VALUES

This area deals with those values that need to be integrated during organizational alliances, mergers and acquisitions, and strategic alliances. So what are these dilemmas that are created in a cross-border alliance? The main dilemmas we have found within mergers and acquisitions (and strategic alliances) are the following:

1.   Core values versus Local values
2.   Centralization of systems versus Decentralization of processes
3.   Integration of businesses versus Differentiation of businesses

4. Short-term versus Long-term focus of integration process
5. Shareholder value versus Stakeholder value

There are differing views on the prime role of the free enterprise corporation in society, and let's look at dilemma 2 again here:

On the one hand...	On the other hand...
The prime process of our corporation is the integration of goods, processes, and services in order to create best value for our customers. The corporation is instrumental to the harmonization of different sectors of the business in order to create synergies.	The prime purpose of the corporation is to allow for enough differentiated activities so one can specialize and be close to the customer. The corporation is instrumental to the deepening of the business in order to create specializations that serve customers best.

1. *Which of these approaches do you personally prefer?*

2. *Which approach prevails at your organization in: (a) Asia, (b) Europe, (c) America?*

Refer to Figure 9.2. Suppose you could allocate 0–10 points to Viewpoint A, "integration," and 0–10 points to Viewpoint Z, "differentiation." Where on the grid would you locate your organization currently ? (Place an X in that square.) To where would you like to see it move? (Place an O there.)

3. *What organizational measures can the firm implement to move closer to the 10/10 position?*

4. *What individual steps can you as a professional take to move closer to the 10/10 position?*

5. *Compare the answers that individual (syndicate) group members have given to the questions above.*

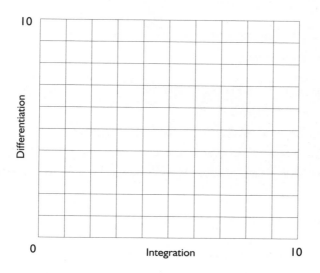

Figure 9.2 Integration–differentiation grid

The above logic can be extended to all the golden dilemmas described here, and indeed to any other dilemma.

LEADERSHIP DILEMMAS IN FUNCTIONAL AREAS

As discussed in previous chapters, the increasing internationalization of business has caused many functional disciplines to redefine and rethink their essence. The HR professional, for example, is up against one dilemma after another. HR professionals are becoming increasingly aware of the limitations of the Anglo-Saxon approaches developed in North-West Europe and the US. Similarly marketing managers become increasingly aware that the outcome of the global–local fight is essential to their own survival. Finally, let's consider aspects of the service function and of a knowledge management culture. Here too, many dilemmas arise such as those between an internal and external focus, implicit or tacit and explicit or codified knowledge.

The principal generic dilemmas we found related to specific functional areas are these:

1. Global versus Local clients and branding
2. R&D versus Marketing
3. Centralization of HR systems versus Decentralization of HR processes
4. Implicit or tacit versus Explicit or codified knowledge
5. Specific service culture versus Holistic integration of service culture

Here we'll look at R&D versus Marketing.

There are differing views on how an organization can be most effective. One view is that success is best guaranteed by pushing its core technologies while a contrasting view would rather focus on the pull of the market.

On the one hand...	On the other hand...
The most fundamental process is that of pushing core technologies, thereby ensuring that advantage over customers is made by having continuously renewed products. They will create the necessary markets.	The most fundamental process is that of being pulled by the market, thereby ensuring that we are close to the customer and able to respond quickly to their needs. That information will create the products needed.

We invite participating leaders to complete the same grids as shown in the two full examples above and consider the same basic questions as a means of eliciting the underlying issues behind the dilemma, and thereby the route to reconciliation.

LEADERSHIP DILEMMAS CONCERNED WITH GLOBALIZATION

Different approaches to reconciling the global–local challenge in different parts of the world are taken as examples. For the Japanese, the only way to survive seems to be internationalizing their business from their high-contextual local environment. In the matrix type of organizations, the quintessence of a structural dilemma – which has little success outside the Anglo-Saxon world – has been raised frequently. It was as early as the beginning of the 80s that André Laurent wrote an article in which he examined why the matrix organization had failed in France. But what is the alternative?

These main dilemmas in globalization processes are raised:

1. Face-to-face management versus Managing remotely
2. Global versus Local
3. Business unit versus Shared responsibilities in matrix
4. Global policies versus Local best practices
5. One definition of integrity worldwide versus Local interpretations

There are differing views of what constitutes good leadership, so let's examine the dilemma between face-to-face management and managing remotely and just in time.

On the one hand ...	On the other hand ...
One leads best when direct reports are physically close to the leader and can discuss positive and negative issues face-to-face. There is nothing more important in effective communication than being close to each other.	One leads best when direct reports operate remotely and use all kinds of media such as e-mail, telephone, and videoconferencing to keep communication at an optimal level.

LEADERSHIP DILEMMAS FROM DIVERSITY

The topic of diversity has become increasingly important and it becomes apparent that we need a diverse approach to diversity across the globe. But the issues are the same.

The diverse roles of women are often raised. One is the question of why women prefer to compromise in business; while outside business they reconcile more effectively than men, looking more often for creative solutions than is the norm in the monolithic business community.

Here are the main dilemmas raised in diversity programs:

1. Similarity of gender versus Different roles
2. Global diversity approach versus Locally-adapted approach
3. Diversity of values versus Inclusion
4. Convergence versus Divergence
5. Equal opportunities versus Cultural diversity.

There are differing views on how important it is to have equal opportunities in a corporation, or how important it is to have greater diversity of values and cultures, so we'll look at that dilemma.

On the one hand...	On the other hand...
A company is most effective when there is a level playing field with equal opportunities to succeed. In this way, the most able get to the top by fair competition, regardless of their origins.	A company is most effective if it can call upon the diversity of particular people and cultures. In this way, many special values and exceptional capacities can be joined to enrich products and processes.

LEADERSHIP DILEMMAS OF CORPORATE IDENTITY, CULTURE AND CHANGE

In Chapters Four and Five we commented on how often cultural background is ignored in both business and scientific discourse. How and why is the Anglo-Saxon model so dominant in the literature on the management of change? Is it because it starts from task orientation and from the idea that one should forget the old as soon as possible? This might work in the UK and the US. The role of core values also gives rise to dilemmas in this area. Can an international or multi-divisional organization share core values? What is valued in one country or division can be seen as totally undesirable in another. And core values should not degenerate into abstract statements to which people pay only token allegiance.

As previously explained, the effect of corporate culture must be included when one is seeking to change an organization. You might wish to set new goals in the context of a new vision and fire anyone who doesn't believe in that vision. How does one deal with a cultural environment that doesn't believe in this logic?

Here are the main leadership dilemmas in the field of identity:

1. Change versus Endurance
2. One identity through core values versus Many identities for intimacy of operations
3. Bottom-up values versus Top-down values
4. Values in use versus Espoused values

There are differing views of what constitutes good leadership; here we'll look at bottom-up and top-down values.

On the one hand...	On the other hand...
One leads when direct reports come with the great and less successful ideas and you facilitate them to guide them into actionable items.	One leads when direct reports are being directed on what to do and are given a sense of direction.

LEADERSHIP DILEMMAS IN MANAGING PEOPLE AND HR

The overall issue for HR was raised in Chapter Seven, but we can now summarize the principal leadership dilemmas as these:

1. Objective observation/evaluation versus Subjective observation/evaluation

2. Teamwork and loyalty to management's decisions versus Expression of dissenting personal convictions

3. Priority for HR development versus Productivity

4. BSC as development tool versus BSC as evaluation tool

5. Development as professional versus Development as generalist

6. Importance of commercial success versus Importance of the need to mentor and manage people

7. Taking risks versus Avoiding failures

8. Individual accountability versus Team responsibility

9. Task orientation versus People orientation

10. Entrepreneurship versus Control/accountability

11. Flexibility versus Efficiency

12. Mentoring versus Managing

13. Competing versus Cooperating as more fundamental process of learning

Here we'll examine teamwork and loyalty to management's decisions versus the expression of dissenting personal convictions. Once again, there are of course differing views of what constitutes good leadership.

On the one hand...	On the other hand...
One leads when direct reports support and execute, with skill and discretion, those decisions that the firm has made, throwing their weight behind shared policies and strategies.	One leads when direct reports can express personal dissenting convictions and attempt to change shared policies through their influence, in the hope that subsequent events will vindicate their judgments.

THE MINDSET CHANGE

But that's not all, of course. It would be a mistake to assume that operational level issues involve closed, solvable problems and only the global challenges for senior managers and leaders are characteristically open problems that manifest as dilemmas. The important lesson from our compilation of dilemmas is that all real-world leadership problems are best considered as open problems and represented as dilemmas. Future leaders and managers will therefore benefit from changing their mindset and viewing their challenges as open problems and expressing them as dilemmas. They can then begin to seek a reconciliation of the dilemmas resulting in integration of the seemingly opposing values to integrity. This results in the inclusion of a wider range of interests than would otherwise reappear later.

We have sought to show that existing theories of leadership – trait, behavioral, and situational theories – do not resolve the main dilemmas leaders are facing today. Trait theory claims a "one best set of traits" for the leader and ignores the culture in which they need to operate. Behavioral theory claims that there are different styles of leaders, such as "task" and "followers." The weakness of this approach is that one barely enters the complexity of the relationship between both styles and, again, the cultural context is not taken into consideration. The situational theory of leadership does introduce the cultural context as an important aspect in the effectiveness of leadership, but fails to resolve one major aspect: how a leader can be effective in a multicultural environment. We believe our integration theory throws light onto most black spots in existing leadership theories. We have given conceptual and empirical evidence that one needs to focus on the reconciling competence of leaders.

CHAPTER 10

The reconciling organization

Finally we offer a summary of some of our experiences and approaches in trying to embed the logic of dilemma reconciliation into the heart of an organization.

DOES IT WORK IN PRACTICE?

As Kurt Lewin (1946) said famously "there is nothing so practical as good theory," to which we would add, "there is nothing like professional practice to develop good theory."

The most basic challenge is to see whether we can create an organization in which one can go beyond simply the mapping and reconciliation of existing dilemmas. As authors and consultants we have run more than 5000 workshops over the last 10 years, together with our team. We have mastered the art of mapping dilemmas through interviewing key players, triangulated by the use of WebCue™, and have produced the results described in the previous chapters. As with any such interventions that come under the umbrella of "training," there is a danger that whilst participants are enthusiastic at the workshop event, they make less use of our methodology in a consistent way sustained over time. It is necessary to genuinely embed the methodology in the organization in order to achieve concrete, lasting benefit. We have therefore sought and developed ways in which an organization and its leaders go beyond dilemma reconciliation as a side dish, and make it a fundamental component of the organization.

What an organization should be seeking is integrated reconciliation with a diversity of workforce; only then will they enrich the variety of what they know. Organizations should beware of celebrating reconciliation as an end in itself and seeing it as a colorful Mardi Gras parade. It certainly has its fun and exploratory side, but it also features million-dollar misunderstandings and its true assessment must be sober. It is much easier to celebrate reconciliation than to reach out to people who seem sinister. The hard part starts now!

While offering some caution and highlighting potential dangers and difficulties, there is also good news. So first one needs to be clear about why one is risking integrity and what the benefits are likely to be.

Integrated or reconciled diversities are a competitive advantage for the following reasons:

1.   A company that can most closely match its own internal reconciliation with the external reconciliation of its customers is going to satisfy more people more of the time and prosper as a result.

2.   All companies try to make their rules as "universal" as possible so as to please the greatest number of people, yet only those companies in touch with a larger number of localities can discover how universal their solutions actually are.

3.   All creativity, innovation, or even improvements can come from comparisons of better with worse practices. The genuinely global company has more "remote associations" from which to create, and more diverse practices from which to pick the best. It has the largest array of potential solutions, for the largest number of varying situations.

4.   The real payoff from reconciliation comes from the reconciliation of ideas and values. A person of minority race who conforms totally to the beliefs of the majority culture will tell you nothing new. A white, Anglo-Saxon, Protestant male with original ideas may strain your tolerance. Fortunately most of

those who look different decide they might as well be different too. Hence many kinds of reconciliation contribute to novelty.

Our approach is that we help an organization compose a policy document in which reconciliation permeates every function of the corporation to comprise an overall philosophy. All is lost if you make reconciliation into just an HR responsibility, or if it remains only as an advertised aspiration. Compartmentalize reconciliation and other functions will believe it is your job, not theirs. They do not have to include diverse people; you do.

We must weave reconciliation into strategy, into corporate ethics, into customer and market relationships, into recruitment and career planning, into training and personal policies and activities. The inclusion of reconciliation has to be woven into the fabric of the corporation itself. Every department has to know its challenges and how these should be met. This will take a lot of drafting and a lot of consultation, but it will help solve the problem you will otherwise hear – that line managers do not seem to know what reconciliation means to them, nor what they should do about it. We must not become sentimental about reconciliation. It is a chasm across which we must learn to leap with all our strength. The time to celebrate is when we reach the other side.

Our own approach to reconciliation is more conscious of the challenge and the necessary responses, of the pains that must be endured if the gains are to be realized. Confronting reconciliation is a necessary risk for a company of global scope, but the "million-dollar misunderstandings" must be looked at, long and hard, so as not to repeat them, or even better, so as to learn from the mistakes of others.

APPROACHES TO EMBEDDING RECONCILIATION

Our evidence from research and consulting reveals that the process of embedding will happen through correctly identifying an organization's more successful units, whether the strategy has come top-down or bottom-up, or with help from customers. We learn from and formalize what works best. Individuals, teams, and business units rarely manage to benefit optimally from the value of reconciliation wholly outside their active working environment.

Furthermore, embedding the new way of thinking and doing is best achieved when combined with actual business operations and actions. When acting upon current business priorities and initiatives, coupled with structured self-discovery and reflection, the constant interplay among these elements over time is what creates lasting change.

We often begin with an inventory of current issues and initiatives, discuss the points of entry and prioritize the issues, in order to ensure that some relatively simple added-value suggestions may be included among activities already planned and scheduled. These are intended to create minimal disturbance to existing plans. We can then proceed to some more ambitious projects that would take time to complete and for which there would necessarily be some reorganization and co-development.

In order to create the Reconciling Organization, we can identify a three-phase process:

- Phase 1: *Diagnosing Leadership Strategy and Issues*
- Phase 2: *Transfer and Embedding through work sessions*
- Phase 3: *Transfer and Integration of Learning Loops*

Typically, this could pan out over a period…

Phase 1	Phase 2	Phase 3
2 months	1 month	ongoing
Preparation and Launch →	**Transfer and Embedding Through Work Sessions** →	**Transfer and Integration Learning Loops**
• Research and review • Interview executive board • Interview sponsors and key players • Program designs • Material designs • WebCue™ "interviews" • Planning and scheduling	• Validate tensions and dilemmas for target groups • Two-day reconciliation work sessions • Methodology transfer classes • Life Line coaching of co-facilitators	• ThroughWise™ • Key Initiative sessions • Collections, feedback, evaluation • Competency measurement • Continued LifeLine coaching of facilitators • Next step planning

Figure 10.1 The three-phase process

PHASE 1: DIAGNOSING LEADERSHIP STRATEGY AND ISSUES

The best way we found to begin embedding dilemma reconciliation thinking within an organization is to start with the most senior ally you can find to champion the cause, preferably the CEO, COO, division head or other key strategists. Initially, they do not need to use dilemma reconciliation or be converted to it, but only agree that it illumines their leadership and provides a rationale for it.

Nor does this leader have to have an articulated strategy. It might be even more useful to have issues or challenges that must be met, problems that must be solved, answers that must be found. These are issues or dilemmas facing the whole industry. If the particular organization concerned works out solutions quicker than its competitors, it will prevail.

We often support the identifying and mapping of strategic issues, facilitate the process of working on reconciling the issues, and map the joint action plan. This initial phase has two intrinsic rationales. Firstly, it has the nature of an intervention, namely to identify, map, and work out the issues. Secondly, it is also a way of introducing the reconciling way of thinking and doing so with top leaders in the context of them engaging themselves to solve issues which they relate to. This helps to ensure the support of these top leaders from the very start and gain their commitment to embedding the process in the future.

After this initial process of face-to-face interviews, we cross-validate the finding by our online interactive WebCue™ with a larger number of leaders and senior managers across the organization.

Face-to-face interviews with CEOs and other key strategists

An advantage of starting at the top is that you can develop your mandate from those generating strategy and all your subsequent activities can be a means of fulfilling them. You build the competences demanded by the company's mission and strategy. All those "developed" know why and what they are supposed to do with these new skills.

The dilemma approach helps to spell out for everyone's agreement what this or that policy would entail. It also satirizes any direction pushed to an extreme. Statements by senior persons can be turned into policy maps on which progress can be plotted and gains measured, while you act with the fullest authority.

The advantage of the dilemma format is that leaders get to pose questions and to flag crucial issues, to which the rest of their teams now have the duty of finding answers and solutions. It is becoming increasingly impossible for leaders to be omniscient about every corner of the globe and they should not be encouraged to try. Leaders have to become Inquirers-in-Chief who know what the dilemmas are, but need their people to find solutions. Cross-cultural competence cannot be commanded from on high; it needs to be learned by error and correction. It is increasingly the job of business leaders to define excellence. It is the job of HR and others to help the employees get there. There is genuine respect between leaders and employees where the former want to know about key issues, and the latter – who are closer to customers – can discover the answers. The basis of dialogue is that questions need answering, theories need data to confirm or refute them, dilemmas need reconciliations.

Through our consulting work we have found that the Integration Theory of leadership is effective in a variety of key business processes ranging from selection, team building, and learning. Selection instruments need to be adapted to be able to "scan" intercultural competence in the manner we described in Chapter Seven when we enriched MBTI from a bi-polar instrument to a two-dimensional one that can measure the degree to which the leader concerned has a propensity to reconcile (see also Trompenaars and Woolliams, 2002). We have also found that leaders can be more effective in practice by reconciling dilemmas raised within teams and learning environments.

Use of WebCue™

We have referred previously to the use of our online WebCue™ "interview" tools. In the context of seeking to embed dilemma thinking with the organization, we use these WebCues™ primarily to capture key issues of concern from our clients and participants prior to actual workshop sessions. Our aim is to ensure that we address issues directly relevant to the audience and validate our interviews. Subsequently we analyze the data captured to tailor our workshop presentations and content, and to produce a report for clients and participants.

The capture of extensive raw dilemmas through this process provides a rich source of constructs as an input to Phase 2. We have recently introduced lemmatization and other linguistic techniques to facilitate the clustering of such responses.

PHASE 2: TRANSFER AND EMBEDDING THROUGH WORK SESSIONS

After analyzing the evidence from our face-to-face interviews and the WebCue™ dilemma capture system, we then secure agreement among top leaders as to which of the principal dilemmas they want to address, and there are usually several. We have taken the interactive workshop facilitated by one of our consultants as the main vehicle to start the reconciliation process. Thus the principal issues raised through the interviews and validated by WebCue™ are ready for execution.

Theory into practice

We have repeatedly cited our central premise that the propensity to reconcile seemingly incompatible values is the key competence to have in order to be an effective leader in today's world. That is a fine statement to make, but can we teach leaders and the organizations that are led by them to attain and utilize this integrative mindset?

We normally start developing total groups of 20–30 "internationally mobile" managers who have ownership of the dilemmas gathered in the earlier diagnostic phase. They will also have completed our ILAP (Inter-Cultural Leadership Assessment Profiler) online questionnaire in advance. We distribute their personal profile to them so that their own values can be explained in the context of the methodology. It is most important that they know what each one of them contributes to their relationship with diverse values.

We use the earlier sessions in the workshops to develop participants in the recognition, framing, and reconciliation of the dilemmas. We place an emphasis on going beyond basic instruction-led input briefings to have each team tell us what dilemmas they have encountered in their workplaces, and to then work on the reconciliation of their own problems. Typically, the participants working in small teams thereby create 7–10 dilemma maps typical of the culture and subcultures of the organization.

As with any syndicate task in a developmental workshop, there is a danger that the quality of the thinking and analysis might be distracted by the legibility of the handwriting and drawing ability of the appointed scribe who writes on the flip chart. Seriously, we have developed the THT GroupCue (GroupWare) software tool so that each group can structure their dilemma, epithets, and action points using software-guided templates. This input data is then automatically converted to a short PowerPoint presentation of the dilemma so that each group can present to the rest of the audience using the video projector. This has the important side benefit that we can conclude the event with a database of rich dilemma content in computer readable form rather than a bundle of flip chart paper to stuff in our briefcases. Soon initial patterns begin to emerge.

After a series of such workshops for the same organization, certain patterns repeat themselves and it becomes possible to pinpoint dilemmas occurring in various parts of the world. At that stage there is a much clearer view of where dangers and opportunities lurk.

It is important that any kind of leadership training should not become a cul-de-sac or something done on the side but must be related to making a real contribution to the bottom line. There are several initiatives which one can take to secure success in making such development influential. Particularly significant is to have top managers hear the presentations made by teams on the last day and give the best of these teams an extended life as advocates of the changes they propose. Ideally the teams should consult back to their own organization, which they can do without triggering the company's immune system, since they are of the company itself. Our web-based ThroughWise™ system, described later in this chapter, enables the teams to have life after the workshop even if they are located at a distance from each other.

Among the objectives of these intervention sessions are the following:

- Create a coherent value system, grounded in reconciliation, and hence friendly to the value systems already in the room.
- Establish a firm connection between wealth creation and values reconciliation. Value is added rather than integrated.
- Develop a realistic understanding of culture shock and the development of the emotional muscles necessary to learning from it. Make cool appraisals of just how expensive cultural mis-involvements can be.
- Develop the capacity to go beneath a culture and grasp its core assumptions. You can then see its conduct as a pattern anchored in those assumptions. (We never make lists of do's and don'ts.) You can then anticipate its response to novel requests.

- To respect and adapt to another culture without abandoning your own convictions, but rather by unifying the integrities of both parties.

- Use the knowledge and experience of the selected managers to discover the half-dozen, recurrent, system-wide dilemmas confronting the client and perhaps twice as many regional dilemmas.

- Make the strongest possible case for the inclusion of diverse persons in general, which must logically extend to minorities given a hard time in the countries in which the client is located.

- Ask senior management to throw down a challenge on occasions to appropriately qualified teams.

- Measuring and assessing learning goals. It is not enough to urge transcultural competence upon people, without them asking "how would we know we were achieving it?" What Balanced Scorecards are available?

Effectiveness of the reconciling mindset

In order to illustrate some of these ideas we now give some examples of feedback we have received. Overall there has been considerable praise for the dilemma-centered workshops, which were described as "enlightening," "profound," "impressive," etc., although we have identified that several people struggled with implementation on arriving back at their normal job location. The following remarks were typical:

"Personally I like dilemma theory. It is refreshingly realistic, all about life as it is, which is never 100% right or wrong. The dilemma logic is very useful and should be spread around so others use it."

I think the workshops were well timed. It opened people up at just the moment when they needed to think more broadly, but the time has now come to follow up on what was learned…It's time to stop learning and start solving real problems. The time has come to execute, not to study. Our executive workshop was most impressive but can it help us implement and execute while the window of opportunity is still open?"

Interestingly all dilemmas were not seen as being equally important.

"I actually preferred the more philosophical dilemmas, because these generalize far and wide, while some we started with were too simplistic. My team chose the "big" dilemmas and concentrated on those. Now is the time to cascade these down, and I don't mean the answers but the dilemmas themselves, for resolution at each level. It is our role to identify these "big" dilemmas and get our people working on these. It is going to take high quality facilitation, because people have to work through the dilemmas and find answers for themselves."

Once committed to the dilemma approach, participants are hungry to apply it to real problems they face and demand answers, as this piece of feedback reveals:

"We, in the company, start with the belief in trade-offs and compromises. You convinced us that in the wider world synergies are possible, but you did not point out our own synergies. Where are they? How do we find them? We need concrete examples drawn from our experiences."

So let us practice what we preach !

We are now in a position to describe a dilemma, not just a dilemma within the company, although it is present there, but a dilemma in the relationship between ourselves and the client.

On the one hand...	On the other hand...
We need to avoid the "sorites" dilemma which is the name given to a class of paradoxical arguments (also known as little-by-little arguments) which arise as a result of the indeterminacy surrounding the limits of application of the predicates involved.	
The knowledge world	The business world
The quest for a robust framework	Can the client apply the framework effectively to be of practical use?
How can we constantly improve and make more rigorous the process and theory for eliciting dilemmas?	What are concrete ways of executing and implementing the judgments arising from the workshops?

After the workshops were over, the participants found themselves badly skewed towards the first axis of this dilemma, as shown in Figure 10.2.

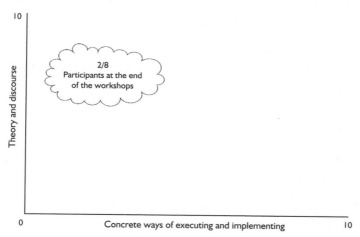

Figure 10.2 Theory versus Execution

We are about 2/8 on the Culture Space represented by this dual axis, much stronger on discourse than on execution. Of course, many training events conclude like this, whatever the subject presented. But at least we were prepared to recognize and face this challenge and do something about it. In a sense this is to be expected. You talk about something and then you walk your talk, but our respondents and participants were impatient for this next phase and felt they needed our help to execute it effectively. As one interviewee put it:

"The important thing is to come together to take pride in performance rather than whining about obstacles and frustrations. This collective pride is beginning to happen. People are saying 'We did it! Here's how.' But we're not there yet. What we need is a further roll out of this system, but it has to be a roll-up studded with examples of our own best performances. It has to be demonstrated through the work of our own people."

Satisfying a quantitative component or rationale

Many organization systems today are based on numbers and unless these numbers are embedded in a dilemmas context they tend to be unilinear, extending single dimensions even further. Numbers are favored to give some objectivity and performance measure to the systems, whatever they may be.

Here is what we were told in a financial institution:

"We tend to be numbers driven, so there is a lot of talking and fighting about what the numbers should say and, of course, this mitigates the significance of those numbers. Perhaps we need something like a Balanced Scorecard."

"People who add value outside areas upon which our numbers are focused do not get the credit they deserve. I personally reward good moves, even where I had not asked for or expected them, but I have to cheat a bit on the numbers to do so. I have the right to make qualitative judgments and I use this to compensate for the arbitrariness of the numbers."

"The numbers are all supposed to add up, so that my own performance con-

tract is the sum of the performances of those reporting to me. I am held accountable. I hold them accountable. You have to beware of 'single number tyranny'."

"I am in Trading and this consists of very clear either/or decisions, taken instantly and beyond recall. They are black and white. Press the wrong key and it could cost millions. Now people who succeed in this, in fast calls and big bets, are not well prepared to see both sides of an issue and to reconcile conflicts. They typically have a great deal of trouble shifting to managerial ways of thinking about people."

"Our management system is purely quantitative with some qualitative discretion thrown in. But I don't regard this as satisfactory. Didn't we hear that quantification is about some quality? And if qualities are properly defined they should not require qualification after the fact... can't you combine numbers with dilemma theory?"

"Our reward mechanisms do not really work. The bonus pool should go not just to quantitative achievements but to certain qualities of work which the client needs to learn and to master."

Let's be clear what people are telling us. Far from the numbers settling conflicts, they actually start them and there are arguments about what they should say but don't! People who do well in ways not anticipated in advance find that there is no way of recording that performance. The numbers are felt to be tyrannical and qualitative judgments require people to "cheat a bit." Another interviewee told us that despite unambiguous numbers people leave meetings with "differing interpretations of what they mean."

These differences dilute shared conviction and concerted action, so the numbers, despite their clarity and factual nature, do not unite people in quick and determined action. This is because the numbers, however precise, give only a partial picture of what the company must do. Moreover there is a serious disconnection between the multilateral nature of dilemma theory and the unilateral nature of current performance indices.

The dilemma can be thought of as shown in Figure 10.3.

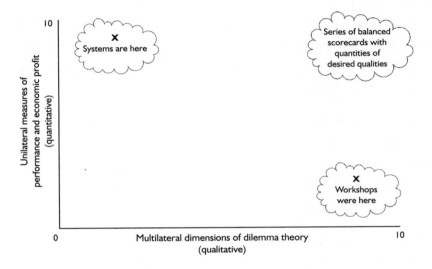

Figure 10.3   Unilateral quantity versus multilateral quality

This client (financial institution) could adopt performance systems and ways of estimating Economic Value for the whole company, so that these reflect not single yardsticks but balanced objectives, between which synergies can be found and reconciliations wrought. To this end we must turn to specific issues, the solution of which is being impeded by unilinear measurement systems. We believe we can help this client over this next hurdle in a number of ways.

Dilemma theory as the validation of "good judgment" and the need to explain success

Several people picked up on the point that dilemma theory was "not new," or that if it was, then its novelty lay in its power to explain the way we actually think about problems.

"At the risk of being rude I don't think that what you are saying is really new, in the sense that I already do it. It is wonderfully packaged and explained and it takes the lid off what is commonly called 'good judgment' or 'intuition,' but the longer I listen the more I feel I've always done this but what I have now is a good way of explaining my own decisions."

We agree that dilemma theory is a compound name for common sense, but it is also a way of improving it. Yet the implications of this insight are important. If good judgment is really a form of dilemma reconciliation, then we should find these reconciliations wherever the client has been unusually successful. Indeed we can use dilemma theory in order to embed successful practice by explaining why and how it was accomplished.

The dilemma is shown in Figure 10.4.

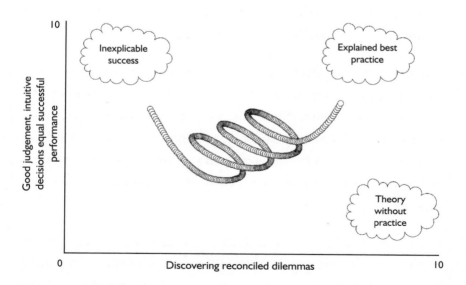

Figure 10.4 *Ex post facto* explanations of good executive judgments

The problem with intuition and good judgment is that these are exercised and then vanish. We are left applauding the person but not knowing what to emulate or what lessons to draw. This confronts us with Inexplicable Success (top left). The problem with reconciled dilemmas is that these may or may not engage with practical business issues. If they do not, we have Theory without Practice (bottom right). What we need is Best Practice explained by dilemma theory so all can learn from this (top right).

From Opportunity to Strategy: Embedding the Dilemma Resolutions of Best Practice

We saw above how important execution and implementation are. Dilemma theory would not embed itself within the organization until people had done it. Perhaps they have been doing it all the time, but have simply been unable to clarify the accuracy of their own decisions and the guiding light of their own high performance… If this is so, then a good explanation of best practice might be found to lie within dilemma theory itself.

"We often stumble over the truth," wrote Winston Churchill, "but we pick ourselves up and hurry along as if nothing had happened." The value of dilemma theory is that you can use it to examine what you stumbled over. Say some unit has had a huge success in Indonesia, then why? Can we somehow capture this achievement and learn from it? Even if it was achieved by intuition, can it be imitated or elaborated with conscious purpose?

When we asked interviewees about the relative salience of strategic thinking versus seizing opportunities, and whether or not these were part of their company's strategy, nearly all opted for seizing opportunities. Here is what clients told us:

"I do agree that Opportunity versus Strategy is a dilemma for us and that we are way over at the opportunity end of the continuum. We do what clients ask and this changes us, usually without anyone's permission. We just go for it. But there has to be a pattern to our successes and discovering what this is, what values are being reconciled by our most successful units is a way of deriving strategy from discoveries of what we are good at. What we can learn from examining successes is what our own culture does best. We can then discover our core competencies and pursue these."

"I think you'd be wise to start with an opportunity seized, ask what dilemmas were reconciled and draw out the strategic lessons for the rest of the organization. But I would warn you that client business is formidably complex. You would have to give these a lot of time, detail, and care. Your suggestion to use students is a smart one, because you would need to study hard what we already know before you could account for it in your terms."

"Strategies are rarely spelled out and hung on the wall, but they can be inferred from what people do (or did). I would like to see some of our outstanding achievements explained. Do that and embedding dilemma theory in this organization would not be so difficult."

The idea of seeking out success stories, publicizing these and then getting the protagonists themselves to present them is a good one. It will make abstractions concrete, and it will show that your ideas are both practical and relevant. In our view some of the best examples come from Asia. Our small presence in some of those countries makes the collaboration of national offices necessary, so you have some good examples of bridging reconciliation.

"Is it possible to express strategies and the contents of performance contracts as dilemmas? Were this possible then dilemma reconciliation could be embedded in our systems. We need to be able to create strategies for new client groups, so drawing out the dilemmas from successful practice could

be very useful indeed. A performance contract should test the strategy of which it is a part."

"Strategies can be broken down into performance initiatives, yet those initiatives may be more than the mere addition of their parts. If all our systems had similar logic and these had more or less successful outcomes, then we could learn a lot about ourselves."

"Why are we doing better in certain industries than others, why in mid-sized companies than in really large ones, why in some countries more than others? If we could 'learn from successes' and generalize the lessons, we'd be in a strong position."

Several interviewees were blunt in advising us to move away from "HR-type" and "trainer-type" presentations because these were regarded, perhaps unfairly, as marginal to real clienting. Nor should we push ourselves to the fore. Rather we should let those who had succeeded expound on their own successes, while making sure that dilemma reconciliation accounted for this. If resolving dilemmas could clearly explain good performance then clients would internalize this logic quickly. Otherwise they would resist. Here it is in their own words.

"Fruitful dialogues between SBUs won't just happen. I would ask each to come up with a success story to shape with the other or others, then explain that success in terms common to all."

"You should ask people in your workshops 'Do you believe in this, yes or no?' If the person said 'yes' then you should use that person as a champion and an exemplar of dilemma theory. Then ask them to present their story as a successful dilemmas resolution. This would fully operationalize your theory."

"In addition to a successful BU you could study a highly successful perfor-

mance contract and ask the protagonist how he or she did it. If we can somehow think together this impels action and drives agendas."

"I think you would be wise to talk to one of our colleagues, who is one of our best 'thinkers about action' and has some responsibility for outstanding successes in Brazil, Chicago, and the Netherlands. I think he would appreciate any efforts to model successful action to show just where we were succeeding and why."

"I think, or hope, that I used dilemma theory correctly the other day. A recurrent dilemma is the need to save on costs versus the need to invest in the company for future growth. As I saw it we could reconcile by investing in cost-saving processes [see Figure 10.5].

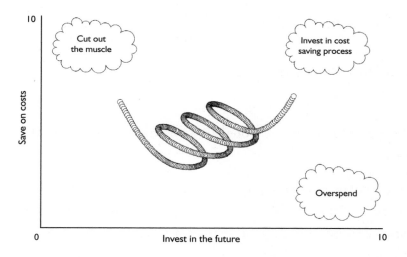

Figure 10.5 Costs or value?

"I presented this to 100 financial analysts and guess what? Our share price climbed in the days and weeks that followed. They were really impressed. We made a quantum leap and served our shareholders."

These interviewees are all telling us that the company leans away from designed strategy towards opportunistic initiatives, as shown in Figure 10.6.

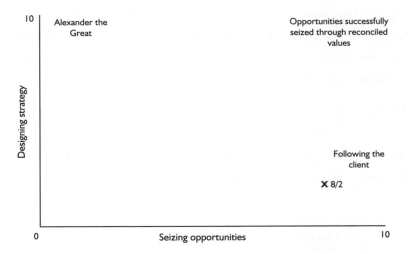

Figure 10.6 Strategy versus opportunism

One respondent with responsibility for strategy was especially eloquent:

"The point of having a strategy is as a framework for resource allocation, but our selling tends to be client driven and not strategic. I'm all for the entrepreneurial initiative of decentralized units, but surely these persons should have consistent strategic implications in mind so that their search for opportunity is methodical and random."

He went on to point out that the tension between strategy and opportunity never goes away:

"As far as I am concerned there is a perpetual dilemma between strategy and opportunity. If this opportunity is not within our strategy, then why not? Perhaps it is not such a good opportunity after all, or perhaps it should

be in our strategy. This tension is healthy. Our strategy should be guiding us to opportunities, not screening us off. I agree that strategic implications should emerge from the consistent patterns of our success."

PHASE 3: TRANSFER AND INTEGRATION OF LEARNING LOOPS

The problem with any new logic, like dilemma logic, is that it only operates in small oases, such as the classroom, the department, the section, the team, etc. When it encounters the company's traditional ways of thinking it fails to communicate, gets ignored and finally withers away.

It is an old adage that what gets measured gets rewarded and what gets rewarded gets done. So dilemma resolution needs to be reinforced by the way the HR department and eventually the whole company is structured.

We cannot ignore current or past initiatives and therefore we would firstly make an inventory of existing tools, instruments, processes, and initiatives, like leadership development, diversity programs, appraisal, and promotion processes. Secondly we would act to harmonize the internal consistency of these in order to support and reinforce the reconciliation logic to be lived and sustained in every part of the organization.

Among the most sophisticated clients, reconciliation is made into the centerpiece of strategy, which is very ambitious and exciting. That said, such a vision of reconciliation is not "wrong," but it is still incomplete, and often a number of people have only scant ideas of what it means.

The danger of starting with an inspired advertising or missionary campaign and then striving to live up to the reputation you've constructed is that the very real dangers of reconciliation are under-emphasized.

Ideally there should be Strategy Maps agreed by your leaders. There should be acquired Competence Maps designed to train leaders for these strategies. Assessment Maps can record agreements between supervisors and supervisees. Coaching maps can plot the paths of self-discovery. Recruiting Maps can guide the selection of employees and Balanced Scorecards can steer the company and measure progress of people, teams, departments, and functions.

These "maps" could be iterated on printed forms, on software, on overheads or on PowerPoint. The choice of values to pursue is yours and yours alone. Diversity and Integration are in the structure of these maps themselves – see Figure 10.7.

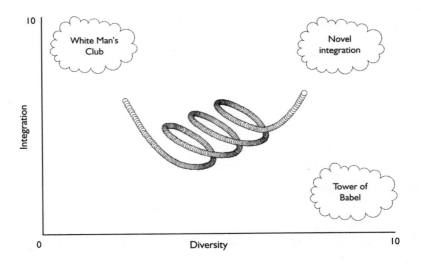

Figure 10.7 Novel integration

Too much reconciliation without integration brings about Babel. Cozy integration without reconciliation leads to a White Men's

Club. It is only when we integrate diverse ideas and lifestyles from across the globe that we get Novel Integration (top right).

Teams play a very important part in reconciliation development. Putting people who were formerly very diverse into a close proximity team setting connects intimacy with reconciliation. The problems such teams gain insight into, because they know and trust each other, can stop whole continents of commerce drifting apart, and can guide the process of mergers and acquisition so that no one is affronted. Team members represent the cultures from which they are drawn and can therefore explain major differences of opinion and judgment. This can suggest solutions acceptable to all, pre-tested in the intimacy of team dynamics.

Teams can help reconcile many kinds of reconciliation. Among these are the view from the center versus the view from the periphery, top-down versus bottom-up, new ideas versus existing rules, etc. If a whole team champions a new development this gives it far more momentum and persuasiveness than does the lone voice of its originator. Individuals are confident and persist because co-workers have given them confidence.

Team sponsorship is an important skill for leaders. Can they delegate and empower a team to investigate key issues and report back? Can they do this in a way that avoids two ways of wasting money? In the first of these the team is really a "front" for what the leader wants to do and is seeded with their agents; in the second, the team is so "creative" that it rewrites its own remit and comes up with a "brilliant" plan which is wholly impractical, for reasons not shared with the organization.

To brief a team so that it truly understands the issue and what a solution must accomplish is a difficult art to master. A team must be genuinely autonomous yet responsive to the task set for it. These kinds of skills could be practiced in workshops.

THE ROLE OF HUMAN RESOURCES IN CREATING A RECONCILING ORGANIZATION

We are often invited to suggest ways of embedding a developmental process of dilemma resolution into the heart of an organization, so that its internal systems of assessing employees, recruiting them, compensating them, mentoring and coaching them, managing knowledge and keeping score, are all internally consistent with each other.

The reasons for this are well known. All processes within a company have an underlying rationale, even where this is tacit and taken for granted. Introducing a new way of thinking into a company with existing rules, structures, and procedures can lead to the new logic being rejected, not because it is wrong, but because it is different. Such a process of rejection is analogous to a body rejecting a tissue graft from someone else.

If you wish the graft to take, it must be compatible with existing structures, and key alterations need to be made to systems that will interact with this new logic so that these recognize it as friendly and consistent. The isolation and encapsulation of a new logic, by confining it to some sub-system, is the beginning of the end. It will expire from its inability to make itself understood by the larger organization.

The legitimacy of HR innovation

Unlike departments with a highly specialized function such as R&D, IT, or Finance, where respect is a result of employees' own limitations, HR specializes in something we all must do – relate to other human beings. Because few people think they are deficient in this area, even if they are, HR finds itself in the rather awkward position of claiming special expertise over processes most of us regard as common sense.

We have all had good and bad relationships in our lives, yet these relationships are not readily improved when one party claims special expertise concerning what both parties share. Relationships are improved by mutual adjustments, not by one person telling another how to communicate better. It follows that claims by HR to important new insights into the human condition are likely to be treated with skepticism, while the explanation of a new piece of software may gain greater credibility.

None of this means that HR cannot successfully innovate, but it is grounds for caution and also grounds for enlisting the help of leaders and all those with deserved reputations for social effectiveness.

So do we really need it? We think so, because corporations are too big for everyone to act intuitively and not have those actions explained, measured, or assessed. You can do this in a start-up company where everyone is on a first-name basis, but not in larger-scale organizations. We do not recommend dilemma theory as a sure-fire formula, nor as a substitute for human judgment, but rather as a way of guiding, testing, recording, and understanding the import of these judgments and as frameworks for shared decisions.

One means of enabling this next phase is to develop illustrative maps such as these:

- Maps that portray strategies.
- Maps for cultural changes.
- Maps for managing diversity.

- Maps for measuring cross-cultural competence.
- Maps for leadership development.

The more clear an organization is about what it needs to do, the clearer will be the list of maps it requires, and the elicitation of the dilemmas it faces.

Leaving the organization self-sufficient in dilemma reconciliation

The need for sharing the thinking about the different dilemmas after any consulting intervention is the point at which THT would plan to leave an organization. But to help our support live on after a formal contact may be complete (at the end of any assignment), we developed our web-based ThroughWise™ system. Developed mainly to provide a way for participants to maintain a close dialogue after the series of workshop events, it was also realized that this could play a major part in providing a vehicle for participants to interact with other participants in an inter-workshop mode as well as intra-workshop.

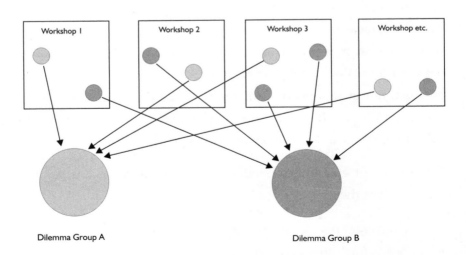

Dilemma Group A   Dilemma Group B

Figure 10.8   Inter- and intra-workshop group interaction

As we have demonstrated, the real benefits of applying dilemma reconciliation methodology to transforming and enhancing business practices will actually be realized after the sessions as the participants return to their business units. In order to leverage and entrench the learning, the ThroughWise™ software technology provides networking between participants who have common dilemma interests (see Figure 10.9).

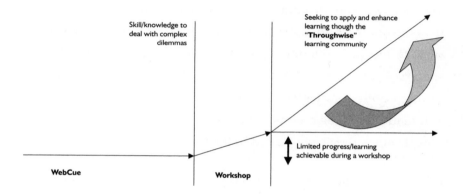

Figure 10.9 Ensuring that learning from the workshop is continued and applied

ThroughWise™ is a closed network for a given client group which provides a number of tools to facilitate the elicitation, capturing, and structuring of dilemmas and thereby codifying the components of dilemmas and action points for their reconciliation so that it can be developed, shared, and exchanged between group members.

Thus the approach is to start developing a learning community as soon as possible. In the first instance, we seed the dilemma database with the output of the dilemma reconciliation exercise at recent sessions.

We immediately start to involve the members of each sub-group in the ThroughWise™ network. This process works in a similar way to WebCue™, but is automated. Members of other sub-groups can also monitor progress of the range of dilemmas in which they might have or develop an interest.

Once the ThroughWise™ web-based learning community repository is in place, the interactive discussion forum is activated. This discussion forum is structured so as to enable continued comments, together with the formulation and reconciliation of dilemmas. Participants are able to enter comments, strategies for implementing steps to reconcile dilemmas, and to report progress, obstacles, and successes. They are also able to view all discussions and comments through both a structured tree or search facility. They can opt to automatically receive e-mail comments from other participants to the questions they have posted in the forum.

It is critical to the success of this type of learning community that it should be supported by a dedicated ThroughWise™ facilitator, especially during the early stages. Given the competing demands placed on top leaders, offering a solution based solely on them being invited to use web communication technology is insufficient. We often, therefore, suggest that a team of two such facilitators – one from the client, and one from our consulting group – would jointly execute this crucial role.

They work together to assume the following responsibilities:

- To steer the initiation and development of the learning community, especially in the early stages, and thereby act as the overall project "champion."
- To capture and formulate an initial series of dilemmas to seed the learning community to ensure a rapid take up, particularly

using the dilemmas identified in the previous sessions, and linking these to other client documents and reports.

- To organize and mobilize membership of sub-groups in the learning community based on common interests (dilemmas), inviting them to join the process.
- To consolidate and collate comments and inputs from members of sub-groups.
- To monitor and report on progress made.

THE FINAL DILEMMA

We have identified many dilemmas throughout our work and cited the important ones in this book. We have sought to show the need for the Reconciling Organization and how this can be developed. So with whom does the ultimate responsibility lie to seek out and elicit dilemmas and reconcile them? Should they be considered from the perspective of the organization or from the perspective of the individual leader? If you have followed us in our journey you will have noticed that the previous sentence contains the word "or" and is – of course – a dilemma.

In other words, how can we reconcile the dilemmas of the organization and the dilemmas of the individual in today's world of work?

We'll leave that one for you as an exercise!

Notes and bibliography

Chapter 2

1. Fons Trompenaars and Charles Hampden-Turner, *21 Leaders for the 21st Century*, Capstone, 2001.
2. Charles Hampden-Turner and Fons Trompenaars, *The Seven Cultures of Capitalism*, Piatkus, 1994.

Chapter 3

3. "Keeping close to the Customer", p. 315 in Trompenaars and Hampden-Turner, *21 Leaders for the 21st Century*, Capstone, 2001.

Chapter 7

4. Richard Donkin, "More than just a job: a brief history of work" in "Mastering People Management," *Financial Times*, 2001, 15 Oct., pp. 4–5.
5. See Isabel Myers, *Gifts Differing*, CPP Inc., 1995.

Chapter 8

6. For further background information, see A. Gordon, "Re-appraising management information flows," Ph.D. thesis, 2002, Anglia University, UK and J. Davies, "Towards the adjustment of accounts for insurance companies," Ph.D. thesis, 1997, University of East London, UK

Bibliography

Ackoff, R.L. (1978) *On Purposeful Systems*, Wiley.

Altman, E.I. (1968) "Financial ratios: the prediction of corporate failure," *Journal of Finance*, September, pp. 589 *et seq.*

Bagwell, L.S. and Bernheim, B.D. (1996) "Veblen effects in conspicuous consumption," *American Economic Review*, June, pp. 349–373.

Belbin, R.M. (1996), *Management Teams: Why They Succeed or Fail*, Butterworth-Heinemann.

Bennis, W. (1999) *The Leadership Advantage*, The Leader to Leader Institute (formerly The Drucker Foundation, New York).

Bennis, W. and Nanus, B. (1985) "From transactional to transformational leadership," *Organization Dynamics*, Winter, pp. 19–31.

Blake, R. and Mouton, J. (1964) *The Management Grid*, Gulf Publishing.

Broom, N. (2003) DBA thesis, APU University, UK (in preparation).

Cameron, K. and Quinn, R. (1999) *Diagnosing and Changing Organizational Culture*, Addison-Wesley.

Chambers, R.J. (1976) "The possibility of a normative accounting standard," *Accounting Review*, July.

Cottle, T. (1967) "The circle test: an investigation of perception of temporal relatedness and dominance," *Journal of Projective Technique and Personality Assessment*, no. 31, pp. 58–71.

Darke, P., Chattopadhyay, A. and Ashworth, L. (2002) "Going with your gut," Working paper, INSEAD.

Deal, T. and Kennedy, A. (1982) *Corporate Cultures: The Rights and Rituals of Corporate Life*, Addison-Wesley.

Deming, W.E. (2000) *Out of the Crisis*, MIT Press.

Demski, J.S. (1976) "General impossibility of normative accounting," *Accounting Review*, pp. 653–656.

Durkeim, E. discussed in Pickering, W. (1999) *Durkheim and Representations*, Routledge.

Etzioni, A. (1998) *The Essential Communitarian Reader*, Rowman & Littlefield.

Fielder, F. (1967) *A Theory of Leadership Effectiveness*, McGraw-Hill.

Goodstein, R. and Burke, S. (1991) cited in French, W., Bell, C. and Zawacki, R. (1994) *Organization Development and Transformation: Managing Effective Change*, 4th edn, Irwin.

Greenleaf, R. K. (1996) *On Becoming a Servant-Leader*, Jossey-Bass.

Hall, E. and Hall, M. (1990) *Understanding Cultural Differences*, Intercultural Press

Hampden-Turner, C. and Trompenaars, F. (1993) *Seven Cultures of Capitalism*, Piatkus

Hampden-Turner, C. and Trompenaars, F. (2000) *Building Cross-Cultural Competence*, Wiley.

Handy, C. (1978) *The Gods of Management*, Souvenir Press.

Harrison, P. (1972) "Understanding your organization's character," *Harvard Business Review*, May–June

Hord, S. (1999) *Facilitative Leadership*, Southwest Educational Development Laboratory, Austin, TX.

House, R. (1971) "A path-goal theory of leader effectiveness," *Administrative Science Quarterly*, vol. 16, pp. 321–339.

Jung, C.G. (1971) *Psychological Types*, Routledge & Kegan Paul.

Kaplan, R.S. with Norton, D.P. (1991) *Relevance Lost: The Rise and Fall of Management Accounting*, Harvard Business School Press.

Kohler, H. (2000) The perils of globalisation, *The Banker*, vol. 150, i.893, p. 16.

KPMG Corporate Finance Survey (1999) KPMG Corporate Finance, July: www.KPMG.com.

Lawrence, P. and Lorsch, J. (1986) *Organization and Environment*, Harvard Business School Press

Laurent, A. (1983) "The cultural diversity of Western conceptions of management," *International Studies of Management and Organization*, X111(1–2), Spring–Summer, pp. 75–96.

Lewin, K. (1946) "Frontiers in Group Dynamics" [republished in Schultz, D.P. and Schultz, S.E. (2000), *A History of Modern Psychology: Gestalt Psychology*, 7th edn, pp. 368–370, Harcourt Brace College Publishers].

Mark, M. and Pearson, C.S. (2001) *The Hero and the Outlaw, Building Extraordinary Brands through the Power of Archetypes*, McGraw-Hill.

May, R.G., Mueller, G.G. and Williams, T.H. (1976), *A New Introduction to Financial Accounting*, Prentice Hall.

de Mooij, M. (1997) *Global Marketing and Advertising*, Sage.

Pettigrew, A.M. (1985) *The Awakening Giant*, Blackwell.

Pugh, D.S. and Hickson, D. J. (1976) *Organizational Structure in Its Context: The Aston Programme One*, Lexington Books.

Rapaille, G.C. (2001) *Seven Secrets of Marketing in a Multi-Cultural World*, Executive Excellence Publishing.

Ries, A. and Trout, J. (1989) *Bottom-Up Marketing*, Plume.

Roselender, R. (1995) "Accounting for strategic positioning," *British Journal of Management*, vol. 6, pp. 45–47.

Rosinski, P. (2003) *Coaching Across Cultures: New Tools for Leveraging National, Corporate and Professional Differences*, Nicholas Brealey.

Rotter, J.B. (1966) "Generalised expectations for internal versus external control of reinforcement," *Psychological Monograph*, 609, pp. 1–28.

Sapir, E. (1929) "The status of linguistics as a science," *Language*, 5, pp. 207–214.

Schein, E.H. (1996) "Culture: the missing concept in organization studies," *Administrative Science Quarterly*, pp. 229–240.

Schein, E.H. (1997) *Organizational Culture and Leadership*, Jossey Bass.

Schutz, A. (1972) *Alfred Schutz on Phenomenology and Social Relations*, ed. Wagner, H.R., University of Chicago Press.

Silvester, J., Anderson, N. and Patterson, F. (1999) "Organizational culture change: an inter-group attributional analysis," *Journal of Occupational and Organizational Psychology*, March.

Smeaton-Webb, H. (2003) DBA thesis, APU University, UK, in preparation.

Solomons, D. (1986) *Making Accounting Policy: The Quest for Credibility*, Oxford University Press.

Southwest Educational Development Lab (1992) "Facilitative leadership: the imperative for change," www.sedl.org/change/facilitate/approaches.html.

Stouffer, S.A. and Toby, J. (1951) "Role conflict and personality," *American Journal of Sociology*, LUI-5, pp. 395–406.

Tannenbaum, R. and Schmidt, W. (1973), "How to choose a leadership pattern," *Harvard Business Review*, May–June, pp 162–175.

Trice, H. and Beyer, J. (1984), "Studying organizational cultures through rites and ceremonies," *Academy of Management Review*, 9(4), pp. 653–669.

Taylor, F.W. (1998) *The Principles of Scientific Management*, Engineering & Management Press.

Trompenaars, F. (2003), *Did the Pedestrian Die?* Capstone.

Trompenaars, F. and Hampden-Turner, C. (1997), *Riding the Waves of Culture*, 2nd rev. edn, McGraw-Hill.

Trompenaars, F. and Hampden-Turner, C. (2001) *21 Leaders for the 21st Century*, Capstone.

Trompenaars, F. and Woolliams, P. (2001) *When Two Worlds Collide* in *The Financial Times Handbook of Management*, 2nd edn, FT Publishing.

Trompenaars, F. and Woolliams, P. (2002) "Just typical: avoiding stereotypes in personality testing," *People Management*, December, pp. 3–35.

Usunier, C. (1996) *Marketing Across Cultures*, 2nd edn, Prentice Hall.

Vink, N. (1996) "The challenge of institutional change," Ph.D. thesis, Royal Tropical Institute, Amsterdam.

Vroom, V. and Yeton, P. (1973) *Leadership and Decision Making*, University of Pittsburgh Press.

Weber, M.: see Kalberg, S. (2001) "The 'spirit' of capitalism revisited: on the new translation of Weber's Protestant Ethic (1920)," *Max Weber Studies*, 2(1), 41–58.

Wilson, T. (2001) "Rewards that work: mastering people management," *Financial Times*, Nov. 5.

Woolliams, P. and Dickerson, D. (2001) *Werbung und Verkauf*, European Technical Literature Publishing House GmbH.

Woolliams, P. and Trompenaars, F. (1998) *The Measurement of Meaning*, Early-Brave Publications.

Index

archetypes
  caregiver 211
  creator 211–13
  explorer 205
  heroes 207–9
  innocent 205
  jester 206
  lover 206
  magician 210–11
  outlaw 210
  regular guy/gal 206
  ruler 213–16
  sage 205–6
  meaning across cultures 202–17
  reconciliation of systems 216–17
  successful 206–7
  see also marketing
promotions *see* advertising/promo-
    tions
public/private space 63–6
Pugh, Derek 15

Rapaille, Clotaire 200, 203, 204
recognition 7–8, 25–8, 32, 105
reconciliation 7–8, 105
  approaches to embedding 320–1
  cultural difference 29–31
  diagnosing leadership
      strategy/issues 321–2
    face-to-face interviews 322–3
  use of WebCue 323–4
  human resources
    leaving organization
        self-sufficient 344–7
    legitimacy of innovation 342–4
    role of 343
  internal–external control 96
  in practice 317–19
  time orientation 89–91
  transfer/embedding through work
      sessions 324
    dilemma theory as validation of
        good judgment 332–4

effectiveness of reconciling
    mindset 327–30
  opportunity-strategy/resolutio
      ns of Best Practice 334–9
  satisfying quantitative
      component/rationale
      330–2
  theory into practice 324–7
  transfer/integration of learning
      loops 339–42
  values 55–6, 58, 70–1, 75–7
recruitment 246–9
  dilemmas 256–8
  process/culture 249–55
research and development (R&D)
    66–7, 84, 92
respect 7–8, 28–9, 105
reward systems 266
  appraisal qualities 263–6
  balanced scorecard 262
  categories 266–7
  choosing 270
  combinations 267
  dilemmas 267–9
  integrated scorecard 263
  see also human resources
Ries, Al 200–1
Roethlisberger, Dick 14
Rolex 198

Sankyung 213
Sanyo 210–11
Scientific Management 13, 14, 242
Sematech 51
sequential–synchronous 31, 85–8
  appointments 86
  bombarded by stimuli 89–90
  reconciling 89–91
  salami case 87–8
  time orientation 77–84
Sesame Street 216
Siemens 209
situational theory 295

Trompenaars Hampden-Turner
Culture for Business

Trompenaars Hampden-Turner provides consulting, training, coaching and (un) learning services to help leaders and professionals manage and solve their business and culture dilemmas. Our clients are primarily Global Fortune 500 companies. We are based in Amsterdam, The Netherlands and Boston, USA. In addition, we have a network of associates throughout the world.

We particularly focus on cross-cultural consulting services around:

- Mergers and acquisitions integration
- Globalization
- Corporate vision and values

We take pride in using the client's own language and discourse, although we make subtle changes to its underlying structure to render it more coherent. Topics may include diversity, communication, learning, training, teamwork, culture, coaching, knowledge management, leadership development, integrity and balanced scorecards. For us these are all parts of a system. We also aim to introduce you to a paradoxical logic of human and organizational development. We aim for minimalist interventions yielding maximum results.

Introduction to our offerings

We work with all business implications of culture. These may be part of an organization's globalization process, external growth and integration strategies, corporate identity and corporate communications, international change management, or the worldwide 'roll-out' of building cross-cultural competencies.

We work with organizations through a highly customized and integrated approach including:

Consulting on culture-for-business management
- Conduct cross-cultural due diligence
- Facilitate your vision and value to strengthen your corporate identity
- Surface cultural challenges and dilemmas which may be creating obstacles
- Systematically reconcile cultural differences in order to maximize the business value of cultural diversity
- Assist in creating a business climate of mutual respect and trust in order to link people from different cultures in productive and positive ways

Global leadership development
- Create top-of-mind recognition of and respect for cross-cultural issues
- Develop culture-for-business competencies into competitive advantage
- Help leaders solve critical culture-for-business dilemmas
- Ascertain awareness of and respect for cross-cultural diversity
- Develop the ability to leverage global diversity

Executive coaching
- Cross-cultural executive coaching helps leaders and managers with wider perspectives, cultural sensitivity and the ability to work with diversity in a productive and innovative way to achieve organizational goals.
- Cross-cultural coaching helps the individual or team assess its own strengths and challenges. It assists with positive changes

in behaviour and perception. It also helps individual integration without sacrificing diversity and integrity, within the organization

Employee training and (un) learning

- Raise awareness of how culture-for-business competencies can help improve bottom line
- Build awareness and respect for cross-culture and diversity issues
- Provide support in "unlearning" negative cultural attitudes and stereotypes
- Develop the ability to value and work with diversity

Amsterdam office:
A.J. Ernststraat 595D
1082 LD Amsterdam,
The Netherlands,
Tel: +31 20 301 6666   fax: +31 20 301 6555
email: info@thtconsulting.com

USA office:
14 Arrow Street, Suite 10
Cambridge, MA 02138- 5106,
USA
Tel: +1 617 876 5025   fax: +1 617 876 5026